THE HISTORY OF AL-ṬABARĪ

AN ANNOTATED TRANSLATION

VOLUME III

The Children of Israel

The History of al-Ṭabarī

SUNY

SERIES IN NEAR EASTERN STUDIES

Said Amir Arjomand, Editor

The preparation of this volume was made possible in part by a grant from the National Endowment for the Humanities, an independent federal agency.

Bibliotheca Persica
Edited by Ehsan Yar-Shater

The History of al-Ṭabarī

(Ta'rīkh al-rusul wa'l mulūk)

VOLUME III

The Children of Israel

translated and annotated
by

William M. Brinner

University of California, Berkeley

State University of New York Press

Published by
State University of New York Press, Albany

Printed in the United States of America

For information, address State University of New York
Press, State University Plaza, Albany, N. Y. 12246

Library of Congress Cataloging in Publication Data

Ṭabarī, 838?–923.
[Ta ʾrīkh al-rusul wa-al-mulūk. English. Selections]
The Children of Israel / translated and annotated by William M. Brinner.
p. cm.—(The history of al-Ṭabarī = Ta ʾrīkh al-rusul wa ʾl mulūk : v. 3) (Bibliotheca Persica) (SUNY series in Near Eastern Studies)
Translation of extracts from: Ta ʾrīkh al-rusul wa-al-mulūk.
Includes bibliographical references (p.) and index.
ISBN 0–7914–0687–3 (alk. paper).—ISBN 0–7914–0688–1 (pbk. : alk. paper)
1. Jews—History—to 953 B.C. 2. Bible. O.T.—History of biblical events. 3. Prophets, Pre-Islamic. 4. Iran—History—To 640. I. Brinner, William M. II. Title. III. Series: Ṭabarī, 838?-923. Ta ʾrīkh al-rusul wa-al-mulūk. English ; v. 3.
IV. Series: Bibliotheca Persica (Albany, N.Y.) V. Series: SUNY Series in Near Eastern Studies.
DS38.2.T313 1985 vol. 3
[DS121.55]
909'.1 s--dc20 90-10264
[933'.01] CIP

10 9 8 7 6 5 4 3 2 1

Preface

THE HISTORY OF PROPHETS AND KINGS *(Ta'rīkh al-rusul wa'l-mulūk)* by Abū Jaʿfar Muḥammad b. Jarīr al-Ṭabarī (839–923), here rendered as *The History of al-Ṭabarī,* is by common consent the most important universal history produced in the world of Islam. It has been translated here in its entirety for the first time for the benefit of non-Arabists, with historical and philological notes for those interested in the particulars of the text.

Al-Ṭabarī's monumental work explores the history of the ancient nations, with special emphasis on biblical peoples and prophets, the legendary and factual history of ancient Iran, and, in great detail, the rise of Islam, the life of the Prophet Muḥammad, and the history of the Islamic world down to the year 915. The first volume of this translation will contain a biography of al-Ṭabarī and a discussion of the method, scope, and value of his work. It will also provide information on some of the technical considerations that have guided the work of the translators.

The *History* has been divided into 39 volumes, each of which covers about two hundred pages of the original Arabic text in the Leiden edition. An attempt has been made to draw the dividing lines between the individual volumes in such a way that each is to some degree independent and can be read as such. The page numbers of the original in the Leiden edition appear on the margins of the translated volumes.

Al-Ṭabarī very often quotes his sources verbatim and traces the chain of transmission *(isnād)* to an original source. The chains of transmitters are, for the sake of brevity, rendered by only a dash (—)

between the individual links in the chain. Thus, "according to Ibn Ḥumayd—Salamah—Ibn Isḥāq" means that al-Ṭabarī received the report from Ibn Ḥumayd, who said that he was told by Salamah, who said that he was told by Ibn Isḥāq, and so on. The numerous subtle and important differences in the original Arabic wording have been disregarded.

The table of contents at the beginning of each volume gives a brief survey of the topics dealt with in that particular volume. It also includes the headings and subheadings as they appear in al-Ṭabarī's text, as well as those occasionally introduced by the translator.

Well-known place names, such as, for instance, Mecca, Baghdad, Jerusalem, Damascus, and the Yemen, are given in their English spellings. Less common place names, which are the vast majority, are transliterated. Biblical figures appear in the accepted English spelling. Iranian names are usually translated according to their Arabic forms, and the presumed Iranian forms are often discussed in the footnotes.

Technical terms have been translated wherever possible, but some, such as dirham and imām, have been retained in Arabic forms. Others that cannot be translated with sufficient precision have been retained and italicized as well as footnoted.

The annotation aims chiefly at clarifying difficult passages, identifying individuals and place names, and discussing textual difficulties. Much leeway has been left to the translators to include in the footnotes whatever they consider necessary and helpful.

The bibliographies list all the sources mentioned in the annotation.

The index in each volume contains all the names of persons and places referred to in the text, as well as those mentioned in the notes as far as they refer to the medieval period. It does not include the names of modern scholars. A general index, it is hoped, will appear after all the volumes have been published.

For further details concerning the series and acknowledgments, see Preface to Volume 1.

Ehsan Yar-Shater

Contents

Abbreviations

EI:[2] *Encyclopaedia of Islam,* 2nd ed., I–. Leiden: Brill, 1960–.

EJ: *Encyclopaedia Judaica,* I–XVI. Jerusalem: Keter Publishing House, 1972.

Enc. Ir.: *Encyclopaedia Iranica.* I–. London: Routledge and Kegan Paul, 1982–

GAL: C. Brockelmann, *Geschichte der arabischen Litteratur.* 2 vols. and Supplement, 3 vols. Leiden: E. J. Brill, 1937–49.

GAS: F. Sezgin, *Geschichte des arabischen Schrifttums.* Leiden: E. J. Brill, 1967–.

ABBREVIATIONS

Translator's Foreword

This volume continues the accounts of the prophets of ancient Israel and of ancient Arabian tradition, and further illustrates al-Ṭabarī's efforts at the historical synchronization of these accounts with ancient Iranian foundation myths. In this difficult process, al-Ṭabarī shows again and again his striving for historical accuracy, despite the heavy odds against him. Lacking the requisite linguistic knowledge and the "primary sources" that are the *sine qua non* of modern scholarship, al-Ṭabarī trained his critical and quite skeptical eye on the tales transmitted by various traditionists, accepting some, questioning or rejecting others.

In this ongoing story, several key figures loom especially large: the mysterious al-Khiḍr, whose identification with the prophet Elijah al-Ṭabarī rejects; Moses; David; and Solomon, David's son. Tales about these figures make up the bulk of this volume, although stories of other individuals are included in briefer form as well: Balaam, Korah, Elijah, Elisha, Ezekiel, the Judges of Israel, Samuel, Saul, and Goliath, not to speak of ancient Iranian figures, including the story of how the boundary between the Iranians and the Turks was determined. Perhaps serving as a bridge between these traditions, there is the enigmatic figure of Dhū al-Qarnayn, who is mentioned in the Qurʾān. Al-Ṭabarī sees the name as encompassing two individuals: one the semimythical figure of the *Alexanderroman*, living at the time of Moses, who accompanies al-Khiḍr on his strange journey, and the later Dhū al-Qarnayn, the historical Alexander, whose exploits will be recounted in the next volume of this series.

In rendering Qur'ānic quotations into English, I have relied on M. M. Pickthall's *The Meaning of the Glorious Koran,* both for the English translation and the numbering of verses. I have, however, modified his biblical style and, in places where an alternative translation seemed more apposite, have turned to A. J. Arberry's *The Koran Interpreted.*

In his Introduction to Volume XXXVIII of this translation series Franz Rosenthal stresses the need for a new, critical edition of the Arabic text of al-Ṭabarī. Lacking that, one is left with some difficult textual problems, some of which may be solved by references to the works of such other medieval Muslim writers as al-Thaʿlabī, who used some, though not all, of the same sources as al-Ṭabarī, or Ibn al-Athīr, who, centuries later, used this text as the basis for his own, much-abbreviated rendition of these tales.

In dealing with some of these problems, I have been greatly aided by the advice and suggestions of several colleagues and friends, but, above all, by the knowledge of Iranian matters of Prof. Martin Schwartz and Dr. P. O. Skjærvø and the meticulous editing of Dr. Everett K. Rowson. I wish to thank them for their assistance in preventing some egregious errors. Those that remain are my own responsibility. I also wish to express my sincere thanks to my student assistant, Amy Forga, for her devoted work in the preparation of the manuscript for publication.

William M. Brinner

The Tale of al-Khiḍr[1] and His History; and the History of Moses and His Servant Joshua[2]

[414]

Abū Jaʿfar[3] said that al-Khiḍr lived in the days of Afrīdhūn the king, the son of Athfiyān,[4] according to the report of the majority of the

1. See *EI*², s.v. "al-Khaḍir" (al-Khiḍr), lit. "the green man, the green." In popular folklore in the Islamic world he is primarily connected, as here, with Qurʾān 18:61–83, although not mentioned by name there. In the Qurʾānic tale he is referred to simply as *ʿabd min ʿibādinā* "one of Our worshipers, servants," whom Mūsā (Moses) and his servant (*fatā*) meet on a journey in search of the "meeting place of the two seas." Elements of the story are based on three sources: the Gilgamesh epic, the Alexander romance (especially its Syriac version), and the Jewish legend of Elijah and Rabbi Joshua ben Levi; see *EI*², s.v. "al-Khaḍir," 902. The latter story is recorded in the Judeo-Arabic collection of tales by Nissim b. Jacob of Kairouan (ca. 990–1062), known in Hebrew as *Ḥibbur Yafeh me-ha-Yeshuʿah* (orig. *al-Faraj baʿda al-shiddah*), trans. W. Brinner as *An Elegant Composition Concerning Relief after Adversity,* 13–16. Joshua b. Levi seems to have been confused with the biblical Joshua, hence his identification as the "servant of Moses." Muslim scholars debated whether this was the biblical Moses or Mūsā b. Mīshā (Manasseh), a descendant of Joseph. Al-Khiḍr is identified with Elijah (Ilyās) in some Muslim stories, but al-Ṭabarī seems not to accept this identification; see nn. 19, 665, below. See also I. Friedlaender, *Die Chadirlegende und der Alexanderroman.*

2. Qurʾān 18:61 says simply "Moses and his servant," not mentioning Joshua by name. This story is found in al-Thaʿlabī, *Qiṣaṣ al-anbiyāʾ*, 192–94, 199–203. Biblical names will be given in their usual English equivalents when actually referring to biblical figures, as here. Joshua: Yūshaʿ.

3. Abū Jaʿfar is the *kunyah* of al-Ṭabarī, the author of this work, and this is his usual manner of interpolating his own views.

4. Afrīdhūn, Middle Persian Frēdōn, Avestan Θraētaona, a Persian mythical hero

first scriptuaries, and before[5] the days of Moses b. Amram.[6] Still others say he was over the vanguard of Dhū al-Qarnayn the Elder,[7] who lived in the days of Abraham, the Friend of the Merciful.[8] Dhū al-Qarnayn passed judgment in favor of Abraham in Beersheba,[9] at an arbitration Abraham brought before him concerning a well that he had dug for his cattle in the desert of Jordan.[10] Abraham brought them for arbitration before Dhū al-Qarnayn, about whom it was mentioned that al-Khiḍr was over his vanguard during the days when he journeyed in the lands; the dispute arose when a group of people of Jordan also claimed this same land. Also, al-Khiḍr reached the River of Life and drank its water unawares; Dhū al-Qarnayn and

---

(see F. Justi, *Iranisches Namenbuch*, 331; M. Mayrhofer, *Die altiranischen Namen*, 81–82 no. 312). He defeated the three-headed dragon or dragon king, Avestan (Aži) Dahāka, Middle Persian Aždahāg, Persian Ẓaḥḥāk/Ẓoḥ(ḥ)āk, Arabic al-Ḍaḥḥāk (see al-Ṭabarī, I, 226–30, trans. Brinner, 23–27; see also Aždahā ii, in *Enc. Ir.* III/2, esp. 195–96). The name *Athfiyān*, Middle Persian *Aspiyān* (cf. B. T. Anklesaria, *Zand-Ākāsīh*, 292–95, chap. 35.8), is from Avestan *Āθwyāna-*, a patronymic meaning "descendent of Āθwya" (see Justi, *op. cit.*, 49; Mayrhofer, *op. cit.*, 30 no. 75; *Enc. Ir.* I/3, p. 248, s.v. Ābtīn, with additional bibliography in *Enc. Ir.* III/1 p. 27, s.v. Āθviya). In the Avesta, in *Yasna* 9.7 (the *Hōm yašt*), Āθwya is said to have been the second human to have pressed the Haoma (cf. n. 639, below), for which he received the fortune of fathering Θraētaona, who killed the dragon.

5. Text has *wa-qīla* "and it was said," but Ibrāhīm, *Taʾrīkh al-Ṭabarī*, I, 365, and Ibn al-Athīr, *al-Kāmil fī al-taʾrīkh*, I, 160, read *qabla* as "before."

6. Arabic: Mūsā b. ʿImrān.

7. Lit. "the two-horned." Generally identified by Muslim and modern Western scholars with Alexander the Great (356–23 B.C.); see *EI*², s.v. "al-Iskandar." Here *al-akbar* "the elder" is used to distinguish a hypothetical, more ancient figure from the historical Alexander, who lived much later. For the connection of this story with the Alexander romance, see no. 1, above. It is significant that the only Qurʾānic mention of Dhū al-Qarnayn is immediately after this story, in 18:84–99. He was considered a *muʾmin* in Islamic tradition, but scholars disputed whether or not he was a prophet. His deeds, like the search for the River of Life, are recorded in collections of tales of the prophets; see al-Thaʿlabī, *op. cit.*, 322–32. See also Friedlaender, *op. cit.*, 276–301. The life of the "historical" Dhū al-Qarnayn is recorded by al-Ṭabarī, I, 692–703, (trans. Perlmann, 87–95).

8. Arabic: Ibrāhīm. Traditionally known in Islam as "the friend of Allah." Al-Ṭabarī here attempts to coordinate early Israelite and Persian chronology and will later attempt to do the same with Greco-Roman and Persian chronology.

9. Arabic: Biʾr al-Sabaʿ; See Genesis 21:22–34 for the story of Abraham and his covenant with Abimelech, king of Gerar, at Beersheba.

10. Al-Urdunn, the name usually used in Arabic for the district (*jund*) west and southwest of the Damascus district, comprising Galilee and the Jordan valley down to the Dead Sea. The area west and south of this, including Beersheba, the Roman Palaestina Prima, was known by the Arabs as Filasṭīn; see G. Le Strange, *Palestine under the Moslems*. 24ff.

his companions did not know [that he drank it]. So he became immortal and remains alive until now.[11]

A scholar claimed that al-Khiḍr was the offspring of a man who believed in Abraham, the Friend of the Merciful, and followed him [415] in his religion, emigrating with him from Babylon when Abraham emigrated.[12] He [also] said that his name was Baliyā b. Malikān[13] b. Peleg b. Eber b. Shelah b. Arphachshad b. Shem b. Noah and that his father was a powerful king. Others say that Dhū al-Qarnayn, who lived in the era of Abraham, was Afrīdhūn b. Athfiyān,[14] and that over the vanguard of Dhū al-Qarnayn was al-Khiḍr.

ʿAbdallāh b. Shawdhab[15] said about him what ʿAbd al-Raḥmān b. ʿAbdallāh b. ʿAbd al-Ḥakam al-Miṣrī[16] related to us — Muḥammad b. al-Mutawakkil[17] — Ḍamrah b. Rabīʿah[18] — ʿAbdallāh b. Shawdhab: Al-Khiḍr was of the progeny of Persia, while Elijah was an Israelite.[19] The two met every year during the annual festival season.[20]

---

11. The story of the River of Life, bathing in which makes creatures immortal, is an element of the Syriac Alexander romance, in which Alexander's cook, Andreas, sees a salted fish he is washing in a spring come to life and swim away. Andreas jumps in and gains immortality, but Alexander's later efforts to find the spring fail; see *EI*², s. vv. "Iskandar Nāma," "Idrīs" (i.e., Andreas). In Jewish tradition the River of Life flows out of Paradise; see L. Ginzberg, *The Legends of the Jews,* V, 92 n. 51.

12. An effort to place al-Khiḍr in history as a contemporary of Abraham. See n. 8, above.

13. MS BM without pointing, also possibly *Yaliyā.* These two names, unlike the remainder of those given here, are not biblical. In Genesis 11:19 Peleg's son is Reu, as also in al-Ṭabarī, I, 217 (trans. Brinner, 16). The genealogy given here would make Baliyā a contemporary of Nahor, the grandfather of Abraham.

14. Here the attempt is made to associate "the elder" Dhū al-Qarnayn with Persian mythical history.

15. ʿAbdallah b. Shawdhab, mentioned as coming from Beirut by Yāqūt, *Kitāb muʿjam al-buldān,* I, 785. Possibly the son of Shawhab Abū Muʿādh, who is mentioned without biographical notice in Ibn Saʿd, *Kitāb al-ṭabaqāt,* VI, 248. As ʿAbdallāh is at the beginning of the *isnād* given here, he must have lived at the end of the second/eighth or the very beginning of the third/ninth century.

16. ʿAbd al-Raḥmān b. ʿAbdallāh b. ʿAbd al-Ḥakam, d. 257/871. A Malikī jurist and the noted historian of the Muslim conquest of Egypt and the Maghrib. See *GAL,* I, 148, Suppl. I, 227; B. Dodge, ed., *The Fihrist of al-Nadīm,* II, 940.

17. Muḥammad b. al-Mutawakkil b. ʿAbd al-Raḥmān al-Luʾluʾī al-Baṣrī Ruways, d. 238/852. See *GAS,* I, 13

18. Ḍamrah b. Rabīʿah, d. 202/817–818, a reliable transmitter, according to Ibn Saʿd, *op. cit.,* VII/2, 173.

19. A clear effort by al-Ṭabarī to separate al-Khiḍr from the association with Elijah, whose story is found in the Bible, 1 Kings 17–2 Kings 2.

20. *Mawsim,* either an annually recurring festival or a regular assembly or reunion; see Dozy, *Supplément aux Dictionnaires arabes,* II, 813–14, s.v. *wsm.*

Ibn Isḥāq[21] said about al-Khiḍr — Ibn Ḥumayd[22] — Salamah[23] — Ibn Isḥāq: God appointed to rule over the Israelites a man named Josiah b. Amon,[24] and He sent al-Khiḍr to them as a prophet. He said that al-Khiḍr's name, according to what Wahb b. Munabbih[25] claimed, on the authority of the Israelites, was Jeremiah b. Hilkiah
[416] from the tribe of Aaron b. Amram.[26] Between this king, whom Ibn Isḥāq mentioned, and Afrīdhūn there was a period of more than one thousand years.

The words of the one who said that al-Khiḍr lived in the days of Afrīdhūn and Dhū al-Qarnayn the Elder before Moses b. Amram are nearer to the truth[27] — *unless* we accept the other report, that he was over the vanguard of Dhū al-Qarnayn, the companion of Abraham, and drank the water of life. Then, however, he was not sent as a

21. Muḥammad b. Isḥāq b. Yasār al-Muṭṭalabī al-Madanī, 85–150/704–67. A famous and reliable traditionist and biographer of the Prophet. Ibn Saᶜd, *op. cit.*, VII/2, 67; *GAL*, I, 134, Suppl. I, 205; *GAS*, I, 288–90; *EI*², s.v. "Ibn Isḥāk." See biography and evaluation of his work by G. D. Newby, *The Making of the Last Prophet*, 5–25.

22. Muḥammad b. Ḥumayd b. Ḥayyān al-Rāzī, d 248/862. A frequently cited transmitter of tradition, especially, as here, from Salamah—Ibn Isḥāq. See Ibn Ḥajar, *Tahdhīb al-tahdhīb*, IX, 127–31; *GAS*, I, 29, 30, 79, 242, 253; Kh. al-Ziriklī, *al-Aᶜlām*, VI, 343.

23. Salamah b. al-Faḍl al-Anṣārī, al-Abrash, d. 191/807. Traditionist, historian of *maghāzī*, and judges in al-Rayy. A companion of Ibn Isḥāq, from whom he was a trusted transmitter. See Ibn Saᶜd, *op. cit.*, VII/2, 110; Ibn Ḥajar, *op. cit.*, IV, 153–54. Briefly noted in *GAL*, Suppl. I, 205.

24. Nāshiyah b. Amūṣ. Perhaps a scribal error for Yāshiyah b. Amūn (MS BM without pointing), i.e., Josiah b. Amon, king of Judah in 640–609 B. C. E., who, together with Hilkiah the priest, carried out the religious revival in Judah known as the Josianic reformation. Elijah prophesied in the kingdom of Israel under the Omrid dynasty — Omri, Ahab, Ahaziah, and Joram, 876–42 B. C. E. — or two hundred years earlier. See 2 Kings 21:24–23:30. The substitution of *Amūṣ* for *Amūn* may have been influenced by the patronymic of the prophet Isaiah (Arabic: Shaᶜya b. Amūṣ); see n. 26, below.

25. A major authority for biblical lore based on the text of the Bible, postbiblical Jewish legends, and Islamic (often Qurʾānic) material. See R. G. Khoury, *Wahb ibn Munabbih*. See also *GAL*, Suppl. I, 101; *GAS*, I, 305–7.

26. Jeremiah the prophet b. Hilkiah the priest lived in Judah during the reigns of its last kings, from Josiah to Zedekiah 597–87 B. C. E., hence about one hundred years after Isaiah and more than two hundred years after Elijah. Note the occurrence of the name Hilkiah, which may be the link to Josiah (Nāshiyah). There seems to be confusion between Josiah (b. Amon)/Yūshiya (b. Amūn) (al-Ṭabarī, I, 643 [trans. Perlmann, 40]) and Shaᶜya/Yāshiyah (Isaiah) b. Amūṣ/Amoz (al-Ṭabarī, I, 657–58 [trans. Perlmann, 55]).

27. *Ashbahu bi-al-ḥaqq*. Ibn al-Athīr, *op. cit.*, I, 161, has *ashbahu li-al-ḥadīth al-ṣaḥīḥ*, "nearer to the sound tradition."

prophet in the days of Abraham, but during the days of Josiah b. Amon, because Josiah b. Amon, whom Ibn Isḥāq mentioned as being king over the Israelites, lived during the era of Bishtāsb b. Luhrāsb.[28] Between Bishtāsb and Afrīdhūn were eras and periods of which everyone knowledgeable about human history and its accounts is aware. I shall mention the sum of that when we reach the account of Bishtāsb, God willing.

We have said that the words of the one who said that al-Khiḍr was before Moses b. Amram were closer to the truth than the words of Ibn Isḥāq. The latter related from Wahb b. Munabbih only because of the account narrated from the Messenger of God by Ubayy b. Kaᶜb,[29] that the companion of Moses b. Amram, who was a learned man whom God commanded Moses to seek out because he thought that there was no one on earth more knowledgeable than he, was al-Khiḍr. The Messenger of God was the most knowledgeable of God's creatures regarding past, as well as future, events.[30] [417]

That which Ubayy b. Kaᶜb narrated to us about [al-Khiḍr] from him is what Abū Kurayb[31] related — Yaḥyā b. Ādam[32] — Sufyān b.

28. Bishtāsf b. Luhrāsb (in Arabic texts also written Bistāsf or Yastāsb, see al-Ṭabarī, I, 416 n. *e*; in Persian the form Gushtāsp is also frequent), is Middle Persian [Kay] Wištāsp or Kay Wištāsp, son of Luhrāsp (cf. Anklesaria, *op. cit.*, 296–97, chap. 35.35), Avestan Vištāspa, or Kavi Vištāspa, son of Aurvaṯ.aspa (*Yašt* 5.105 [*Ardwīsūr yašt*]; see Justi, *op. cit.*, 372; Mayrhofer and Schmitt, *op. cit.*, 26 no. 57, 97 no. 379). The Avestan Vištāspa, who was Zarathustra's patron, became confused in the later tradition with Old Persian Vištāspa, Greek Hystaspes, the father of Darius I (see M. Boyce, *A History of Zoroastrianism* II, 41, 68). According to the *Shāhnāmah* Luhrāsb was the fourteenth king to rule over Iran. For al-Ṭabarī's account of Luhrāsb and Bishtāsb, see I, 645–49 (trans. Perlmann, 43–47). The point of this paragraph is that, if we accept the story of al-Khiḍr's drinking the Water of Life, we can accept *both* synchronisms: with Abraham and Dhū al-Qarnayn, as well as with Josiah.

29. Ubayy b. Kaᶜb, d. 21/642, associate of the Prophet and one of the earliest transmitters of prophetic traditions. See Ibn Saᶜd, *op. cit.*, III, 2, 59; *GAS*, I, 3, 5, 14, 29, 404; al-Ziriklī, *op. cit.*, I, 78; Dodge, *op. cit.*, II, 1116.

30. This statement both bolsters the authority of traditions linking al-Khiḍr with the Qurʾānic tale and emphasizes the superiority of the Prophet Muḥammad over other prophets; hence al-Ṭabarī's preference for this version of the story of al-Khiḍr. See the study of this story in H. Schwarzbaum, "The Jewish and Moslem Versions of Some Theodicy Legends."

31. Muḥammad b. al-ᶜAlāʾ, one of the earliest traditionists, lived in al-Kūfah. See Ibn Saᶜd, *op. cit.*, VI, 289; Dodge, *op. cit.*, II, 1033.

32. Yaḥyā b. Ādam b. Sulaymān, Abū Zakariyā, d. 203/818–19, a jurist and authority on tradition. See Ibn Saᶜd, *op. cit.*, VI, 281; Dodge, *op. cit.*, II, 1124.

ʿUyaynah[33] — ʿAmr b. Dīnār[34] — Saʿīd:[35] I said to Ibn ʿAbbās[36] that Nawf[37] claimed that al-Khiḍr was not the companion of Moses. He said, "The enemy of God has lied! Ubayy b. Kaʿb related to us from the Messenger of God, saying that Moses rose to preach among the Israelites. Someone said, 'who of the people knows best?' and he replied, 'I do.' God reproved him when he did not attribute knowledge to Him, so He said, 'Nay, but I have a servant at the meeting place of the two seas.'[38] Moses said, 'O Lord! How can I find him?' He replied: 'Take a fish and put it in a basket. When you miss it, he will be there.'[39] Moses took a fish and put it in a basket. Then he said to his servant, 'If you miss this fish, tell me.' They set out walking along the shore of the river until they reached a large stone, where Moses went to sleep. The fish stirred in the basket, got out, and fell into the sea. God held the flow of the water so that it became like an opening and a tunnel for the fish. It was a wonder to both Moses and his servant, and then they set out.

When it was time for breakfast, Moses said to his servant: *'Bring us our breakfast. Verily we have become weary from our journey.'*[40]

---

33. Sufyān b. ʿUyaynah b. Abī ʿImrān, Abū Muḥammad, 107–99/725–814, a scholar of Qurʾān and law, famed for his piety. See Ibn Saʿd, *op. cit.*, VI, 364–65; Dodge, *op. cit.*, II, 1103.

34. ʿAmr b. Dīnār, 46–126/666–743, a jurist in Mecca of Persian origin and a trusted transmitter of tradition. See Ibn Ḥajar, *op. cit.*, VIII, 30; al-Ziriklī, *op. cit.*, V, 245; *GAS*, I, 800.

35. Here Saʿīd b. Jubayr al-Asadī, Abū ʿAbdallāh, 45–95/665–714. Studied with Ibn ʿAbbās and ʿAbdallāh b. ʿUmar. One of the most learned and important of the generation after that of the Prophet. One of the earliest Qurʾānic commentators. Executed by al-Ḥajjāj. See Ibn Saʿd, *op. cit.*, VI, 178–87; *GAS*, I, 28–29; Dodge, *op. cit.*, II, 1089.

36. ʿAbdallāh b. al-ʿAbbās, usually known as Ibn ʿAbbās, ca. 69–88/620–87. A cousin of the Prophet, involved in the political life of the early Muslim community but owing his renown to his knowledge of tradition, jurisprudence, and Qurʾānic exegesis. He was a controversial figure in his political life, and many forged traditions were attributed to him as well; see n. 237, below. See *EI²*, s.v. "ʿAbd Allāh b. al-ʿAbbās" 40–41. See also G. H. A. Juynboll, *The Authenticity of the Tradition Literature*, for modern Muslim discussions on this issue.

37. Nawf al-Bikālī b. Faḍālah al-Ḥimyarī, son of the wife of Kaʿb (al-Aḥbār), d. ca. 95/714, a traditionist mentioned in the two *Ṣaḥīḥ*s and a narrator of *qiṣaṣ* (tales). See Ibn Saʿd, *op. cit.*, VII/2, 160; al-Ziriklī, *op. cit.*, IX, 31.

38. *ʿInda majmaʿ al-baḥrayn*, lit. "at the joining (or gathering) of the two seas, or rivers." Variously interpreted in Islamic sources as "the place where the Persian Ocean unites with the Roman Sea" or the junction of the Roman Sea with the (Atlantic) Ocean. See *EI²*, s.v. "al-Khaḍir," 903–4; Friedlaender, *op. cit.*, pp. 302–4.

39. Based on Qurʾān 18:59, 18:64.

40. Qurʾān 18:63.

Moses did not become weary until he went beyond where God had commanded him. *Moses said: 'Did you see that, when we took refuge on the rock, I forgot the fish — and none but Satan caused me to forget it — and it found its way into the water by a marvel?' He said, 'This is what we have been seeking.' So they retraced their steps."*[41]

He relates that they came to the rock and "behold! there was a man sleeping, covered with his garment. Moses greeted him with peace, and the man said, 'Whence does this greeting come in our land?'[42] He said, 'I am Moses.' The man responded, 'Moses of the Israelites?' Moses replied, 'Yes.' The man continued, 'O Moses! I possess what God taught me of His knowledge that you do not know, while you possess what God taught you of His knowledge that I do not know.' Moses said, *'May I follow you, so that you may teach me the right conduct which you have been taught?'*[43] He said, *'If you go with me, do not ask me anything until I myself mention it to you.'*[44] So they set off, walking on the shore and lo! there was a sailor in a ship who knew al-Khiḍr, so he carried him without charge. A bird came and alighted on [the ship's] edge and pecked or picked[45] at the water. Al-Khiḍr said to Moses, 'My knowledge and yours are not less than God's knowledge, except for the amount that this bird pecks or picks at in the sea.' [Abū Jaʿfar said: I am uncertain, but I have taken the reading *nqr* as "pecks" in my book.][46] [418]

While they were on the ship, Moses was startled when al-Khiḍr drove a peg or pulled out a board.[47] Moses said to him: 'He carried

---

41. Qurʾān 18:64–65. *Saraban*, translated "by a marvel" by M. M. Pickthall, "in a wondrous sort" by J. M. Rodwell, "took its way freely" by G. Sale, "in a miraculous fashion" by N. J. Dawood, "in a manner marvelous" by A. J. Arberry, is translated by M. Kasimirski "par une voie souterraine." The latter is in keeping with E. W. Lane, *An Arabic-English Lexicon*, 1341–42: "a subterranean excavation."

42. *Wa-annā bi-arḍinā al-salām.* Perhaps "From whom comes [this greeting of] peace in our land?" See Schwarzbaum, *op. cit.*, 151. See, n. 68, below.

43. Qurʾān 18:67.

44. Qurʾān 18:71.

45. *Naqara aw naqada;* both words mean "to peck or pick at," as of a bird, though *naqada* also has the meaning of "to pick and separate." See Lane, *op. cit.*, 2836–37, s.v v. *nqd, nqr*.

46. *I.e.*, al-Ṭabarī reads *naqara*, rather than *naqada*. This is phrased more clearly below, p. 13, where the bird takes water from the sea.

47. *Takht;* see *Glossarium*, CXLIX, "tabula (planche)"; al-Nuwayrī has *lawḥ;* see al-Ṭabarī, I, 418 n. *m*.

us without charge. *Did you make a hole in this ship to drown the people? You have indeed done a dreadful thing.'* Al-Khiḍr replied, *'Did I not tell you that you could not bear with me?'* Moses said, *'Do not be angry with me that I forgot.'*[48] This was the first instance of Moses' forgetting.[49] Then the two of them got off the ship and
[419] went walking. When they saw a boy playing with other boys, al-Khiḍr took him by the head and slew him. Moses said to him: *'What! Have you slain an innocent soul who has slain no one? Verily you have done a horrid thing.'* Al-Khiḍr replied, *'Did I not tell you that you could not bear with me?'* Moses said: *'If I ask you about anything after this, do not keep company with me. You have received an excuse from me.'*[50]

They continued their journey until they reached a town where they asked the people to feed them, and found no one who would feed them or give them anything to drink. *They found there a wall about to fall into ruin and he (al-Khiḍr) repaired it* with his hand."[51] The narrator said: "He touched it with his hand. Moses said to him: 'They showed us no hospitality, nor did they give us shelter. *If you had wished, you could have taken payment for it.' He said, 'This is the parting between me and you.'*"[52] The Messenger of God said, "I would have liked him to have been patient so that he could have told us their story."

Al-ʿAbbās b. Al-Walīd[53]—my father—al-Awzāʿī[54]—al-Zuhrī[55]—

---

48. Qurʾān 18:72–74.

49. I.e., his promise, above, not to ask about anything until al-Khiḍr himself had mentioned it to him. Other instances follow.

50. Qurʾān 18:75–77.

51. Qurʾān 18:78.

52. Qurʾān 18:78–79. See the slightly different details in the Judeo-Arabic version; Nissim, *op. cit.*, 13–16.

53. Al-ʿAbbās b. al-Walīd b. Mazyad al-Āmulī al-Bayūtī. *Index*, 313. Not further identified.

54. Al-Awzāʿī, ʿAbd al-Raḥmān b. ʿAmr b. Yuḥmid, Abū ʿAmr, 88–157/707–74, founder of the Awzāʿī legal school, favored by the Umayyads in Syria and Spain. Transmitted from Qatādah and al-Zuhrī. *GAS*, I, 516–17; *GAL*, Suppl. I, 307; al-Ziriklī, *op. cit.*, IV, 94.

55. Al-Zuhrī, Muḥammad b. Muslim b. ʿUbaydallāh b. ʿAbdallāh b. Shihāb, Abū Bakr, ca. 50–124/670–742. A traditionist, historian, and expert in poetry, he played a leading role in the transmission and organization of prophetic *Ḥadīth* based on personal contact with the earliest links in the chain of transmitters. *GAS*, I, 280–83; *GAL*, I, 65, Suppl. I, 102.

ʿUbaydallāh b. ʿAbdallāh b. ʿUtbah b. Masʿūd[56]—Ibn ʿAbbās, who said that he and al-Ḥurr b. Qays b. Ḥiṣn al-Fazārī[57] had a dispute about the companion of Moses, and Ibn ʿAbbās said that he was al-Khiḍr. Ubayy b. Kaʿb passed by them, and Ibn ʿAbbās called him over, saying, "This companion of mine and I are disputing about the companion of Moses, who asked for the way to meet him. Did you hear the Messenger of God mention this matter?" [Ubayy] said, "Yes, I heard the Messenger of God say: 'While Moses was among a [420] crowd of the Israelites, a man came up to him and said, "Do you know where there is someone who knows more than you do?" Moses said, "No." Thereupon God inspired Moses, "Yes, Our servant al-Khiḍr." Moses inquired about the way to meet him. So God made the fish a sign, saying, "When you have forgotten the fish, return, for you will meet al-Khiḍr." Moses then followed the traces of the fish and said, *"This is what we have been seeking." So they retraced their steps,*[58] and they found al-Khiḍr. Their meeting was as God has related in His Book.'"

Muḥammad b. Marzūq[59] related to me—Ḥajjāj b. al-Minhāl[60]—ʿAbdallāh b. ʿUmar al-Numayrī[61]—Yūnus b. Yazīd:[62] I heard al-Zuhrī relating traditions, saying: ʿUbaydallāh b. ʿAbdallāh b. ʿUtbah b. Masʿūd—Ibn ʿAbbās that he and al-Ḥurr b. Qays b. Ḥiṣn al-Fazārī were disputing about the companion of Moses; his account was similar to the report of al-ʿAbbās on the authority of his father.[63]

Muḥammad b. Saʿd[64]—my father—my uncle—my father—his father—Ibn ʿAbbās, about His words: *And when Moses said to his*

---

56. ʿUbaydallāh b. ʿAbdallāh b. ʿUtbah b. Masʿūd al-Hudhalī, Abū ʿAbdallāh, d. 98/716. A jurist of Medina and a noted poet, he was a teacher of the caliph ʿUmar II. Al-Ziriklī, *op. cit.*, IV, 350.

57. Al-Ḥurr b. Qays b. Ḥiṣn al-Fazārī. *Index*, 126. Not further identified.

58. Qurʾān 18:65.

59. Muḥammad b. Marzūq. *Index*, 528. Not further identified.

60. (Al-)Ḥajjāj b. al-Minhāl al-Anamāṭī, Abū Muḥammad, d. 217/832, a reliable transmitter of many traditions. Died in al-Baṣrah. Ibn Saʿd, *op. cit.*, VII/2, 53.

61. ʿAbdallāh b. ʿUmar al-Numayrī. *Index*, 332. Not further identified.

62. Yūnus b. Yazīd b. Abī al-Nijād al-Aylī, Abū Yazīd, d. ca. 158/775. A student and transmitter of al-Zuhrī. See Ibn Saʿd, *op. cit.*, VII/2, 206; *GAS*, I, 519.

63. *I.e.*, the account in the previous paragraph by al-ʿAbbās b. al-Walīd—Ubayy.

64. Muḥammad b. Saʿd b. Manī al-Baṣrī, Abū ʿAbdallāh, Kātib al-Wāqidī, 168–230/784–845. His major work, *Kitāb al-ṭabaqāt al-kabīr*, is one of the main sources for the life of the Prophet and for the major traditionists up to the year of his death. *GAS*, I, 300–1; *GAL*, I, 136, Suppl., I, 208; Dodge, *op. cit.*, II, 1058.

servant, I will not give up until I reach the point where the two rivers meet ... [65] [Ibn ʿAbbās] said, When Moses and his people were victorious over Egypt, his people settled in Egypt. When their residence there became fixed, God revealed to Moses: "Remind them of the days of God."[66] So he preached to his people and mentioned the
[421] good that God had given them, as well as the pleasure. He reminded them that God had saved them from the people of Pharaoh, [how] their enemy had perished, and also how He had appointed them vicars in the land. Then Moses said: "God spoke to me, your prophet, in speech, chose me for Himself, and sent revelation to me out of His love. God has brought you everything you have asked of Him. Your prophet is the best of the people of the earth, and you are reading the Torah." Moses did not leave one kindness that God had shown them unmentioned, reminding them of everything.

One of the Israelites said to him: "It is so, O Prophet of God! We know what you are saying. But is there on earth anyone who knows more than you, O Prophet of God?" Moses said, "No." So God sent Gabriel to Moses, who said, "Verily, God says, "How do you know where I have placed My knowledge? Indeed, there is a man on the shore of the sea who knows more than you.'" Ibn ʿAbbās said that this is al-Khiḍr. Moses asked his Lord to show this man to him, so God inspired him: "Go to the sea, and you will find a fish on the shore. Take it and give it to your servant; then stay on the shore of the sea. But if you forget the fish and it disappears from you, then you will find the pious servant whom you seek."

When the journey of Moses, the Prophet of God, became long and he became tired, he asked his servant about the fish, and his servant —his young man—said to him: *"Did you see that, when we took refuge on the rock and I forgot the fish, none but Satan caused me to forget to mention it* to you?" The servant said to him, "I saw the fish when *it took its way into the waters by way of a marvel."*[67] This
[422] caused Moses to wonder, and he turned back until he came to the rock and found the fish. The fish began to move in the sea, and Moses followed it. He began to use his staff to stir the water away from the fish, in order to follow the fish. Whatever the fish touched

65. Qurʾān 18:61.
66. *I.e.,* in which He manifested His justice or mercy.
67. Qurʾān 18:64. See n. 41, above.

dried up and became a rock. God's prophet wondered at this, until the fish led him to one of the islands of the sea, where he met al-Khiḍr. Moses greeted him with peace, and al-Khiḍr said: "And upon you be peace. Whence comes this [greeting of] peace in this land?[68] And who are you?" Moses replied, "I am Moses." Al-Khiḍr said to him, "The master of the Israelites?" He responded, "Yes." Then al-Khiḍr welcomed him and said, "What has brought you?" He said, "I came *so that you may teach me the right conduct that you have been taught."* He replied, *"Lo! you cannot bear with me"*[69]—saying "You cannot do that." Moses said, *"God willing, you will find me patient, and I shall not contradict you in anything."*[70] So he went with al-Khiḍr, who said to him: *"Do not ask me about anything* I do until I explain its matter to you"—for that is His word: *"until I mention it to you myself."*[71] They sailed on a ship, desiring to cross over to the dry land, but al-Khiḍr arose and made a hole in the ship. Moses said to him: *"Have you made a hole in this ship to drown its people? Verily you have done a dreadful thing."*[72] Then [Ibn ʿAbbās] mentioned the rest of the story.

Ibn Ḥumayd—Yaʿqūb al-Qummī[73]—Hārūn b. ʿAntarah[74]—his father—Ibn ʿAbbās: Moses asked his Lord, saying, "O Lord! which of Your servants is most beloved by You?" He responded, "The one who remembers Me and does not forget Me." Moses said, "And which of Your servants is best in judging?" He responded, "He who judges with right and does not follow his fancy." Moses continued, "O Lord! which of Your servants is the wisest?" He responded, "The one to whose knowledge the people's knowledge aspires, so that it [423] might attain a word that will lead one to guidance or turn one away from evil." Moses said, "Lord! is there anyone on earth?" Abū Jaʿfar said, "I think he meant 'Who knows more than I?'" God said, "Yes." Moses said, "Lord! who is he?" He replied, "al-Khiḍr." Moses asked,

68. *Wa-annā yakūnu hādhā al-salām bi-hādhihi al-arḍ;* see the similar statement, n. 42, above.

69. Qur'ān 18:67–68.

70. Qur'ān 18:70.

71. Qur'ān 18:71.

72. Qur'ān 18:72.

73. Yaʿqūb b. ʿAbdallāh al-Ashʿarī al-Qummī, mentioned by name only; Ibn Saʿd, *op. cit.,* VII/2, 111.

74. Hārūn b. ʿAntarah. *Index,* 605. Not further identified.

"Where shall I seek him?" He replied, "On the shore at the rock where the fish will get away."

Then Moses began seeking al-Khiḍr, until he met up with him at the rock, as God had mentioned would happen. Each greeted the other, and Moses said to him, "I want you to take me along as a companion." Al-Khiḍr responded, "You will not be able to bear my company." He said, "Yes, I can." Al-Khiḍr said, "If you accompany me, do not ask me about anything until I mention it to you." They set out until, when they were sailing on the ship, al-Khiḍr made a hole in it, and Moses said: *"Have you made a hole in this ship to drown its people? Verily you have done a dreadful thing."*[75] Al-Khiḍr replied, "Did I not say to you that *you cannot bear with me?*"[76] Moses said, *"Do not be angry with me because I forgot, and do not be hard on me for my fault."* They set out until they met a young lad, whom al-Khiḍr slew. Moses said: *"What! Have you slain an innocent soul who has slain no one? Verily you have done a horrid thing."* [(Al-Khiḍr) said, *"Did I not tell you that you could not bear with me?"* (Moses) said, *"If I ask you anything after this, do not keep company with me.*] *You have received an excuse from me."*[77]

Moses' words regarding the wall were for himself and for his seeking some gain in this world, while his words regarding the ship and the lad were for the sake of God. Al-Khiḍr said, *"This is the parting between you and me! I will announce to you the interpretation of what you could not bear with patience."*[78] Then he related to him: *"As for the ship [it belonged to poor people working on the river. I wished to mar it because there was a king behind them who is taking every ship by force]. And as for the lad [his parents were believers, and we feared that he would oppress them by rebellion and disbelief. And we intended that their Lord should change him for them for one better in purity and closer to mercy]. And as for the wall [it belonged to two orphan boys in the city. There was a treasure beneath it belonging to them, and their father had been pious, and your Lord intended that they should come to their full strength*

75. Qur'ān 18:72.
76. Qur'ān 18:68.
77. Qur'ān 18:74–77. The section in brackets is omitted in the text, with the phrase "to where He said" indicating that the educated Muslim would know the omitted portion.
78. Qur'ān 18:79.

and should bring forth their treasure as a mercy from their Lord; and I did not do it on my own command. Such is the interpretation of what you could not bear."[79] He continued: Then he journeyed on the sea with him, until they reached the meeting place of the two [424] seas, than which no place on earth has more water. He said, "Your Lord sent the swallow, and it began to take water with its beak." Al-Khiḍr said to Moses, "How much do you think this swallow takes away from this water?" He said, "How little it diminishes it!" Al-Khiḍr said, "O Moses! My knowledge and your knowledge are to God's knowledge like the quantity of this water that this swallow drinks." Moses had thought to himself that there was no one wiser than [this man] or who had uttered [anything like] this, and for that reason he had been commanded to go to al-Khiḍr.

Ibn Ḥumayd related to us—Salamah—Muḥammad b. Isḥāq—al-Ḥasan b. ʿUmārah[80]—al-Ḥakam b. ʿUtaybah[81]—Saʿīd b. Jubayr: I was sitting with Ibn ʿAbbās and several People of the Book, and one of them said: "O Abū al-ʿAbbās, Nawf, the son of the wife of Kaʿb, mentioned on Kaʿb's authority that Moses the prophet, who searched for the sage, was none other than Moses b. Manasseh."[82] Saʿīd said, "Then Ibn ʿAbbās replied, 'Did Nawf say that?'" Saʿīd said, "I told him, 'Yes, I heard Nawf say that.' Ibn ʿAbbās said, 'You heard him, O Saʿīd?' He replied, "I said, 'Yes.' Ibn ʿAbbās said, 'Nawf lied.' Then Ibn ʿAbbās said, ʿUbayy b. Kaʿb related to me—the Messenger of God that Moses, the prophet of Israel, asked his Lord saying, "O Lord, if there is among Your servants one who knows more than I, lead me to him." God replied, "Yes, among My servants is one who knows more than you." Then He described his location and gave Moses permission to meet him. Moses set out, his servant accompanying him, with a salted fish about which he had been told,

---

79. Qurʾān 18:80–83. Texts in brackets omitted by al-Ṭabarī, who writes after the first words of each verse "*al-āya,*" i.e., "[the rest of] the verse."

80. Al-Ḥasan b. ʿUmārah. *Index,* 134. Not further identified.

81. Al-Ḥakam b. ʿUtaybah al-Asadī (al-Kindī), Abū ʿAbdallāh, d. 113/731. *GAS,* I, 65; Ibn Saʿd, *op. cit.,* VI, 231.

82. Mūsā b. Mīshā b. Yūsuf. According to al-Thaʿlabī, *op. cit.,* 126, and Ibn al-Athīr, *op. cit.,* I, 160, while some Israelites thought that he and not Moses b. Amram was the companion of al-Khiḍr, other scholars generally held that it was the latter Moses. Al-Thaʿlabī states that Mūsā b. Mīshā was a messenger, who called his people back to the worship of God and performance of His commandments two hundred years before the birth of Moses b. Amram.

[425] "If this fish comes to life in a certain place, then your companion is there too, and you will have attained your desire." So Moses went forth with his servant, both carrying the fish. He traveled until the journey exhausted him, reaching the rock and the water. Since the water was the water of life, whoever drank of it became eternal, and no dead thing could draw near to it without life entering it, making it alive. When they settled down there and the fish touched the water, it became alive, and *it took its way into the waters, being free,*[83] and it swam away. When they had gone beyond a day's journey, Moses said to his servant, *"Bring us our breakfast. Verily we are fatigued from our journey."* The servant spoke, saying, *"Did you see, when we took refuge on the rock, and I forgot the fish—none other than Satan caused me to forget to mention it—it took its way into the waters by a marvel."*[84]

Ibn ʿAbbās said: "Moses became aware of the rock as they reached it, and lo! there was a man there wrapped in a garment. Moses greeted him, and he returned the greeting, saying, 'Who are you?' He replied, 'I am Moses b. Amram.' The man asked, 'Master of the Israelites?' He replied, 'Yes, I am the one.' So he said, 'What has brought you to this land, for you must be busy with your people?' Moses said to him, 'I have come to you so you can teach me the right conduct which you have been taught.'[85] The man said to him, *'Lo! you cannot bear with me.'*[86] He was a man who used esoteric knowledge[87] that he had learned. Moses said, 'I certainly can.' He said, *'How can you bear with what you cannot encompass in knowledge?'*[88] In other words, 'You know only what is obvious about
[426] justice, but you have not encompassed the esoteric knowledge that I know.' Moses said, *'God willing, you will find me patient, and I shall not contradict you in anything,* even though I see something that offends me.' The man replied, *'If you go with me, do not ask me about anything until I mention it to you myself.'*[89] In other words,

83. Qurʾān 18:62.
84. Qurʾān 18:63–64. See discussion of *saraban,* n. 41, above.
85. Based on Qurʾān 18:67.
86. Qurʾān 18:68.
87. *Yaʿmalu ʿalā al-ghayb.* See *Glossarium,* CCCXCIII.
88. Qurʾān 18:69.
89. Qurʾān 18:70–71.

'Don't ask me about anything even if you disapprove of it, until I mention it to you.'

The two of them set out walking along the shore of the sea, encountering people and seeking someone to provide them with transportation, when a new, reliable ship passed by, a ship better than any that had passed by them, more beautiful and more trustworthy. They asked the people on the ship to carry them, and they agreed. When they felt secure on the ship and it set out upon the sea, al-Khiḍr took out a chisel and a mallet he carried with him. He made his way to a section of the ship, where he struck the side with the chisel until it made a hole. Then he took a plank and covered the hole, sitting upon it to patch it. Moses said to him: 'What can be more abominable than this? *Have you made that hole to drown the people? You have indeed done a dreadful thing.*[90] The people carried us, giving us shelter in their ship, unlike any other ship on the sea. Why did you pierce it?' He replied, *'Did I not tell you that you could not bear with me?' Moses said to him, 'Do not be angry with me because I forgot*—namely, I abandoned your agreement—*and don't be hard on me for my fault.'*[91]

Then they left the ship, walking until they came to the people of a town, and lo! there were boys playing. Among them was a boy who was more handsome, more delicate, cleaner than the other boys. Al-Khiḍr took him by the hand, grabbed a stone, and hit him on the head until he killed him. Thus Moses saw something abominable, which he could not bear: He had taken a young lad without wrongdoing or sin. So Moses said, *'Have you slain an innocent soul who has slain* [427]
no one?—namely, someone small who has killed no one—*Verily you have done a horrid thing.'* Al-Khiḍr replied, *'Did I not tell you that you could not bear with me?' He replied: 'If I ask you about anything after this, do not keep company with me. You have received an excuse from me'*[92]—that is to say, 'You have been excused regarding a matter concerning me.'

The two of them continued on until, when they came to the people of another town, they asked them for food, but they refused to

90. Qur'ān 18:72.
91. Qur'ān 18:73–74.
92. Qur'ān 18:75–77.

extend hospitality to them. Then the two of them found a wall threatening to fall down, which [al-Khiḍr] set upright.[93] He proceeded to destroy it, and then he began to rebuild it. Moses was exasperated by what he saw al-Khiḍr doing, and such hypocrisy he could not bear. *He said, 'If you had wished, you could have been paid for it'*[94]—meaning: 'We asked the people for food, but they did not feed us; we asked them for hospitality, and they did not extend it; then you began to work without pay, when, if you had wished, you could have been paid for it.' *He said: 'This is the parting between me and you! I will give you the interpretation of those events that you could not bear with patience. As for the ship, it belonged to poor people working on the river. I wished to mar it because there was a king behind them who is taking every ship by force.'"*[95]—the reading of Ubayy b. Kaʿb has *"every useful ship by force"*—"'but I marred it only to avert him from taking it. It was safe when he saw the defect that I caused. *As for the lad, his parents were believers, and we feared that he would oppress them by rebellion and disbelief. And we intended that their Lord should change him for one better in purity and closer to mercy. And as for the wall, it belonged to two orphan boys in the city. There was a treasure beneath it be-*
[428] *longing to them, and their father had been pious'* . . . to . . . *'what you could not bear.'"*[96]

Ibn Ḥumayd related to us—Salamah—Muḥammad b. Isḥāq—al-Ḥasan b. ʿUmārah—his father—ʿIkrimah:[97] Someone said to Ibn ʿAbbās, "We have not heard any mention of an account about the servant of Moses, although he was with him." Ibn ʿAbbās mentioned the narrative of the servant, saying, "The servant drank the water of eternal life and became immortal. The learned sage took him, fitted him with a ship, then sent him out to sea. The ship will rock on the sea with him until the Day of Resurrection, because he drank from the river, which he should not have done."

---

93. Qurʾān 18:78.
94. Qurʾān 18:78.
95. Qurʾān 18:79–80.
96. Qurʾān 18:81–83. For the full text of the last verse, see pp. 12–13, above.
97. ʿIkrimah b. ʿAbdallāh al-Barbarī al-Madanī, Abū ʿAbdallāh, 25–105/645–723. A slave of Ibn ʿAbbās, later set free, he became an expert on the life of the Prophet, the Qurʾān, and the *maghāzī*. *GAS*, I, 23, 24, 26, 81, 91, 243, 285; *GAL*, Suppl. I, 691; Ibn Saʿd, *op. cit.*, V, 212–16; al-Ziriklī, *op. cit.*, V, 43–44.

Bishr b. Muʿādh[98] related to us — Yazīd[99] — Shuʿbah[100] — Qatādah[101]: His words: *And when they reached the point where the two met, they forgot their fish.*[102] It was mentioned to us that, when the Prophet of God, Moses, split the sea and God saved him from the people of Pharaoh, he gathered the Israelites and addressed them, saying "You are the best people on earth and the most learned. God has destroyed your enemy, has made you cross the sea, and has revealed the Torah to you." Someone said to him, "There is a man wiser than you." So he and his servant Joshua b. Nun set out to seek him. They were supplied with provisions of a salted fish in a large basket. Someone said to them, "When you forget what you have, you will meet a learned man who is called al-Khiḍr." When they came to that place, God restored life to the fish, and it crawled from the shore[103] until it swam into the sea. Then it journeyed on, and every road it traversed became solid water. He continued: Moses and his [429]
servant went on. God says, "*And when they had gone farther, he said to his servant: 'Bring us our breakfast. Verily we have become tired from our journey*... to where He says... '*[Then they found one of Our servants, unto whom We had given mercy from Us and] had taught him knowledge from Our Presence.*'"[104] The two of them met a wise man called al-Khiḍr. It has been mentioned to us that the Prophet of God said: "Al-Khiḍr was called green, because he sat on a white fur and it shimmered green with him."

---

98. Bishr b. Muʿādh al-ʿAqadī al-Baṣrī, Abū Sahl, d. ca. 245/859. An authority on *Ḥadīth,* who taught al-Ṭabarī. Ibn Ḥajar, *op. cit.*, I, 458; *GAS*, I, 32, 92.

99. Yazīd b. Hārūn b. Zādān al-Wāsiṭī, Abū Khālid, 118–206/736–821. A *mawlā* of the Banū Sulaym, he wrote a commentary on the Qurʾān and was a traditionist. *GAS*, I, 40; Ibn Ḥajar, *op. cit.*, XI, 366–69. Ibn Saʿd, *op. cit.*, VII/2, p. 62; al-Ziriklī, *op. cit.*, IX, 247; Dodge, *op. cit.*, II, 1127.

100. Shuʿbah b. al-Ḥajjāj b. al-Ward al-ʿAtakī al-Azdī, Abū Bisṭām, 82–160/701–76. One of the earliest *Ḥadīth* scholars to order them systematically and to treat the biographies of the traditionists in a scholarly manner. *GAS*, I, 92; Ibn Saʿd, *op. cit.*, VII/2, 60–118/280–81; al-Ziriklī, *op. cit.*, III, 241–42; Dodge, *op. cit.*, II, 1100.

101. Qatādah b. Diʿāmah b. Qatādah al-Sadūsī, Abū al-Khaṭṭāb, 60–119/679–736. Blind from birth, noted for his memory in fields of lexicography, Qurʾān exegesis, law, poetry, genealogy, and history, he transmitted from such Companions of the Prophet as Anas b. Mālik and gave the Muʿtazilah their name. Ibn Saʿd, *op. cit.*, VII/2, 229–31; Ibn Ḥajar, *op. cit.*, VIII, 351–56; *GAS*, I, 31–32; *EI*², s.v. "Ḳatāda b. Diʿāma."

102. Qurʾān 18:62.

103. *Min al-jadd.* MS BM has *al-ḥadd* "the edge."

104. Qurʾān 18:63–66. Full text is given above, pp. 6–7.

These accounts that we have mentioned on the authority of the Messenger of God and the scholars among the predecessors make it clear that al-Khiḍr was before and during the days of Moses. This proves the error of the words of those who say that he was Jeremiah b. Hilkiah, because Jeremiah lived during the days of Nebuchadnezzar, and between the days of Moses and Nebuchadnezzar was a period the extent of which is not difficult for scholars of the days of mankind and their accounts to calculate.[105]

We have put mention of him and his account this early only because he lived during the era of Afrīdhūn, according to what is told, even if, according to this account about al-Khiḍr, Moses, and his servant, he lived into the days of Manūshihr[106] and his reign, since Moses became a prophet only during the era of Manūshihr, whose reign came after the reign of his grandfather Afrīdhūn. Everything we have mentioned about the individuals in these tales, from the period of Abraham to the account of al-Khiḍr, all that—so it is reported—took place during the reigns of Bīwarāsb[107] and Afrīdhūn, the stories of whose lives, their scope, and the span of each we have mentioned previously.

[430] Now we will return to the account concerning Manūshihr, his relations, and the events that took place during his time.

---

105. Compare with the previous discussion, pp. 2–5, above, and see the identification of Jeremiah with al-Khiḍr in the next volume; al-Ṭabarī, I, 658 (trans. Perlmann, 55).

106. Manūshihr, Avestan Manuš.čiθra, son of Airyāva the just (*Yašt* 13.131 [*Farvardīn yašt*]); in the *Bundahishn* Manuščihr is said to be the great-great-grandson of Ērič (cf. Anklesaria, *op. cit.*, 294–95, chap. 35.16; and see n. 119, below; see also Justi, *op. cit.*, 191; Mayrhofer, *op. cit.*, 61 no. 219).

107. Bīwarāsb, Middle Persian Bēwarāsp, literally "having ten thousand horses" (cf. Justi *op. cit.*, 60–61), another name for al-Ḍaḥḥāk (see n. 4, above, and al-Ṭabarī, I, 201–10; trans. Brinner, 1–10). The name is not attested in Avestan, but it may be noted that in *Yašt* 5, 28–31, Aži Dahāka is a figure in the mythical history of Iran, who sacrifices "a hundred stallions, a thousand oxen, and ten thousand sheep" to Anāhitā in order to obtain a wish.

Manūshihr

After Afrīdhūn b. Athfiyān Burkāw,[108] Manūshihr, who was a descendant of Īraj b. Afrīdhūn,[109] ruled. Someone has claimed that Fārs[110] was named Fārs for this Manūshihr. He was Manūshihr, great king, according to the genealogists of the Persians, son of Manushkharnar b. Wayrak[111] b. Sarūshank b. Athrak b. Bitak b. Farzū- [431]
shak b. Zūshak b. Farkūzak b. Kūzak b. Īraj b. Afrīdhūn b. Athfiyān Burkāw. These names are pronounced unlike these formulations. One of the Magians claimed that Afrīdhūn had intercourse with the daughter of his son Īraj, who was named Kūshak,[112] and she bore him

108. Athfiyān Burkāw, Middle Persian Aspiyān ī Purgāw (cf. Anklesaria, *op. cit.*, 292–95, chap. 35.8), literally "(the?) Aspiyān who possesses many cattle" (from Avestan *pouru.gav-*, C. Bartholomae, *Altiranisches Wörterbuch*, 899).

109. Īraj b. Afrīdhūn, Middle Persian Ērij (Ērič), son of Frēdōn, the eponymous progenitor of the Iranian peoples (see n. 123, below). In the Avesta the father of Manuš.čiθra was Airyāva the Just; the original meaning of this name may be "he who brings help to the Aryas" (cf. Justi, *op. cit.*, 11(2); Mayrhofer, *op. cit.*, 18 no. 11).

110. Fārs (from Old Persian Pārsa, which the Greeks knew as Persis) was originally the name of a province in southern Iran but was later extended to include the entire country; see Yāqūt, *op. cit.*, II, 835–38. The fact that coins of three rulers of Fārs called Mančihr have survived from the 2nd century C.E. (M. Alram, *Nomina Propria Iranica in Nummis*, 180–83) may be connected with the tradition cited here by al-Ṭabarī.

111. Manshakhurnar, Middle Persian Manushxwarnar, son of Manushxwarnāk, whose mother was Gūzag according to the *Bundahishn*, but Vīrak in the *Pazand Jāmāspnāmag;* see Anklesaria, *op. cit.*, 294–95, chap. 35.16; *Indian Bundahishn*, tr. E. W. West, 133–34).

112. Kuzak, above, from Guzak (Gučak); see Justi, *op. cit.*, 123(2).

a girl named Farkūshak;[113] then he had intercourse with this Farkūshak, and she bore him a girl, named Zūshak;[114] then he had intercouse with this Zūshak, and she bore him a girl named Farzūshak;[115] then he had intercouse with this Farzūshak, and she bore
him a girl named Baytak;[116] then he had intercourse with this Bay-
[432] tak, and she bore him a girl named Athrak; then he had intercourse
with Athrak,[117] and she bore him Īzak; then he had intercourse with
Īzak,[118] and she bore him Wayrak; then he had intercourse with Wayrak, and she bore him Manushkharfāgh, whom some call Manushkhwārnāgh, and a girl named Manushkhorak.[119] They say that
Manushkhwārnāgh had intercourse with Manushkhorak, and she
bore him Manushkharnar and a girl named Manushrāzūk;[120] and

---

113. Instead of Farkūzak, above, from Fragūzak; see Justi, *op. cit.*, 101.

114. Zūshak; see Justi, *op. cit.*, 388.

115. Frazūshak; see Justi, *op. cit.*, 105.

116. Instead of Bitak, above, which is correct. See Justi, *op. cit.*, 69.

117. Unclear in MSS, except Tn, which has Ayrak (al-Ṭabarī, 433 n. *a*), but *Bundahishn* has Ērak daughter of Thritak, possible conflation of *ʾθrtk* and *ʾyrk*?; hence the names here should probably be Athrak and Irak; see Justi, *op. cit.*, 23.

118. For Īrak? Not listed in the genealogy above, where Sarūshank (Srūshenk) is named as the child of Athrak; see Justi, *op. cit.*, 23.

119. Manushkharnāgh is probably the correct form, as the *Bundahishn* has the popular etymology "Manuš ī xwaršēd pad wēnīg: Manush, who has the sun on his nose" (i.e., khar = Mid. Pers. xwar = xwaršēt "sun" and nāgh = Mid. Pers. *nāg = wēnīk "nose"). See also *Addenda*, DLXXXII. The genealogical information given by al-Ṭabarī may be compared with that of the *Bundahishn*:

Bundahishn	al-Ṭabarī-I	Magians according to al-Ṭabarī
Frēdōn	Afrīdhūn	Afrīdhūn
Ērij	Īraj	—
Gūzag	Kūzak	Kūshak
Fragūzag	Farkūzak	Farkūshak
Zūšag	Zūshak	Zūshak
Frazūšag	Farzūshak	Farzūshak
Bidag	Bitak	Baytak
Θritag	Athrak	Athrak
Ērag	Sarūshank	Īzak
Gūza	Wayrak	Wayrak
Manushxwarnāk	—	Manushkharfāgh, -nāgh + Manushkhorak
Manushxwarnar	Manushkharnar	Manushkharnar + Manushrāzūk
Manuščihr	Manūshihr	Manūshihr

120. *Manūskh*^{w}*arnar* in *Bundahishn*. The girl's name should probably be Manushrārūk; see Justi, *op. cit.*, 193. These twins represent a pattern repeated in the mythical genealogies.

that Manushkharnar had intercourse with Manushrāzūk, and she bore him Manūshihr.

One scholar says that Manūshihr's birthplace was in Danbāvand,[121] while another says that she was born in al-Rayy,[122] and that Manushkharnar and Manushrāzūk, when Manūshihr was born to them, concealed his birth for fear of Tūj[123] and Salm.[124] When Manūshihr grew up, he went to his grandfather Afrīdhūn. When he entered to see him, Afrīdhūn saw promising signs in him, and he placed in Manūshihr's custody the domain that he had formerly assigned to his grandfather Īraj, crowning him with his crown. A certain historian has asserted [rather] that this Manūshihr was Manūshihr b. Manushkharnar b. Ifrīqīs[125] b. Isaac b. Abraham. He also asserted that rule was transferred to him after Afrīdhūn, after nineteen hundred and twenty-two years of the era of Jayūmart[126] had passed. He cited as witness to the truth of that these verses of Jarīr b. ʿAṭīyah:[127] [433]

---

121. The highest summit of the Elburz mountains in Iran and a town on its slopes. Early Persian manuscripts show this spelling, but the word is today pronounced Damāvand. See Yāqūt, *op. cit.*, II, 606–10, s.v. "Dunbāwand." See also W. Eilers, *Der Name Demawand.*

122. An important medieval city, southwest of Damāvand and just outside present-day Tehran. See Yāqūt, *op. cit.*, II, 892–901.

123. Tūj, also Tūr (Justi, *op. cit.*, 329), eponymous ancestor of the Turanians, or Turks, whose conflict with the descendents of Iraj, the Iranians, occupies the whole of the mythical portion of the *Shāhnāmah*. See Boyce, *op. cit.*, 104 and n. 128 for further references.

124. Also written Sarm, from Avestan Sairima, representing the western lands and peoples; see Justi, *op. cit.*, 289; Boyce, *op. cit.*, 104.

125. The name *Ifrīqīs* may be an arabicized form of *Ferengīs,* which, in the *Shāhnāmah,* is the name of the daughter of Afrāsiāb (on whom see *Enc. Ir.* I/6, 570–76). In the *Bundahishn* the names of several daughters of Afrāsiyāb are mentioned (Anklesaria, *op. cit.*, 294–95, chap. 35.20–22), among them one whose name is traditionally read Wispān-friyā, though Wispān-friy, literally "dear to all," may be a more probable Middle Persian reading. Justi, *op. cit.*, 371, speculated that Ferengīs might be a distortion of this name (cf. A. Christensen, *Les Kayanides,* 85 n. 4); it is also possible, however, that al-Ṭabarī is here reporting the name of Wispānfriy's sister, Frīgīz ī Čūr (thus Anklesaria; West, *op. cit.*, 135, and Justi, *op. cit.*, 104, read this name as Frasp-i čūr).

126. *Gaya-maretan,* lit. "mortal man"; Justi, *op. cit.*, 108. Identified at times with Gomer, the biblical son of Japheth, and as the first of the mythical Persian rulers; see al-Ṭabarī, I, 216, 353 (trans. Brinner, 15, 133); Christensen, *Les types du premier homme . . .*, esp. I.

127. Jarīr b. ʿAṭīyah b. al-Khatafa (Hudhayfa) b. Badr, d. ca. 110/728. One of the great court poets of the Umayyad period, a master of *hijāʾ*, or satirical verse. See *EI*², s.v. "Djarīr."

The sons of Isaac were lions when they girded themselves
with the sword belts of death, clothed in armor,
And when they claimed descent they numbered al-Ṣibahbadh[128] to be of them and Chosroes,[129] and they counted Hurmuzān[130] and Caesar.[131]
Scripture and prophecy were among them,[132]
and they were kings of Iṣṭakhr[133] and Tustar.[134]
There unites us and the noble ones, sons of Fāris,[135]
a father after whom it matters not to us who comes later.
Our forefather is the Friend of Allah,[136] and Allah is our Lord.
We are pleased with what God has bestowed and has decreed.

As for the Persians, they disclaim this genealogy, and they know no kings ruling over them other than the sons of Afrīdhūn and acknowledge no kings of other peoples. They think that, if an intruder of other stock entered among them in ancient times,[137] he did so wrongfully.

I was informed—Hishām b. Muḥammad:[138] Between themselves

---

128. *Ṣibāhbadh/ṣabāhbadh*, perhaps for *iṣbāhbadh*, the title of the foremost military leader in ancient Iran, from **spādapati: ispehbed*. Justi, *op. cit.*, 306; see also *EI*², s.v. "Ispahbadh."

129. Arabic: *kisrā*. Title given to all pre-Islamic Persian rulers in later Arabic literature, based on the name of the mythical ruler Kay Khusrau in the *Shāhnāmah*.

130. Al-Hurmuzān, for Persian Hormiz(d)ān. Persian governor and defender of Khūzistān against the Arabs 16–19 or 21/637–640 or 642. Taken prisoner by the Arabs at Tustar and slain by ʿUbaydallāh b. ʿUmar at Medina in 23/644. See *EI*², s.v. "al-Hurmuzān."

131. A generic title for Roman and Byzantine rulers in Arabic literature. All of the above names are used as general categories. Hence "We are descended from Isaac but also from military commanders, kings of the Persians and of the Byzantines; thus we unite Abrahamic descent with descent from the two other major ancient civilizations."

132. Prophecy and kingship were special gifts of God to the Children of Israel, but both disappeared from them with the coming of the Persians and the Byzantines; see al-Ṭabarī, I, 353 (trans. Brinner, 133).

133. Iṣṭakhr, near Iṣfahān, one of the great frontier cities of medieval Iran, as well as a district; Yāqūt, *op. cit.*, I, 299.

134. Šuštar, the greatest city of Khūzistān in southwestern Iran; Yāqūt, I, 847–50.

135. In Jarīr's *Dīwān* (Jarīr b. ʿAṭīyah, *The Naḳāiḍ of Jarir* ...) and in Yāqūt, *op. cit.*, I, 299, s.v. "Iṣṭakhr," we find here *sārah* (i.e., descent from Abraham?), but this should be *sādat* "dominion," as in Abū al-Faraj, *Kitāb al-Aghānī*, according to al-Ṭabarī, I, 433 n.*e*.

136. *Khalīl allāh*, the traditional Muslim epithet for Abraham. See n. 8, above.

137. *Qabl al-Islām* "before Islam" is inserted here in MS BM.

138. Hishām b. Muḥammad b. al-Sāʾib, Abū al-Mundhir al-Kalbī, called Ibn al-Kalbī, ca. 119–204 or 206/737–819 or 821. An immensely learned and prolific au-

Tūj and Sarm[139] ruled the earth for three hundred years after they had slain their brother Īraj. Then Manūshihr b. Īraj b. Afrīdhūn ruled for one hundred and twenty years. Then a son of the son of Tūj the [434]
Turk pounced upon Manūshihr, exiling him from the land of Iraq for twelve years. Manūshihr, in turn, replaced him, exiled him from his land, and returned to his rule, reigning for an additional twenty-eight years.

Manūshihr was described as just and generous. He was the first who dug trenches[140] and collected weapons of war, and the first who set up *dihqāns,*[141] imposing a *dihqān* over each village, making its inhabitants his chattels and slaves, clothing them in garments of submission, and ordering them to obey him.

It is said that Moses the Prophet appeared in the sixtieth year of his reign. It has been mentioned by someone other than Hishām[142] that, when Manūshihr became king, he was crowned with the royal crown, and he said on the day of his enthronement, "We will strengthen our fighting force and promise them to take vengeance for our forefathers and drive the enemy from our land." Then he journeyed to the land of the Turks, seeking to avenge the blood of his grandfather Īraj b. Afrīdhūn. He slew Tūj b. Afrīdhūn and his brother Salm, achieving his revenge; then he left.

He also mentioned Frāsiyāb b. Fashanj b. Rustam b. Turk[143] (from [435]
whom the Turks claim descent) b. Shahrāsb[144] (or, as some say, the son of Arshāsb) b. Tūj b. Afrīdhūn the king, (Fashak is also called Fashanj b. Zāshamīn).[145] [Frāsiyāb] did battle with Manūshihr sixty years after the latter had slain Tūj and Salm, and [he] besieged him in Ṭabaristān. Then Manūshihr and Frāsiyāb reached an agreement

---

thor of books in many branches of knowledge, especially Arab history. *EI*², s.v. "al-Kalbi"; *GAS,* I, 268–71; Dodge, *op. cit.,* II, 1027, s.v. "Kalbī."

139. An alternative writing of Salm; see n. 124, above.

140. Referring, perhaps, to irrigation channels.

141. Head of a village and member of the lesser Sasanian nobility, representing the government to peasants and responsible for collecting taxes. See *EI*², s.v. "*Dihḳān.*"

142. Text has ʿ*an* "according to," but Ibrāhīm, I, 379, has *ghayr* "other than," which fits the context.

143. Also called Frāsiāf, Afrāsiāb from old Iranian Fraṅrasyan. See Justi, *op. cit.,* 103; see also *Enc. Ir.* I/6, 570–76. Cf. n. 623, below.

144. Šērāsp, son of Arūšāsb (Dūrōšāsp). See Justi, *op. cit.,* 295.

145. Pashang (or Pesheng), Middle Persian Pašang, son of Zaēšim (the latter in Avestan letters; Anklesaria, *op. cit.,* 294–95, chap. 35.17). In al-Ṭabarī, above, the father's name is mistakenly written Rustam (see Justi, *op. cit.,* 245).

that they would set a boundary between their two kingdoms at the distance of an arrow shot by a man from among Manūshihr's companions named Arishshibaṭīr[146] (but sometimes one shortens his name and calls him Īrash): Wherever his arrow fell from the place where it was shot, adjacent to the land of the Turks, would be the boundary between them, which neither of them was to cross to the other side. Arishshibaṭīr drew an arrow in his bow, then released it.
[436] He was given strength and power so that his shot reached from Ṭabaristān to the river of Balkh.[147] Because the arrow fell there, the river of Balkh became the boundary between the Turks and the children of Tūj, and the children of Īraj and the region of the Persians. In this way, through Arishshibaṭīr's shot, wars were ended between Frāsiyāb and Manūshihr.

They have mentioned that Manūshihr derived mighty rivers from al-Ṣarāt,[148] the Tigris, and the river of Balkh. It is said that he was the one who dug the great Euphrates and commanded the people to plow and to cultivate the earth. He added archery to the art of warfare and gave leadership in archery to Arishshibaṭīr, owing to the shooting he had performed.

They say that, after thirty-five years of Manūshihr's reign had passed, the Turks seized some of his outlying districts. He reproached his people and said to them: "O people! Not all those you have sired are people;[149] for people are only truly people so long as they defend themselves and repel the enemy from them, but the Turks have seized a part of your outlying districts. That is only because you abandoned warfare against your enemy and you lacked concern. But God has granted us dominion as a test of whether we

---

146. Arishshibaṭīr, corrected from Arishshiyaṭīr (*Addenda*, DLXXXIII), "shortened" form Īrash, a mythical archer; in Middle Persian his name must have been *Arš *Šēbāg-tigr "Arš with the swift arrow," attested in the anonymous *Mujmal al-tawārīkh wa-al-qiṣaṣ* (520/1126), 190, as Ārash shiwā-tīr, a rendering of Avestan Ərəxša xšwivi-išu (*Yašt* 8.6; see *Enc. Ir.* II/3, 266–67, s.v. "Āraš i"). See also al-Bīrūnī, *al-Athār al-bāqiyah*, 205; J. Darmesteter, *Le Zend-Avesta*, II, 415–16 n. 24; Boyce, *op. cit.*, 75.

147. The river of Balkh, the Jayḥūn, the classical Oxus, today the Amu Darya, is the boundary between Īraj and Tūj, hence between the Iranians and the Turks.

148. A canal watering the Baghdad area dating back to Sasanian times. See Yāqūt, *op. cit.*, III, 377–79; J. Lassner, *The Topography of Baghdad in the Early Middle Ages*, 277 n. 4.

149. *Lam talidū al-nāsa kullahum.* See *Glossarium*, DLXVI, s.v. *wld.*

will be grateful, and He will increase us, or will disbelieve and He will punish us, though we belong to a family of renown, for the source of rule belongs to God. When tomorrow comes, be present!" They said they would and sought forgiveness.

He dismissed them, and when the next day came, he sent for those possessing royalty and the noblest commanders.[150] He invited them and made the leaders of the people enter: he invited the Chief Magus,[151] who was seated on a chair opposite his throne. Then Manūshihr rose on his throne, with the nobles of the royal family and the [437] noblest commanders rising to their feet. He said: "Be seated! I stood up only to let you hear my words." They sat down, and he continued:

> O people! All creatures belong to the Creator; gratitude belongs to the One Who grants favors, as does submission to the All-Powerful. What exists is inescapable, for there is none weaker than a creature, whether he seeks or is sought; there is no one more powerful than a creator or anyone more powerful than He who has what He seeks [already] in His hand or one weaker than one who is in the hand of His seeker. Verily, contemplation is light, while forgetfulness is darkness; ignorance is misguidance. The first has come, and the last must join the first. Before us there came principles of which we are derivative—and what kind of continued existence can a derivative have after its purpose disappears?
>
> Verily God has given us this dominion, and to Him belongs praise. We ask Him to inspire us with integrity, truth, and certainty. For the king has a claim on his subjects, and his subjects have a claim on him, whereas their obligation to the ruler is tht they obey him, give him good counsel, and fight his enemy; the king's obligation to them is to provide them with their sustenance in its proper times, for they cannot rely on anything else, and that is their commerce. The king's obligation to his subjects is that he take care of them, treat them kindly, and not impose on them what they cannot do. If a calamity befalls them and diminishes their gains

150. *Ahl al-mamlakah wa-ashrāf al-asāwirah.*

151. *I.e.,* the high priest of the Zoroastrian faith, the *mobedh al-mobedhān.* See al-Ṭabarī, I, 436 n. *k.*

because a heavenly or earthly evil comes upon them, he should deduct from the land tax that which was diminished. If a calamity ruins them altogether, he should give them what they need to strengthen their rebuilding. Afterward, he
[438] may take from them to the extent that he does not harm them, for a year or two years.

The relationship of the army to the king is of the same status as the two wings of a bird, for they are the wings of the king. Whenever a feather is cut off from a wing, that is a blemish in it. Likewise in the case of the king, for he is equally dependent on his wings and feathers. Moreover, the king must possess three qualities: first, that he be truthful and not lie, that he be bountiful and not be miserly, and that he be in control of himself in anger, for he is given power with his hand outstretched and the land tax coming to him. He must not appropriate to himself what belongs to his troops and his subjects. He must be liberal in pardon, for there is no king more long-lasting than a king who pardons or one more doomed to perish than one who punishes. Moreover, a man who errs regarding pardon and pardons is better than one who errs in punishing. It is necessary that a king be cautious in a matter involving the killing of a person and his ruin. If a matter requiring punishment is brought to him regarding one of his officials, he must not show him favor. Let him bring him together with the complainant, and, if the claim of the wronged one is proved right against him, the sum is transferred from the official to him.[152] But, if [the official] is unable to [pay], then the king should pay the sum for him and then return the official to his position, requiring that he make restitution for what he extorted. So much for my obligation to you. However, I will not pardon one who sheds blood wrongfully or cuts off a hand without right, unless the aggrieved one pardons. Therefore accept this from me [as my right].

The Turks have coveted you, so protect us and you will only protect yourselves. I have commanded arms and provi-
[439] sions for you. I am your partner in this matter, for I can only

152. See *Glossarium*, CCXVI, s.v. *khrj*.

call myself king as long as I have obedience from you. Indeed, a king is a king only if he is obeyed. For if he is contradicted, he is ruled and is not a ruler. Whenever we are informed of disobedience, we will not accept it from the informer until we have verified it. If the report is true, so be it; if not, we will treat the informer as a disobedient one.

Is not the finest act in the face of misfortune the acceptance of patience and rejoicing in the comfort of certainty? Whoever is slain in battle with the enemy, I hope for him the attainment of God's pleasure. The best of things is the submission to God's command, a rejoicing in certainty, and satisfaction in His judgment. Where is sanctuary from what exists? One can only squirm in the hand of the seeker. This world is only a journey for its inhabitants; they cannot loosen the knots of the saddle except in the other [world], and their self-sufficiency is in borrowed things.

How good is gratitude toward the Benefactor and submission to the One to Whom judgment belongs! Who owes submission more to One above him than he who has no refuge except in Him, or any reliance except on Him! So trust in victory if your determination is that succor is from God. Be confident of achieving the goal if your intent is sincere. Know that this dominion will not stand except through uprightness and good obedience, suppression of the enemy, blocking the frontiers, justice to the subjects, and just treatment of the oppressed. Your healing is within you; the remedy in which there is no illness is uprightness, commanding good and forbidding evil. For there is no power except in God. Look to the subjects, for they are your food and drink. Whenever you deal justly with them, they desire prosperity, [440]
which will increase your land-tax revenues and will be made evident in the growth of your wealth. But, if you wrong the subjects, they will abandon cultivation and leave most of the land idle. This will decrease your land-tax revenues, and it will be made evident in the decrease of your wealth. Pledge yourself to deal justly with your subjects. Whatever rivers or overflows there are, of which the cost [of repair] is the ruler's, hurry to take care of it before it increases. But whatever is owed by the subjects of which they are unable to

> take care, lend it to them from the treasury of the land taxes. When the times of their taxes come due, take it back with their produce tax to the extent that it will not harm them: a quarter [of it] each year, or a third, or a half, so that it will not cause them distress.[153]
>
> This is my speech and my command, O Chief Magus! Adhere to these words, and hold onto what you have heard this day. Have you heard, O people?

They said, "Yes! You have spoken well, and we will act, God willing." Then he ordered the food, and it was placed before them. They ate and drank, then left, thankful to him. His rule lasted one hundred and twenty years.

Hishām b. al-Kalbī claimed—in what has been transmitted to me from him—that al-Rāʾish b. Qays b. Ṣayfī b.[154] Sabaʾ b. Yashjub b. Yaʿrub b. Joktan (Qaḥṭān) was one of the kings of Yemen after Yaʿrub b. Joktan b. Eber b. Shelah and his brothers, and that the reign of al-Rāʾish in Yemen was during the days of Manūshihr. He was only called al-Rāʾish, although his name was al-Ḥārith b. Abī Sadad, be-
[441] cause of the booty he had plundered from people he raided and had taken to Yemen; therefore he was called al-Rāʾish.[155] He raided India, slaying there, taking captives, and plundering wealth; then he returned to Yemen. He traveled from there and attacked the two mountains of Ṭayyʾ,[156] then al-Anbār,[157] then Mosul.[158] He sent out his cavalry from Mosul under the command of one of his companions, a man called Shimr b. al-Aṭāf. He fought against the Turks of the land of Adharbaijān, which belonged to them in those days. He

153. Text has *yatabayyana* "be noticed," here reading instead *yashaqqa* with MS Tn and Ibrāhīm, I, 383. See al-Ṭabarī, I, 440 n. *f*.

154. There may be some generations omitted here; see the genealogies on pp. 98, 156, below. In the last it seems that Bilqīs, the Queen of Sheba, is of the same family.

155. Lit. "the one who accepts or gives bribes" or "one who gives one the property of another"; see Lane, *op. cit.*, 1200, s.v. *rysh*.

156. Two mountains, Ajaʾ and Salmā, in the territory of Ṭayyʾ, a tribe inhabiting the north-central area of the Arabian peninsula in pre-Islamic times. See Yāqūt, *op. cit.*, I, 122–30.

157. A town built by the Sasanian Persians on the left bank of the Euphrates, not far from the present site of Baghdad. *EI*², s.v. "al-Anbār."

158. The great center of northern Iraq across the river from ancient Nineveh. The army of al-Rāʾish moved roughly in a north-by-east direction through al-Ṭayyʾ and al-Anbār to Mosul.

slew the fighters and took the children captive. He engraved on two stones, which are known in Adharbaijān, what had happened on his campaign. Imru᾿ al-Qays[159] said about this:

Did he not inform you that Time is a demon,
  traitor to a pact, gobbling up men?
He caused the "feathered one"[160] to cease his banquets,
  though he had already ruled plains and mountains,
And he attached Dhū Manār to the claws
  and set snares for the strangler.[161]

Dhū Manār, whom the poet mentioned, is Dhū Manār b. Rā᾿ish, the king after his father, and his name was Abrahah b. al-Rā᾿ish.[162] He was called Dhū Manār only because he raided the lands of the west and penetrated them by land and by sea. He feared that his troops might lose their way on their return journey, so he built a lighthouse tower *(manār)* with which to guide them. The people of Yemen claimed that he sent his son, al-ʿAbd b. Abrahah on his raid to the area of the most distant lands of the west, where he plundered and seized their wealth. He brought back to [his father] some *nās-nās,* which had wild and abominable faces.[163] People were frightened [442]
of them and called him Dhū al-Adhʿār (possessor of frightening things). He said further: Abrahah was one of their kings who penetrated deeply in the earth.

I have mentioned these kings of Yemen here because I remembered the words of one who claimed that al-Rā᾿ish was ruler in Yemen in the days of Manūshihr and that the kings of Yemen were governors for the kings of Persia there, which was their dominion before them.

---

159. One of the six great pre-Islamic poets, perhaps the most famous of them, d. ca. 550 C. E. *EI*², s.v. "Imru᾿ al-Kays."

160. The other, more common meaning of the root *rysh* is "to feather (an arrow)"; hence *dhū al-riyāsh* here is "the feathered one."

161. *Al-zarrād,* perhaps an epithet for an historical figure.

162. It is unclear whether this is the Abrahah, a Christian king of South Arabia, who is famous for leading an expedition against Mecca in 570. See *EI*², s.v. "Abraha."

163. *Nāsnās,* a creature jumping or hopping on one leg. Tradition related that a tribe of ʿĀd disobeyed their apostle and that God transformed them into *nāsnās,* each having one arm and one leg, being one-half of a human being; they hopped like birds and pastured like animals. See Lane, *op. cit.,* s.v. *nsns;* another story is given in al-Ṭabarī, I, 214 (trans. Brinner, 13).

The Genealogy of Moses b. Amram, His History, and the Events That Took Place in His Era and That of Manūshihr b. Manushkharnar

We have already mentioned the children of Jacob, Israel of God, their numbers, and their birth dates. Ibn Ḥumayd transmitted to us — Salamah b. al-Faḍl — Muḥammad b. Isḥāq, who said moreover that Levi b. Jacob married Nābitah bt. Mārī b. Issachar, and she bore him Gershon, and Merari, and Kohath. Kohath b. Levi married Fāhī bt.
[443] Masīn b. Bethuel b. Elias, and she bore him Izhar. Izhar married Shamīth bt. Batādīt b. Barakiyā b. Jokshan b. Abraham, and she bore him Amram and Korah. Amram married Jochebed bt. Samuel b. Barakiyā b. Jokshan b. Abraham, and she bore him Aaron and Moses.[164]

Someone other than Ibn Isḥāq said: The life span of Jacob b. Isaac was one hundred and forty-seven years, and Levi was born to him when he was eighty-nine years old. Kohath was born to Levi when he was forty-six years old. Then Izhar was born to Kohath, then Amram to Izhar, and he is ʿImrān [in Arabic]. Izhar lived for one hundred forty-seven years, and Amram was born to him when he was sixty years old. Then Moses was born to Amram, and his mother was Jochebed, and some say that her name was Anāḥīd.[165] His wife

164. There are significant deviations here from the biblical genealogy of Moses. In Exodus 6:18 Amram and Izhar are brothers, both sons of Kohath. Korah was the son of Izhar (Exodus 6:21), hence not the brother of Amram but his nephew. Jochebed, the

was Zipporah bt. Jethro, who is Shuʿayb the prophet.[166] Moses begat Gershom and Eliezer. He left for Midian out of fear when he was forty-one years old and called people to the religion of Abraham. God appeared to him at Mt. Sinai when he was eighty years old. The [444] pharaoh of Egypt in his days was Qabūs b. Muṣʿab b. Muʿāwiyah, the second master of Joseph. His wife was Āsiyah bt. Muzāḥim b. ʿUbayd b. al-Rayyān b. al-Walīd, the first pharaoh of Joseph. When Moses was called, he was informed that Qabūs b. Muṣʿab had died and that his brother, al-Walīd b. Muṣʿab,[167] had taken his place. He was more insolent than Qabūs, more disbelieving, and more boastful. God commanded that Moses and his brother Aaron go to al-Walīd with the message.

It was said the al-Walīd married Āsiyah bt. Muzāḥim after his brother. Amram lived for one hundred and thirty-six years, and Moses was born when Amram was seventy years old. Then Moses went to Pharaoh as a messenger, together with Aaron. Eighty years passed from the time of Moses' birth to his departure from Egypt with the Israelites, whereupon he went to the wilderness, after crossing the sea. Forty years passed from their sojourn there until they went out with Joshua b. Nun. One hundred twenty years passed from Moses' birth to his death in the wilderness.

Ibn Isḥāq said—Ibn Ḥumayd—Salamah—Ibn Isḥāq: God took Joseph, and the king who was with him, al-Rayyān b. al-Walīd, died. The pharaohs had inherited rule over Egypt from the Amalekites. God scattered the Israelites there; when Joseph died, he was buried,

---

mother of Moses and Aaron, was the paternal aunt of Amram (Exodus 6:20). The female names and their genealogies are not given in the Bible.

165. Middle Persian form of Avestan and Old Persian Anāhitā, the important old Iranian river goddess, on whom see, e.g., *Enc. Ir.* II/1, 1003–11. Although it is unclear why she is associated with the mother of Moses, E. R. Goodenough has identified the female figure holding the infant Moses in the Dura Europus synagogue murals as Aphrodite/ Anāhitā. See *Jewish Symbols in the Greco-Roman Period* IX, 6, 10, 83, 165, 200–3; XI, fig. 178; XII, 66, 168, 169.

166. The identification of Qurʾānic Shuʿayb with biblical Jethro is made by later commentators and has no basis in the Qurʾān, except for the connection of both with the land of Midian (Madyan). See below, p. 47, where Jethro is mentioned as a nephew of Shuʿayb. *Shorter Encyclopedia of Islam,* s.v. "Shuʿaib."

167. The traditional Muslim names given to these figures. Compare al-Ṭabarī, I, 378, 412 (trans. Brinner, 154, 184): Qabūs; al-Ṭabarī I, 378, 386 (trans. Brinner, 154, 161): al-Walīd b. al-Rayyān. Āsiyah is close to biblical Asenath, name of the wife of Joseph, not of Pharaoh. In Jewish legend the daughter of Pharaoh is called Bithiah ("daugher of God,") a name given to her by God for her kindness to Moses. See Ginzberg, *op. cit.*, II, 170. For the Islamic view of Pharaoh, see *EI²*, s.v. "Firʿawn."

as was mentioned to me, in a casket of marble in the Nile, in the
[445] midst of the water. The Israelites continued living under the rule of the pharaohs while maintaining of their religion whatever Joseph, Jacob, Isaac, and Abraham had prescribed for them of Islam, holding fast to that until the Pharaoh, to whom God sent Moses, had arrived. Among the pharaohs there was none more insolent than he toward God, or haughtier in speech, or longer-lived in his rule. His name, according to what I have been told, was al-Walīd b. Muṣʿab. There was no pharaoh more ruthless, harder-hearted, or of more evil character toward the Israelites than he. He tormented them and made them slaves and chattels, classifying them in his tasks: one class for building, another class for plowing, another class for his sowing. They were busy with his projects, and whoever among them was not working for him had to pay a poll tax. He *inflicted*[168] upon them, as God said, *"dreadful torment."*[169] Yet they retained remnants of their religion, from which they did not want to depart. The pharaoh had married an Israelite woman named Āsiyah bt. Muzāḥim, from the best of a limited number of women. He was granted a long life among them while he ruled them, and in return he inflicted upon them dreadful torment. When God wanted to release them from their misery, and when Moses had reached maturity, God gave him the message.

The narrator continued: It was told to me that, when Moses' time approached, the astrologers and diviners of Pharaoh came to him and said: "We want you to know that we find according to our lore that a child born to the Israelites, the time of whose birth draws near to you, will deprive you of your rule. He will vanquish you in your dominion, send you out of your land, and change your religion." When
[446] they told him this, he ordered the slaying of every newborn male child who would be born among the Israelites and commanded that they spare the females alive.[170] He gathered the midwives from the people of his domain and said to them, "Do not let a single male fetus of the Israelites come forth at your hands without striking him." They would do this, while he killed those lads who were older. As for the pregnant women, he ordered them to be tormented until they miscarried.

168. Qurʾān 7:137.
169. Qurʾān 2:49.
170. Based on Qurʾān 2:49.

According to Ibn Ḥumayd — Salamah — Muḥammad b. Isḥāq — ʿAbdallāh b. Abī Najīḥ[171] — Mujāhid[172]: I was told that he called for reeds and had them split so they became like sharp blades, which were then lined up one next to another. The pregnant Israelite women were brought and made to stand on them. It cut their feet, so that a woman would miscarry, causing the fetus to fall between her legs. A woman would tread on [the fetus] and thereby avoid the reeds, cutting her feet out of exhaustion from her effort. [Pharaoh] went so far in this that he almost wiped out all of the [Israelites]. Someone said to him, "You have destroyed the people and cut off their progeny, although they are still your slaves and workers." So he commanded that the boys be slain one year and spared the next. Aaron was born in the year during which the boys were spared, and Moses was born in the year during which the boys were slain; Aaron was one year older than Moses.

Al-Suddī[173] told us what Mūsā b. Hārūn[174] related to us — Asbāṭ[175] — al-Suddī, in an account — Abū Mālik[176] and Abī Ṣāliḥ[177] — Ibn ʿAbbās; also from Murrah al-Hamdānī[178] — Ibn Masʿūd;[179] and from people among the Companions of the Prophet: Pharaoh saw a vision

---

171. ʿAbdallāh b. Abī Najīḥ al-Makkī, Abū Yasār, d. 131/748–49. A reliable transmitter of many traditions. Ibn Saʿd, *op. cit.*, V, 355; *GAS*, I, 20–21.

172. Mujāhid b. Jabr, Abū al-Ḥajjāj, ca. 21–104/642–722. One of the most reliable disciples of Ibn ʿAbbās, he also studied with other Companions of the Prophet, wrote a commentary on the Qurʾān, and was active in jurisprudence. *GAS*, I, 29; Ibn Saʿd, *op. cit.*, V, 343–44; al-Ziriklī, *op. cit.*, VI: 161; Dodge, *op. cit.*, II, 1061.

173. Ismāʿīl b. ʿAbd al-Raḥmān b. Abī Karīmah al-Suddī, Abū Muḥammad, d. 127/745. An important Qurʾān exegete and author of *maghāzī* and biographical works, he transmitted from Companions of the Prophet, as well as from many of their successors. *GAS*, I, 32–33; Ibn Saʿd, *op. cit.*, VI, 225; al-Ziriklī, *op. cit.*, I, 313; Dodge, *op. cit.*, II, 1103.

174. Mūsā b. Hārūn, probably Mūsā b. Hārūn al-Hamdānī. Cf. *GAS*, I, 33 n. 2.

175. Asbāṭ b. Naṣr al-Hamadānī, Abū Naṣr, d. 170/786. He transmitted the Qurʾān commentary of al-Suddī and was himself a commentator and transmitter. Ibn Saʿd, *op. cit.*, VI, 341; al-Ziriklī, *op. cit.*, I, 282.

176. Abū Mālik, often linked with Abū Ṣāliḥ, whose name follows, possibly Abū Mālik al-Ghifārī. Ibn Saʿd, *op. cit.*, VI, 206.

177. Abū Ṣāliḥ Bādhām, *mawlā* of Umm Hāniʾ bt. Abī Ṭālib. Ibn al-Kalbī and others transmitted from Umm Hāniʾ. Ibn Saʿd, *op. cit.*, V, 222.

178. Murrah b. Sharāḥīl al-Hamdānī, according to Ibn Saʿd, *op. cit.*, VI, 79.

179. ʿAbdallāh b. Ghāfil b. Ḥabīb al-Hudhalī, known as Ibn Masʿūd, d. 32/653. Of humble origin, he became one of the first Muslims, a famous Companion of the Prophet and reader of the Qurʾān. His *Ḥadīth* and Qurʾān readings were preferred in al-Kūfah and by Shiʿites generally. *EI*², s.v. "Ibn Masʿūd"; *Shorter Encyclopedia of Islam*, 150; *GAS*, I, 3, 5, 14, 86 et passim; al-Ziriklī, *op. cit.*, IV, 280; Dodge *op. cit.*, II, 936.

[447] in his dream. A fire came from Bayt al-Maqdis[180] until it overcame the houses of Egypt; the Egyptians were burned, while the Israelites were left and the houses of Egypt were destroyed. He called for the magicians, soothsayers, prognosticators, and diviners and asked them about his dream. They said to him: "There will come from the land of the Israelites, meaning Jerusalem, a man in whose face one can read the destruction of Egypt." He therefore ordered any boy born to the Israelites to be killed and any girl born to them to be left. He then said to the Egyptians: "Observe your slaves who work outside and bring them in. Put the Israelites in charge of those loathsome tasks." So the Egyptians set the Israelites the tasks of the servants and brought the latter inside. That is where God says: *"Lo! Pharaoh exalted himself in the earth"*—meaning: he acted haughtily on earth— *"and made its people castes"*[181]—meaning the Israelites, when he placed them in loathsome tasks— *"a tribe among them he oppressed, killing their sons. . . . "*[182] It came to be that every male child who was born to the Israelites was slain, and the little ones did not grow up. God sent down death upon the elders of the Israelites, and it hastened among them. Then the heads of the Egyptians entered in to Pharaoh and spoke to him, saying: "Verily, death has befallen this people, and the work will soon fall upon our servants. We slay their sons, and then the little ones do not grow up, and the old ones die off. Perhaps you could let some of their sons live." So he ordered that they kill them one year and let them live the next.

The year in which they did not kill, Aaron was born and was left to live. But during the year of slaying, the mother of Moses was preg-
[448] nant with him. When she wanted to give birth, she grieved for him. God inspired her, saying, *"Suckle him, and when you fear for him, cast him into the river"*— that is, the Nile— *"and fear not nor grieve. Lo! We shall bring him back to you and shall make him one of Our messengers."*[183]

When she had given birth and had suckled him, she called for a carpenter, who made an ark for Moses, placing the key to the ark inside. She placed him in it, casting him into the river. *And she said*

---

180. Lit. "the house of the sanctuary," i.e., the temple in Jerusalem, *beyt hamiqdash* in Hebrew, hence often used to refer either to Jerusalem or to all of Palestine.
181. *Shiyaʿan*, lit. "factions, parties"; Arberry translates it "sects."
182. Qurʾān 28:3–4.
183. Qurʾān 28:7.

to his sister, "Trace him"—that is, "Trace signs of him." *So she observed him from afar, and they did not notice*[184] that she was his sister. The wave carried the ark forward, alternately lifting it up and carrying it down, until a wave took the ark to some trees at Pharaoh's residence. The servant girls of Āsiyah, the wife of Pharaoh, came out to wash themselves and found the ark. They took it to her, thinking there might be some treasure in it. As Āsiyah looked at him, her pity went out to him, and she loved him. When she told Pharaoh about the baby, he wanted to kill him; however, Āsiyah continued speaking to him until Pharaoh left the baby to her. He said, "I am afraid this child is an Israelite and he is the one at whose hands our destruction will occur." For that is God's Word: *"And the family of Pharaoh took him up, that he might become for them an enemy and a sorrow."*[185] They sought wet nurses for him, but he would not suckle from any of them. The women, meanwhile, were vying for the position of wet nurse, so that they might dwell with Pharaoh during the period of nursing. But the baby refused to suckle. And that is God's Word: *"And We had before forbidden wet nurses for him."* So his sister *said, "Shall I show you a household who will rear him for you and show good will to him?"*[186] They took her and said: "You already know this lad, so lead us to his family." She said: [449]
"I do not know him. I only said that they would show good will to Pharaoh." When his mother came, he took her breasts, and she almost said, "This is my son," but God held her back, for that is God's Word: *"And she would almost have betrayed him if We had not fortified her heart so that she might be one of the believers."*[187]

He was called Moses (Mūsā) only because they found him in water and trees, and in Egyptian water is *mū* and tree is *shā*.[188] And that is the Word of God: *"We gave him to his mother that she might be comforted and would not grieve."*[189] Pharaoh took him as a son, and he was called "son of Pharaoh." When he walked, his mother showed him to Āsiyah. While she was swinging and playing with

184. Qur'ān 28:11.
185. Qur'ān 28:8.
186. Qur'ān 28:12.
187. Qur'ān 28:10.
188. Mūsā in Arabic, Mosheh in Hebrew. Contrast this etymology with the biblical "I drew him out of the water," Exodus 2:10, from Hebrew *mashah*, "to draw out."
189. Qur'ān 28:13.

him, she offered him to Pharaoh, saying, "Take him, the delight of my eye and yours!" Pharaoh said, "He is the delight of your eye, not mine."

ʿAbdallāh b. ʿAbbās said: If he had said "and he is the delight of my eye," then He would have entrusted [Moses] to him, but he refused. So, when Pharaoh took him, Moses seized his beard and pulled out hairs from it. Pharaoh said: "Bring me executioners! He is the one!"[190] Āsiyah said: *"Do not kill him. Perhaps he may be of use to us, or we may choose him as a son."*[191] He is only a boy who does not understand. He has done this only because of his childishness. You know that among the people of Egypt there is no woman more adorned than I. I shall make him an ornament of sapphire and place next to it a live coal. If he takes the sapphire, he is aware, so you may kill him. But, if he takes the live coal, he is only a child."[192]
[450] She brought for him a sapphire and placed before him a basin of live coals. Gabriel came and put a live coal in Moses' hand, which he put into his mouth, burning his tongue. This is as God said: *"And loose a knot from my tongue that they may understand my speech."*[193] Because of this incident, she left Moses alone.

Moses grew up and would sail in Pharaoh's boats and dress as he did, and he was known only as Moses, son of Pharaoh. Once, Pharaoh sailed on a boat without Moses. When Moses arrived, he was told that Pharaoh had already set sail, so he set out to sail after him. He reached a town named Memphis[194] at siesta time. Entering at midday, he found its markets were already closed, and no one was in its streets. This is God's word: *"He entered the city at a time when its people were heedless. He found there two men fighting, one of his own faction"*—they mean this was an Israelite— *"and the other of his enemies"*— they mean one of the Egyptians. *"The man of his faction asked him for help against his enemy. So Moses struck him with his fist, killing him. He said, 'This is of the devil's doing. He*

190. *I.e.*, the one who, the astrologers had predicted, would deprive Pharaoh of his rule. See pp. 32–34, above. See also the Jewish legend in Ginzberg, *op. cit.*, II, 272. Al-Thaʿlabī, *op. cit.*, 152, has "he is my enemy who is being sought."

191. Qurʾān 28:9.

192. See the Jewish legend, in which an onyx stone and a fiery coal are mentioned. Ginzberg, *op. cit.*, II, 274.

193. Qurʾān 20:27–28. In the Jewish version, the fiery coal is the reason for his being tongue-tied, or stammering. Ginzberg, *op. cit.*, II, 274.

194. The Arabic has Manf here; also Manfis, Mansaf.

is an enemy, clearly a misleader.' He said, 'My Lord! Lo! I have wronged my soul, so forgive me.' Then He forgave Moses. He is the Forgiving, the Merciful. He said: 'My Lord! since You have favored me, I will nevermore be a supporter of the guilty.' And morning found him in the city, fearing, vigilant"—fearing that he would be apprehended—*"when behold! the man who had asked for his help the day before cried out to him"*—meaning, he asked for his assistance. *Moses said to him, 'Lo! You are indeed a mere hothead.'"*[195] Then Moses approached to aid him. But when he saw Moses approaching him to fall upon the man who was fighting with the Israelite, the Israelite said, fearing that Moses would strike him because [451]
he had spoken rudely: *"O Moses! Would you kill me like you killed a person yesterday? You would be nothing but a tyrant in the land; you would not be one of those who puts things right."*[196] So he left, and the Egyptian circulated the story that Moses was the one who had killed the man, whereupon Pharaoh sought him, saying, "Seek him out, for he is the one." He said to those who were searching for him, "Look for him on the side roads, for Moses is a boy who will not discover the main road." Moses set out on the side roads, and a man came to Moses, informing him that *"the chiefs take counsel against you to kill you; so escape! So he escaped from there, afraid, vigilant. He said: "My Lord! deliver me from the wrongdoing people."*[197]

When Moses set out on the side roads, an angel came to him on a horse, with a javelin in his hand. When Moses saw him, he bowed down to him in fear. The angel said, "Do not bow down to me, but follow me instead." So Moses followed as the angel guided him to Midian. Moses said, turning his face toward Midian, *"Perhaps my Lord will guide me in the right road."*[198] The angel went with him until he brought him to Midian.

Al-ʿAbbās b. al-Walīd related to me—al-Qāsim[199]—Saʿīd b. Jubayr—Ibn ʿAbbās: Pharaoh and his counselors conferred about what God had promised Abraham: that He would appoint among his de-

---

195. Qurʾān 28:15–17.
196. Qurʾān 28:18–19.
197. Qurʾān 28:20–21.
198. Qurʾān 28:22.
199. Probably al-Qāsim b. Abī Ayyūb (for full name, see n. 242 below), called a reliable transmitter of a few traditions by Ibn Saʿd, *op. cit.*, VII, 2, 59.

[452] scendants prophets and kings. Some of them said that the Israelites were awaiting that, not doubting it. They had thought that it might be Joseph b. Jacob, but when he died they said, "God would not have promised Abraham that." So Pharaoh said, "What do you think [we should do]?" Ibn ʿAbbās continued: They deliberated together and reached a common conclusion: Pharaoh would send men carrying knives to circulate among the Israelites; wherever they found a male infant, they would kill him.

When they saw that the old Israelites were dying at their appointed times and the infants were being killed, they said: "You are about to wipe out the Israelites, and you will reach the point where you will have to carry out the tasks and perform the services that they performed for you. So during one year kill every newborn male, and their sons will decrease in number. During the next year do not kill any of them, and let the little ones grow up in place of the old ones who die. They will not become numerous from those whom you let live so that you would have to be afraid of their becoming more numerous than you; nor will they become fewer in number through those whom you kill." On that they agreed.

The mother of Moses became pregnant with Aaron in the year during which they did not kill male newborns, and she gave birth to him openly and safely. In the following year she became pregnant with Moses, with distress and sadness falling on her heart. That was one of the trials, O Ibn Jubayr![200] that entered him [already while still] in the womb of his mother, that was intended for him. So God inspired her: *"Fear not nor grieve! Lo! We shall bring him back to you and shall make him one of Our messengers."*[201] When she gave birth to him, He commanded her to place him in a chest and to cast it into the sea. After she gave birth, she did what she was com-
[453] manded. But then, in the time when her son was concealed from her, Iblīs came to her, and she said to herself, "What have I done with my son? If he were slain while he was with me, I would conceal and bury

200. The phrase *wa-dhālika min al-futūn yā ibna jubayr* recurs four more times. It is an exclamation by the narrator, Ibn ʿAbbās, addressed to the transmitter of his account, Saʿīd b. Jubayr, and is connected with Qurʾān 20:40–(41)... *"We delivered you from great distress and tried you with heavy trials"* (*wa-fatannāka futūnan*). Ibn ʿAbbās thus points to five trials (*futūn*) in his account to Ibn Jubayr. See *Glossarium*, CCCXCVII, s.v. *ftn*.

201. Qurʾān 28:7; cf n. 183, above.

him. I would prefer that to throwing him with my own hands to the fish and beasts of the sea."

The water carried the chest until it brought it ashore at a harbor of the watering place of the slave girls belonging to the family of Pharaoh. They saw it and took it, and they were about to open the chest. But then they said to one another, "There must be treasure in this, and, if we were to open it, the wife of Pharaoh would not believe us when we told her what we found in it." So they carried it just as they found it, not moving anything in it until they presented it to her. When she opened it, she saw the boy. She cast her love onto him, the like of which had never been cast by her on any other person.

And the heart of the mother of Moses became empty[202] of the memory of everything except the memory of Moses. When the executioners heard about him, they approached the wife of the Pharaoh with their knives, wishing to kill him—and that was one of the trials, O Ibn Jubayr. She said to the executioners: "Be gone! This single one will not increase the Israelites. I shall go to Pharaoh and ask the lad of him as a gift. If he gives him to me, you have been kind and done well. If he orders him slain, I will not blame you." When she took him to Pharaoh, she said, *"[He will be] a consolation for me and for you. Do not kill him."*[203] Pharaoh said: "He may be that for you, but as for me, I have no need for him."

The Messenger of God said, "By the One by Whom one swears! Had Pharaoh admitted that Moses would be a consolation to him as she had admitted, God would have guided Pharaoh on his account, as He guided his wife on his account. But God forbade him that."

Then she sent to all the females around her who had milk, in order [454]
to choose a wet nurse. As each woman would take him to nurse, he would not accept her breast. The wife of Pharaoh worried that he would refuse milk and die, and that saddened her. She gave orders regarding him, for a group of people were in the marketplace, to find a wet nurse from whom he would accept [milk], but they did not find anyone.

The mother of Moses awakened in the morning, and *she said to his sister; "Follow him,* and seek him out. Will you hear anything about him? Is my son alive, or did the beasts and fish of the river eat

202. Qur'ān 28:10.
203. Qur'ān 28:9.

him?" She had forgotten what God had promised her. His sister *observed him from afar, but they did not notice.*[204] She said, out of joy when the wet nurses failed them, *"Shall I show you a household who will rear him for you and show good will to him?"*[205] They seized her, and they said: "How do you know what their good will to him is? Do you know him?" Therefore they had doubts about that, and that was one of the trials, O Ibn Jubayr! She said, "Their good will is toward him, and their worry is about him; their desire is for nursing for the king,[206] and their wish to be of use to him." So they left her alone, and she returned to her mother, relating the story to her. Moses' mother came, and when she placed Moses in her bosom, he leaped[207] to her breasts until both sides of him were filled. The messengers went to the wife of Pharaoh to give her the good news: "We have found a wet nurse for your son!" She sent for her, and Moses' mother was brought together with him. When Pharaoh's wife saw how he behaved with her, she said, "Stay with me, and nurse this son of mine, for I have never loved anything as I love him."

[455] Moses' mother said: "I cannot leave my house and my child, for he will perish. If it pleases you to give him to me, I will take him to my house, and he will be with me. I will not neglect anything good for him that you have done. Otherwise, I am unable to leave my house and my child." The mother of Moses remembered what God had promised her, so she treated the wife of Pharaoh harshly and verified that God carries out His promise. Thus she returned to her house with her son that very day.

God made him grow up a strong child and preserved him for what He had predestined for him. Meanwhile, the Israelites, who were gathered in the vicinity of the city, continued to be secure through him from the injustice and forced labor that was upon them. When Moses grew up, the wife of Pharaoh said to his mother, "I want you to show me Moses."[208] She promised Pharaoh's wife a day on which she would show him. Pharaoh's wife said to her nursemaids, wet

---

204. Both italicized passages are from Qurʾān 28:11.

205. Qurʾān 28:12.

206. *Raghbatuhum fī ẓuʾūrat al-malik*. Lane, *op. cit.*, has for *ẓuʾūrah* "inclination to, or affection for, the young one of another," or "the relation in which one stands by being a . . . nurse."

207. *Nazā*, but other MSS (BM, Ca) have *nazala* "he settled down."

208. MS Ca: "my son"; MSS C and Tn: "Show me my son!"; al-Thaʿlabī, *op. cit.*, 151: "I should like you to show me my son."

nurses, and stewards: "None of you is to refrain from receiving my son with a gift and respect, so that he may see it. Meanwhile, I am sending a reliable woman to count what each of you does." He continued to be met by gifts, generosity, and treasures from the time he left his mother's house until he entered to see Pharaoh's wife. When he came, she treated him with respect, honored him, and rejoiced in him. What she saw of his mother's good influence on him pleased her, and she said [to her women], "Take him to Pharaoh so that he may respect and honor him." But when they took him to Pharaoh, placing him on his lap, Moses took hold of Pharaoh's beard and pulled it. One of the enemies of God said, "Do you not see what God promised to Abraham, that He would cast you down and raise you up?" Pharaoh sent for the executioners to kill him, and that was one [456]
of the trials, O Ibn Jubayr! after all the trials with which he was tried and enticed.

Then Pharaoh's wife came hurrying to Pharaoh and said to him, "What happened to you with this boy whom you gave to me?" He said, "Did you not see him claim that he would cast me down and raise me up?" She replied: "Let us set between us something by which the truth will become known. Bring two glowing coals and two pearls, and set them near him. If he falls upon the pearls and avoids the coals, you will know that he is sensible. But, if he takes the coals and does not want the pearls, then realize that no one will prefer glowing coals over pearls if he is sensible." Pharaoh brought these close to him, and Moses took the glowing coals. They were removed from him, for fear that they would burn his hand, but the woman said, "Do you not see?" Thus God turned [Pharaoh] away from [Moses] after what he had intended to do to him. *And God attains His purpose through him.*[209]

When he matured and became a man, he did not permit anyone of Pharaoh's people to treat the Israelites with injustice or forced labor, so they were completely secure from these. However, while he was walking one day in the vicinity of the town, suddenly he came across two men fighting: one of them an Israelite and the other a Pharaonite. The Israelite asked Moses for help against the Pharaonite, and Moses became extremely angry. His anger grew because the man had reached out to him, knowing Moses' standing with the

209. Qurʾān 65:2.

Israelites[210] and his protection of them.[211] Except for the mother of
[457] Moses, no one knew that that was because of anything but his nursing, unless God told Moses [himself] about that what He had told no one else. *Moses struck* the Pharaonite *with his fist and killed him,* but no one saw them except God and the Israelite. When he killed the man, Moses said: *"This is Satan's doing. He is an enemy, a clear misleader."* Then he said: *"My Lord, I have wronged my soul. Forgive me." Then He forgave him, for He is the Forgiving, Merciful One.*[212]

The next morning he arose in the city afraid, waiting for the news to spread. People came to Pharaoh, and he was told that the Israelites had killed a man from the people of Pharaoh, "So demand our due, and do not permit them to take liberties regarding that." He replied, "Seek his killer for me and whoever witnessed it, for it is not right for us to pass judgment without evidence or someone trustworthy." They sought that for him, and, while they were searching and not finding any evidence, Moses passed by the very same Israelite the next day, fighting with a Pharaonite, and the Israelite again asked him for help against the Pharaonite. By chance he had encountered Moses, who had regretted what he had done the previous day and hated what he had seen. Moses became angry and reached out his hand, wanting to strike the Pharaonite. Instead he said to the Israelite, because of what the man had done yesterday and today, *"Verily you are clearly a hothead!"*[213] The Israelite looked at Moses after he had spoken and saw that Moses was as angry as he had been the day before, when he had killed the Pharaonite, and the Israelite feared—after his saying *"Verily, you are clearly a hothead!"*[214]—that [his anger] would be intended for him. But it was not intended for him, only for the Pharaonite. However, the Israelite was afraid and held off the Pharaonite. The Israelite said, *"Would you kill me as you killed*
[458] *a person yesterday?"*[215] He said that only because he feared it was he

210. MS BM has, instead of "with the Israelites," "with Pharaoh. For what Moses did in advising the Israelites sincerely, his responding to them. . . . "

211. MS BM adds here "without knowing that he was an Israelite."

212. Qur'ān 28:15–16.

213. Qur'ān 28:18.

214. Qur'ān 28:18.

215. Qur'ān 28:19.

that Moses had in mind to kill. The two stopped fighting, and the Pharaonite went off to his people, relating to them the report he had heard from the Israelite when the latter said, "Would you kill me as you killed a person yesterday?"

Moses took the main road when Pharaoh sent out the executioners in search of him, certain that he would not escape them. A man from the party of Moses who lived in the farthest part of the city took a shortcut nearby and got to Moses first, informing him of this. And that was one of the trials, O Ibn Jubayr!

The account now returns to that of al-Suddī, who said: When [Moses] reached Midian, *he found there a tribe of men watering*[216] [their flocks]—meaning: a great many of the people watering [their flocks].

Abu ʿAmmār al-Marwazī[217]—al-Faḍl b. Mūsā[218]—al-Aʿmash[219]—al-Minhāl b. ʿAmr[220]—Saʿīd b. Jubayr: Moses left Egypt for Midian, between which lay a journey of eight nights. Saʿīd commented: "It is said to be like [the distance] from al-Kūfah to al-Baṣrah." He had no food except leaves of trees. He had left barefoot and did not reach Midian until the soles fell off his feet.

Abū Kurayb—ʿAththām[221]—al-Aʿmash—al-Minhāl—Saʿīd b. Jubayr—Ibn ʿAbbās, who said something similar.

The account returns to that of al-Suddī: *He found apart from them two women keeping back*—meaning, holding back their flocks of sheep. He asked them, *"What ails you?" The two said,* [459]
"We cannot give our flocks anything to drink until the shepherds go away, and our father is a very old man."[222] Moses had pity on them and went to the well. He took away a stone that was on the well, which it took a group from the people of Midian together to lift

---

216. Qurʾān 28:23.
217. Abū ʿAmmār al-Marwazī. *Index,* 404. Not further identified.
218. Possibly al-Faḍl b. Mūsā al-Sinānī, from the region of Marw. Ibn Saʿd, *op. cit.,* VII, 2, 104.
219. Sulaymān b. Mihrān al-Asadī, nicknamed al-Aʿmash, 61–148/681–765. A traditionist and Qurʾān "reader" from al-Kufah, following the system of Ibn Masʿūd. *EI²*, s.v. "al-Aʿmash"; Ibn Saʿd, *op. cit.,* VI, 238; al-Ziriklī, *op. cit.,* III, 198; *GAS,* I, 9, 81, 310–11, 560.
220. Al-Minhāl b. ʿAmr, cf. *Index,* 574. Not further identified.
221. ʿAththām b. ʿAlī, Abū ʿAlī, d. 195/811, a reliable Kūfan traditionist. Ibn Saʿd, *op. cit.,* VI, 173.
222. Qurʾān 28:23.

up. Moses drew water for them with a bucket, and they gave their flocks water and returned [home] quickly, for usually they watered only from the overflow of the troughs. *Then* Moses *turned aside to the shade* of an acacia tree *and said, "My Lord! I am in need of whatever good You send down to me."*[223]

Ibn ʿAbbās said: As Moses spoke, if a man wanted he could see the greenness of his entrails from his intense hunger. He was only asking God for food.

Ibn Ḥumayd — Ḥakkām b. Salm[224] — ʿAnbasah[225] — Abū Ḥuṣayn[226]—Saʿīd b. Jubayr—Ibn ʿAbbās, about His words: *when he came to the water of Midian*[227] said: He came to the water, and the greenness of plants appeared in his stomach because of his emaciation. Then he said, *"My Lord! I am in need of whatever good You send down for me."*[228] [Ibn ʿAbbās interpreted this as] sufficient food.

The account returns to that of al-Suddī: When the two maidens returned quickly to their father, he asked them about the watering. They told him the story of Moses, so he sent one of them to him, and she came to him *walking shyly. She said, "Lo! my father bids you, that he may reward you with a payment for your having watered*
[460] *the flock for us."*[229] So he arose with her and said, "Go." So she walked before him, and the winds blew on her so he could look at her buttocks. Moses said to her, "Walk behind me, and guide me on the way [from there] if I make a mistake." When he came to the old man *and told him the story, he said: "Fear not! You have escaped from the wrongdoing folk." One of the two women said: "O my father! Hire him! For the best one you can hire is the strong, the trustworthy one."*[230] She was the maiden who had invited him. The old man said: "I had already seen his strength when he took away the stone, but did you see his trustworthiness? What do you know of that?"

---

223. Qurʾān 28:24.

224. Ḥakkām b. Salm al-Rāzī. Ibn Saʿd, *op. cit.*, VII/2, 110.

225. ʿAnbasah b. Saʿīd al-Kūfī, of Umayyad descent, he transmitted from Abū Hurayrah. Ibn Saʿd, *op. cit.*, V, 177.

226. Abū Ḥusayn al-Rāwī. *Index*, 169. Not further identified. Possibly the man mentioned by Ibn Saʿd, *op. cit.*, IV, 2, 19.

227. Qurʾān 28:23.

228. Qurʾān 28:24.

229. Qurʾān 28:25.

230. Qurʾān 28:25–26.

She said, "I was walking in front of him, and he did not wish to wrong me, so he ordered me to walk behind him." The old man said to him; *"I would like to marry you to one of my two daughters, on the condition that you hire yourself to me [for (the term of) eight pilgrimages. Then, if you complete ten, it will be of your own accord, for I would not make it hard for you. God willing, you will find me of the righteous." He said, "That is between you and me], whichever of the two terms I fulfill*—whether eight or ten. *God is Guarantor over what we say."*[231] Ibn ʿAbbās said: The maiden who invited him was the one he married.

Then he ordered one of his daughters to bring him a staff, and she brought it to him. That was the staff that an angel in the form of a man had given to the old man. The maiden entered and got the staff and brought it out to him. When the old man saw it, he said to her, "No! Bring another one." So she threw it down and tried to grab another one, but only that one came to her hand. He kept sending her back, but every time she would come back with that one in her hand. When [Moses] saw this, he approached the staff, took it out, and herded the flocks with it. The old man regretted this, saying, "This was entrusted [to me]." So he went out to meet Moses, and when he [461]
met him he said, "Give me the staff!" Moses replied, "It is my staff" and refused to give it to him. They argued over it, until they came to an agreement that they would appoint the first man who would meet them as an arbitrator. An angel came walking and judged between them, saying, "Place the staff on the ground, and whoever can lift it, it is his." The old man tried but could not lift it. Moses took it in his hand and lifted it up. So the old man left it to Moses, and he herded for the old man for ten years. ʿAbdallāh b. ʿAbbās said: Moses was more worthy of discharging the obligation.

Aḥmad b. Muḥammad al-Ṭūsī[232] related to me — al-Ḥumaydī [Ibn] ʿAbdallāh b. al-Zubayr[233]—Sufyān—Ibrāhīm b. Yaḥyā b. Abī

231. Qurʾān 28:27–28. The section in brackets is omitted in al-Ṭabarī and replaced by "to where He says." In what seems almost a reflex of the story of Jacob's serving Laban for the right to marry his daughter, Shuʿayb has imposed a term of eight to ten years of service in these verses.

232. Aḥmad b. Muḥammad b. Ḥabīb al-Ṭūsī. *Index,* 18. Not further identified.

233. Al-Ḥumaydī (Ibn) ʿAbdallāh b. al-Zubayr b. ʿĪsā, Abū Bakr, d. 219/834, a leading Meccan tradition authority, cited by al-Bukhārī and Muslim. Al-Ziriklī, *op. cit.,* IV, 219; Ibn Ḥajar, *op. cit.,* V, 215; Ibn Saʿd, *op. cit.,* V, 368.

Yaʿqūb[234]—al-Ḥakam b. Ābān[235]—ʿIkrimah—Ibn ʿAbbās that the Messenger of God said: "I asked Gabriel which of the two terms [eight or ten years] did Moses serve, and he replied, 'The fuller and more complete of them.'"

Ibn Ḥumayd related to us — Salamah — Ibn Isḥāq — Ḥakīm b. Jubayr[236] — Saʿīd b. Jubayr, who said: A Jew said to me in al-Kūfah, while I was preparing for the pilgrimage: "Verily, I consider you to be a man who pursues knowledge. Tell me, which of the two terms did Moses complete?" I said: "I do not know. But I am now going to the 'rabbi of the Arabs'[237]—meaning Ibn ʿAbbās—and I will ask him
[462] about that." When I reached Mecca, I asked Ibn ʿAbbās about that, telling him what the Jew had said. Ibn ʿAbbās said: "He completed the greater of the two and the better of them. When a prophet promises something, he does not contradict it." Saʿīd said: I returned to Iraq and met the Jew, telling him about that, and he said, "He is right, but God did not reveal that to Moses."[238] And God is the One who knows best.

Ibn Wakīʿ[239] related to us — Yazīd[240] — al-Aṣbagh b. Zayd[241] — al-Qāsim b. Abī Ayyūb[242] — Saʿīd b. Jubayr, who said: A man from the Christian community asked me which of the two terms Moses completed, and I said, "I do not know," for at that time I did not know. Then I met with Ibn ʿAbbās and mentioned to him what the Christian had asked me, and he said: "Didn't you know that eight were obligatory for him? A prophet cannot decrease this required number. Know that God made Moses keep his promise that he had made, so he completed ten years."

---

234. Ibrāhīm b. Yaḥyā b. Abī Yaʿqūb. *Index*, 10. Not further identified.

235. Al-Ḥakam b. Ābān, d. 154/770. A native of Aden. Ibn Saʿd, *op. cit.*, V, 397.

236. Ḥakīm b. Jubayr al-Asadī. Ibn Saʿd, *op. cit.*, VI, 228. No further information.

237. *Ḥabr/ḥibr al-ʿarab*. Usually used for a non-Muslim religious authority, *ḥabr* is derived from Hebrew *ḥaber*, a title of respect for outstanding rabbinic authorities. Among Arabic-speaking Jews it became a synonym for educated men and scholars, see *EJ* VII, 1491–92. See also *EI*[2] I, s.v. "Ibn ʿAbbās," where Ibn ʿAbbās was called *ḥibr/ḥabr* and *al-baḥr* "the sea" because of the breadth of his learning.

238. Perhaps implying that none of this is included in the biblical account.

239. Sufyān b. Wakīʿ, d. 247/861. Mentioned in Yāqūt, *op. cit.*, III, 276. Not further identified.

240. I.e., Yazīd b. Hārūn. See n. 99, above.

241. Al-Aṣbagh b. Zayd al-Warrāq al-Juhanī (client of al-Juhaynah), d. 159/776, a bookseller who copied Qurʾān texts and a weak transmitter of tradition, according to Ibn Saʿd, *op. cit.*, VII/2, 61.

242. Al-Qāsim b. Abī Ayyūb. See n. 199, above.

Al-Qāsim b. al-Ḥasan[243] related to us—al-Ḥusayn[244]—Ḥajjāj[245]—Ibn Jurayj—Wahb b. Sulaymān al-Dhimārī[246]—Shuʿayb al-Jabāʾī,[247] who said: The names of the two maidens were Liyā and Zipporah, and the wife of Moses was Zipporah bt. Jethro,[248] the priest of Midian; and a priest *(kāhin)* is a rabbi *(ḥabr)*.[249]

Abū al-Sāʾib[250] related to me—Abū Muʿāwiyah[251]—al-Aʿmash—ʿAmr b. Murrah[252]—Abū ʿUbaydah,[253] who said: The one who hired Moses was Jethro, the nephew of Shuʿayb the prophet.

Ibn Wakīʿ related to us—al-ʿAlāʾ b. ʿAbd al-Jabbār[254]—Ḥammād b. Salamah[255]—Abū Ḥamzah[256]—Ibn ʿAbbās, who said: The one who hired Moses was named Jethro (Yathrā), the ruler of Midian.

---

243. Probably al-Qāsim b. al-Ḥasan, al-Hamadānī, d. 272/885, as given in the chain of transmitters in *GAS*, I, 31.

244. Al-Ḥusayn b. Dāwūd al-Maṣṣīṣī, d. 226/840. See *GAS*, I, 31.

245. Al-Ḥajjāj b. Muḥammad al-Aʿwar, Abū Muḥammad, d. 206/821 in Baghdad. A reliable transmitter. *GAS*, I, 31; Ibn Saʿd, *op. cit.*, VII, 2, 75, 186.

246. Wahb b. Sulaymān al-Dhimarī, a scholar from Yemen. Ibn Saʿd, *op. cit.*, V, 391; Dodge, *op. cit.*, II, 1121; Yāqūt, *op. cit.*, II, 129.

247. Shuʿayb al-Jabāʾī, a scholar from Yemen and contemporary of Ṭāwūs b. Kaysān, who died in 106/724. Yāqūt, *op. cit.*, II, 12, s.v. "Jabaʾ."

248. Ṣafūrah bt. Yathrā in Arabic. See n. 166, above, where the question of the identity of Shuʿayb and Jethro is discussed; and see the continued discussion in the text. Liyā (not mentioned in the Bible) may be a reflex of Leah, the first wife of Jacob. See n. 231, above.

249. The Arabic *kāhin* is used for Hebrew *kohen,* with which it is etymologically connected, although the *kāhin* was a diviner or soothsayer, rather than a priest. For *ḥabr,* see n. 237, above.

250. Abū al-Sāʾib Salm b. Junādah. *Index,* 221. Not further identified.

251. Abū Muʿāwiyah al-Ḍarīr, Muḥammad b. Khāzim, 113–94/731–810. A blind memorizer and reliable transmitter of many traditions, who died in al-Kūfah. Ibn Ḥajar, *op. cit.*, IX,137; Ibn Saʿd, *op. cit.*, VI, 273; al-Ziriklī, *op. cit.*, VI, 345.

252. ʿAmr b. Murrah al-Jamalī, d. 116 or 118/734 or 736. From Madhḥij in Yemen. Ibn Saʿd, *op. cit.*, VI, 220.

253. Abū ʿUbaydah Maʿmar b. al-Muthannā, 110–209/728–824. A Baṣran noted for his learning, brought to Baghdad by Hārūn al-Rashīd; an author of numerous works. Ibn Ḥajar, *op. cit.*, X, 246; Yāqūt, *op. cit.*, many citations.

254. Al-ʿAlāʾ b. ʿAbd al-Jabbār al-ʿAṭṭār, a Baṣran who settled in Mecca and transmitted many traditions. Ibn Saʿd, *op. cit.*, V, 367.

255. Ḥammād b. Salamah b. Dīnār, Abū Salamah, d. 164 or 166/781 or 783, at al-Baṣrah. A noted mufti and scholar who transmitted many traditions, often ones that were disapproved. Ibn Saʿd, *op. cit.*, VII/2, 39; Dodge, *op. cit.*, II, 993; al-Ziriklī, *op. cit.*, II, 302.

256. So also in al-Thaʿlabī, *op. cit.*, 154, but Ibrāhīm, *op. cit.*, I, 400, has Abū Jamrah instead of Abū Ḥamzah. If the former, he is Abū Jamrah al-Ḍubaʿī, Naṣr b. ʿImrān, d. 127/745. A noted trusted transmitter of tradition from al-Baṣrah, later Khurāsān. Ibn Saʿd, *op. cit.*, VII/2, 6; Ibn Ḥajar, *op. cit.*, X,431; al-Ziriklī, *op. cit.*, VII, 348.

[463] Ismāʿīl b. al-Ḥaytham Abū al-ʿĀliyah[257] related to me — Abū Qutaybah[258] — Ḥammād b. Salamah — Abū Ḥamzah[259] — Ibn ʿAbbās, who said: The name of the father of Moses' wife was Jethro (Yathrā).

The account returns to that of al-Suddī: *Then, when Moses had fulfilled his term and was journeying with his family,*[260] he erred in the way. ʿAbdallāh b. ʿAbbās said: "It was winter. A fire became visible to him and he thought that it was fire, but it was the light of God. *He said to his family, 'Stay here. Lo! I see in the distance a fire; perhaps I may bring you tidings from it.*[261] And if I do not find any tidings *I shall bring you a borrowed flame so that you may warm yourselves.'"*[262] [Ibn ʿAbbās] said: "[That was] because of the cold. But, when he reached the flame, he was called from the right side of the valley from the tree *in the blessed field.*[263] *'Blessed is whoever is in the fire and whoever is around it.'*[264] And, when Moses heard the call, he was startled and said, 'Praise be to God, Lord of the worlds!' And there was proclaimed: *'O Moses! lo! I, verily I, am God, the Lord of the Worlds.*[265] *What is that in your right hand, O Moses?' He said, 'This is my staff, on which I lean and with which I beat down leaves for my sheep.'*[266] He is saying: 'I would beat the leaves of the trees with it, and they would fall down for the sheep. *'And I have other uses.'*[267] He means to say, 'Other needs.' 'I carry on the staff the provision bag and the waterskin.' God said to him, *'Cast it down, O Moses!' So he cast it down, and lo! it was a serpent gliding.*[268] *But, when Moses saw it writhing as though it were a demon, he turned to flee and did not wait.'*[269] He means to say: 'He did not wait.'[270] It was said to him, *'O Moses! Do not fear! The messengers*

257. Ismāʿīl b. al-Ḥaytham, Abū al-ʿĀliyah. *Index,* 39. Not further identified.
258. Abū Qutaybah. *Index,* 460. Not further identified.
259. Abū Jamrah (?). See n. 256, above.
260. Qurʾān 28:29.
261. Qurʾān 28:29.
262. Qurʾān 27:7.
263. Qurʾān 28:30.
264. Qurʾān 27:8.
265. Qurʾān 28:30.
266. Qurʾān 20:17–18.
267. Qurʾān 20:17–18.
268. Qurʾān 20:19–20.
269. Qurʾān 27:10; 28:31.
270. Qurʾān has *yuʿaqqib,* which al-Ṭabarī glosses by *yantaẓir.*

do not fear in My presence.[271] *Draw near, and do not fear. Verily! you are one of those who are secure. Thrust your hand into the bosom of your robe; [it will come forth white without hurt. And guard your heart from fear.] Then there shall be two proofs from your* [464] *Lord,'*[272] In other words, the staff and the hand are [the] two signs because Moses had prayed to his Lord and said, *'My Lord! Lo! I killed a man among them, and I fear that they will kill me. My brother Aaron is more eloquent than I in speech. Therefore send him with me as a helper to confirm me*—he is saying, 'In order that he confirm me.'— *'for I fear that they will consider me a liar.'*[273] He had said to them, *'I have committed a crime,' and I fear that they will kill me,*[274] meaning, for the slain man. *He said, 'We will strengthen your arm with your brother, and We will give both of you power'*—and the power is the proof— *'so that they cannot reach you because of Our signs. You two, and those who follow you, will be the victors.*[275] Moses and Aaron, come [both of you] to [Pharaoh] and say, *"Verily, we are messengers of the Lord of the Worlds."'*[276]

Ibn Ḥumayd related to us—Salamah: *When Moses completed his term,*[277] he went out—according to what was mentioned to me by Ibn Isḥāq—Wahb b. Munabbih the Yemenite,[278] according to what was mentioned to him about Moses—with his flocks, his fire drill, and in his hand his staff, with which he beat leaves down for his flocks in the daytime. When night fell, he struck a fire with his fire drill and slept near it with his family and flocks. When morning came, he set out with his family and flocks, leaning on his staff, which had, according to what was described to me from Wahb b. Munabbih, two prongs at its top and a hook at its end.

Ibn Ḥumayd related to us—Salamah—Ibn Isḥāq—one of his friends who could not be doubted [as to veracity]—that Kaʿb al-

---

271. Qurʾān 27:10.
272. Qurʾān 28:31–32. The omitted portion of the verse is given here in brackets.
273. Qurʾān 28:33–34.
274. Qurʾān 26:14.
275. Qurʾān 28:35.
276. Qurʾān 26:16.
277. Qurʾān 28:29.
278. Wahb b. Munabbih, Abū ʿAbdallāh, ca. 17–110 or 114, 638–728 or 732. A Yemenite Muslim scholar of Jewish origin who was noted for his acquaintance with pre-Muslim traditions, especially from Jewish sources. Ibn Saʿd, *op. cit.*, V, 395; Ibn Ḥajar, *op. cit.*, XI: 166; *GAS*, I, 305–7; *EJ*, 16, 341–42; al-Ziriklī, *op. cit.*, IX, 150; Dodge, *op. cit.*, II, 1121.

Aḥbār[279] came to Mecca where ʿAbdallāh b. ʿAmr b. al-ʿĀṣ[280] was, and Kaʿb said: "Ask him about three things, and, if he tells you, then he is learned. Ask him about something that God placed on earth for mankind from Paradise; and ask him what was the first thing placed on the earth; and what was the first tree planted in the earth?" ʿAbdallāh was asked about them, and he said: "The first thing God
[465] placed on earth for mankind from Paradise was this Black Corner.[281] As for the first thing placed on earth, it was Barahūt[282] in Yemen, where the corpses of the unbelievers will come. As for the first tree that God planted on earth, it was the boxthorn from which Moses cut his staff." When this reached Kaʿb, he said: "The man is right, a scholar, by God!"

The narrator continued: When the night came on which God wished to show His favor upon Moses and on which He started him on his prophethood and His speaking to him, Moses took the wrong road, so that he did not know where he was going. He took out his fire drill to kindle a fire for his family so that they might sleep around it and in the morning they would awaken and he could determine his path's direction. However, his fire drill became inert and would not strike a fire for him. He continued to strike it until, [when][283] it tired him, a fire glowed. When he saw it, *he said to his family: "Wait! Lo! I discern a fire. Perhaps I may bring you a brand from it or may find guidance at the fire"*[284]—with a brand, so they might warm themselves, and guidance about knowledge of the path on which we were misled by the description of a knowledgeable one.[285] So he moved toward it, and behold! it was in a creeping bush

279. Kaʿb al-Aḥbār b. Mātiʿ, Abū Isḥāq, d. 32/652. A Yemenite Jew who converted to Islam under ʿUmar, he emigrated to Medina, then to Syria, and became a noted source, often quoted, for Jewish and Yemenite traditions. Ibn Saʿd, *op. cit.*, VII, 2, 156; *EI*², s.v. "Kaʿb al-Aḥbār." 17; Ibn Ḥajar, *op. cit.*, VIII, 438–40; *EJ*, 10:488; I. Ben Zeev, *Kaʿb al-Aḥbār*; *GAS*, I, 304–5.

280. ʿAbdallāh b. ʿAmr b. al-ʿĀṣ, 65/616–84. An early convert to Islam and source of many traditions from the Prophet, he served as governor of al-Kūfah briefly under Muʿāwiyah. Ibn Saʿd, *op. cit.*, IV, 2, 8–13; *GAS*, I, 84; al-Ziriklī, *op. cit.*, IV, 250.

281. *Al-rukn al-aswad*, i.e., the corner of the Kaʿbah in which the Black Stone is embedded.

282. MS C has Barahūd. Yāqūt, *op. cit.*, I, 598: a valley in Yemen in which the Prophet said the souls of the unbelievers and hypocrites will be placed.

283. The insertion of *idhā* "when" is suggested by the editor of the Arabic text, al-Ṭabarī, I, 465 n. *f*, and appears in Ibrāhīm, *op. cit.*, I, 402.

284. Qurʾān 20:10.

285. Text has *khabīr*, instead of *khayr* "goodness." See al-Ṭabarī, I, 465 n. *h*; Ibrāhīm, *op. cit.*, I, 402.

—although some among the scriptuaries say it was in a boxthorn. When he came near, it drew back from him. When he saw it draw back, he retreated from it, feeling a sense of fear. When he wanted to leave, it drew near him. Then something was spoken from the bush. When he heard the voice, he listened, and God said to him, *"Take off your shoes, for lo! you are in the holy valley of Ṭuwā,"*[286] and he [466] threw them down. Then He said, *"What is that in your right hand, O Moses?"*[287] [Moses] replied, *"This is my staff on which I lean, and with which I beat down branches for my sheep, and wherein I find other uses'*—that is, other benefits. *He said, "Cast it down, O Moses!" So he cast it down, and lo! it was a serpent gliding.*[288] Its two prongs became the serpent's mouth; its hook became a crest on its back, which shook, and it had fangs. It was as God wished it to be. Moses saw this fearful thing and turned to flee, and he did not wait.

His Lord called to him: "O Moses! Approach, *and fear not. We shall return it to its former state"*—that is, its state as a staff, as it had been. When he approached, He said: *"Grasp it and do not fear.*[289] Put your hand into its mouth." Moses was wearing a long garment of wool, so he wrapped his hand in his sleeve, because he was terrified of the serpent. It was proclaimed: "Cast your sleeve from your hand!" and he cast it off. Then he placed his hand between the serpent's jaws. When he did so, he seized it, and lo! It became his staff, with his hand between its two forks, where he usually grasped it, and its hook in its place. There was nothing of it he did not recognize.

Then it was said to him: *"Thrust your hand into your bosom; it will come forth white without injury"*[290]—that is, without leprosy—for Moses was a ruddy man, hook-nosed, curly-haired, and tall. So he placed his hand into his bosom and then brought it out, white as snow. He returned it to his bosom, and it came out as it had previously been in color. Then He said: *"These shall be two proofs from your Lord to Pharaoh and his chiefs. Lo! They are evil-living people." He said: "My Lord! I killed one of their men, and I fear that they will kill me. My brother Aaron is more eloquent than I in*

---

286. Qur'ān 20:12.
287. Qur'ān 20:17.
288. Qur'ān 20:18–20.
289. Qur'ān 20:21.
290. Qur'ān 20:22; cf. 27:12, 28:32.

speech. So send him with me as a helper to confirm me"—that is,
[467] to explain to them what I say, for he will clarify what they do not understand. *He said: "We will strengthen your arm with your brother, and We will give to you both power, so that they cannot reach you for Our signs. You two, and those who follow you, will be the winners."*[291]

The account returns to that of al-Suddī: Moses returned to his family, and together they journeyed toward Egypt until they arrived during the night. He was given hospitality by his mother, but he did not recognize them.[292] He came to them on a night during which they were eating *ṭifshīl*,[293] and he camped beside the house. Then Aaron came and noticed his guest. He asked his mother about him, and she told him that he was a guest. He invited Moses and ate with him. While they were sitting and conversing, Aaron asked him: "Who are you?" He replied: "I am Moses." So both stood up, and each embraced the other.

When they had become familiar with each other, Moses said to him: "O Aaron! Go to Pharaoh with me, for God has sent us to him." Aaron responded: "I hear and obey!" But their mother arose and shouted, saying, "I beg you by God not to go to Pharaoh, for he will kill you." But they refused and went off to him during the night. They arrived at the gate and knocked. Pharaoh was startled, as was the gatekeeper, and Pharaoh said: "Who is that knocking at my gate at this hour?" The gatekeeper looked down upon them and spoke to them. Moses said to him: *"I am the messenger of the Lord of the Worlds!"*[294] The gatekeeper was frightened, and he went to Pharaoh and informed him, saying: "Here is a madman who claims that he is the Messenger of the Lord of the Worlds." Pharaoh said, "Let him enter." Moses entered and said, "Verily, I am the Messenger of the Lord of the Worlds," and you must *send with me the Children of Israel."* Pharaoh recognized him and said, *"Did we not rear you*

291. Qurʾān 28:32–35.

292. *Yaʿrifuhum* or *yuʿrifuhum* "he had not informed them." But Ibn al-Athīr, *op. cit.*, I, 180, has *wa-lā yaʿrifūnahu* "and they did not recognize him." See the very different account in al-Thaʿlabī, *op. cit.*, 160.

293. A dish of grains. See the note in *Glossarium*, CCCXLI, s.v. *ṭafshīl*. See al-Ṭabarī, trans. Perlmann, 66 n. 171, where it is related to the Aramaic *tabshīla*, a kind of broth.

294. Qurʾān 43:46.

among us as a child? And you spent many years of your life among us, and you did your deed that you did. You are one of the unbelievers [468] together with us in our religion, which you denounce!" Moses said: *"I did it then when I was one who is astray. Then I fled from you when I feared you. My Lord gave me rule* (and this rule is prophecy) *and appointed me one of the messengers. And this is a favor with which you reproach me, that you have enslaved the Israelites*[295] and you reared me previously as a child."

Pharaoh said: "What is the Lord of the Worlds?[296] *And who is your Lord, O Moses?" He replied: "Our Lord is He who gave everything its nature, then guided it."*[297] He means to say: He gave every beast its mate, then guided it to mate. Pharaoh said to him: *"If you have brought a sign, then bring it forth, if you are one of the truthful."*[298] This was after he had said to him some words that God had mentioned. Moses said: *"Even though I bring you something plain?" Pharaoh said: "Bring it, if you are one of the truthful." Then he flung down his staff, and it became clearly a serpent*[299] (the serpent is a male snake), which opened its mouth and placed its lower jaw on the ground and its upper on the walls of the palace. It then turned toward Pharaoh to seize him. When Pharaoh saw it, he was terrified and jumped up, voiding excrement, although he had not previously done so.[300] He screamed, "O Moses! Seize it and I will believe in you. I will send the Israelites with you." So Moses grabbed the serpent, and it became a staff once more. *And he drew forth his hand*—bringing it out of his bosom—*and lo! It was white to the beholders.*[301] Moses left his presence after that, and Pharaoh refused to believe in him or to send the Israelites with him. Instead, he said to his people: *"O Chiefs! I do not know that you have a god other than me, so kindle a fire for me, O Haman,*[302] *to bake the mud; and set* [469]

---

295. Qur'ān 26:17–22.

296. Qur'ān 26:23.

297. Qur'ān 20:50.

298. Qur'ān 7:106.

299 Qur'ān 26:30–32.

300. This was supposedly a sign of Pharaoh's superhuman nature. See p. 55 and nn. 314–16, below.

301. Qur'ān 26:33, 7:106.

302. One of the prototypical figures of evil in the Qur'ān and Islamic lore, Haman is transferred from his biblical locale in Persia to the palace of Pharaoh. See *EI*², s.v. "Hāmān."

up a lofty tower so that I may look at the god of Moses."[303] When the lofty edifice was built for him, he climbed to the top of it, called for an arrow, and shot it toward heaven. It returned to him, stained with blood. So he said, "I have killed the God of Moses."[304]

Bishr b. Muʿādh—Yazīd b. Zurayʿ[305]—Saʿīd—Qatādah: *So kindle a fire for me, O Haman, to bake the mud;*[306] he said [this means] he was the first to bake the bricks with which to build a tower.

As for Ibn Isḥāq, he said what Ibn Ḥumayd related—Salamah—Ibn Isḥāq: Moses went out when God sent him until he reached Egypt and Pharaoh, both he and his brother Aaron, until they stood at Pharaoh's gate, requesting to enter, saying: "We are two Messengers of the Lord of the Worlds, so permit us to see this man." According to what we have heard, they remained for two years, spending mornings and evenings at his gate, while Pharaoh knew nothing of this, for no one had the audacity to inform him. This continued until a jester of his, one who amused him and made him laugh, entered to him and said: "O King! At the gate there is a man who says something strange, claiming that he has a god other than you." Pharaoh said: "Let him be brought in!" So Moses entered, with his brother Aaron; and in his hand was his staff. When he stood before Pharaoh, he said to him: *"I am the Messenger of the Lord of the Worlds."*[307] But Pharaoh recognized him and said, *"Did we not rear you among us as a child? And you dwelt many years of your life among us. And you did your deed that you did, and you are one of the unbelievers." He replied: "I did it then when I was one [who is] astray."*[308]—that is, erring—"I did not wish to do that." Then Moses approached him, denying to Pharaoh what he mentioned of his favor to Moses while he was with him, and said: *"And this is a favor with which you reproved me, that you have enslaved the Israelites*[309]—
[470] that is, you regarded them as slaves, taking their sons from them,

303. Qurʾān 28:38.

304. See the story of Nimrod, who also wanted to reach God in heaven. Al-Ṭabarī, I, 321–23 (trans. Brinner, 107–9).

305. Yazīd b. Zurayʿ, Abū Muʿāwiyah, 102–82/720–98. A Baṣran considered a trustworthy transmitter of *Ḥadīth*. Ibn Saʿd, *op. cit.*, VII/2, 44; Ibn Ḥajar, *op. cit.*, XI, 325–28; al-Ziriklī, *op. cit.*, IX, 235.

306. Qurʾān 28:38.

307. Qurʾān 7:104.

308. Qurʾān 26:18–20.

309. Qurʾān 26:22. Probably to be understood as "and this is a 'favor' you granted me? That you enslaved. . . . "

stealing from whomever you wished, and killing whomever you wished. Indeed, only this brought me to your house and to you." *Pharaoh said: "And what is the Lord of the Worlds?"*[310] That is, he asked him to describe his God Who sent him, or "What is this God of yours?" *Moses said: "Lord of the heavens and the earth and all that is between them, if only you had sure belief." Pharaoh said to those around him* of his chiefs, *"Do you not hear?"*[311]—namely, disputing what he had said—"He has no god but me." *Moses said: "Your Lord and the Lord of your forefathers*[312] Who created your forefathers and created you from your fathers." *Pharaoh said: "Lo! Your messenger, who has been sent to you, is indeed a madman"*—that is, this is not true when he claims that you have a god other than me. *Moses said: "Lord of the East and the West and all that is between them, if you would only understand"*—that is, He is creator of the East and the West and all created things between them, if you would only understand. *Pharaoh said: "If you choose a god other than me*—to worship other than me and abandon my worship—*I shall certainly place you among the prisoners." He replied: "Even if I show you something plain?"*—that is, by which you will acknowledge my truth and your falsehood. *Pharaoh said: "Produce it then, if you are truthful!" Then he flung down his staff, and it became a serpent manifest*[313] and filled all that was between the two ranks of Pharaoh's men, its mouth open. The crook of the staff had become a crest on its back, and the people scattered before it. Pharaoh left his throne, adjuring Moses by his Lord. Then Moses placed his hand in his bosom and withdrew it white as snow. Then he returned it to its [471]
condition. Moses placed his hand between the serpent's jaws, and it became a staff in his hand, the latter being between its prongs and its crook at the bottom as it had been. Pharaoh was unable to control his bowels, although they claim he used to remain for five or six days not seeking the privy—meaning the latrine—as other people do, and that was one of the things that induced him to say that there was not like him anyone among the people.[314]

---

310. Qur'ān 26:23.
311. Qur'ān 26:24–25.
312. Qur'ān 26:26.
313. Qur'ān 26:27–32.
314. For other references to Pharaoh's bowels and his reactions to these events, see p. 53 and n. 300, above.

Ibn Ḥumayd related to us — Salamah — Ibn Isḥāq: I was told by Wahb b. Munabbih the Yemenite that [Pharaoh] had diarrhea[315] for twenty-odd nights until he almost expired; then it ceased.[316] He said to his chiefs: *"Lo! This is verily a sage wizard"*—that is, there is no wizard more competent at magic than Moses — *[who would drive you out of your land by his magic.] "Now what do you counsel?*[317] Shall I kill him?" *And a believer of Pharaoh's family [who hid his faith] said* — a pious servant whose name was, as they assert, Ḥabrak — *"Would you kill a man because he said: 'My Lord is Allāh,' and has brought you clear proofs from His Lord*[318] with his staff and his hand?" Then he made them afraid of God's punishment and warned them of what had happened to peoples before them, saying: *"O my people! Your dominion is today the uppermost in the land. But who would save us from the wrath of God should it reach us?"* *Pharaoh said: "I only show you what I think, and I only guide you to a wise policy"*[319] The chiefs of his people said, the power of God having disenchanted them, *"Put him off, him and his brother, and send into the cities summoners, who will bring to you every knowing wizard"*[320] — that is, outnumber him with wizards. "Perhaps
[472] you may find among the wizards someone who can perform what he does."

Moses and Aaron had left Pharaoh after Moses had shown them some of God's powers. Pharaoh immediately[321] sent throughout his domain and did not leave a single sorcerer under his rule whom he did not have brought. I have been told, but God knows best, that he gathered fifteen thousand sorcerers, and when they assembled before him he gave them his command, saying: "A sorcerer has come to us unlike any we have seen before. If you are able to outdo him, I shall honor you and prefer you and bring you nearer than all the people of my kingdom." They said: "Will all that indeed be ours if we outdo him?" He replied, "Yes." They said, "Then set a date for us to come together, the sorcerer and us."

---

315. *Fa-mashā* (Ms Tn adds *baṭnuhu*). See *Glossarium*, CDLXXVI, s.v. *mshy: alvi profluvio laboravit;* Dozy, *op. cit.*, II, 604, *aller à la selle.*

316. *Istamsaka.* See *Glossarium*, CDLXXXIV, s.v. *msk: se sustinuit, se cohibuit. MS C has istaballa* "was cured."

317. Qurʾān 26:34–35. Words in brackets omitted in text.

318. Qurʾān 40:28. Words in brackets omitted in text.

319. Qurʾān 40:29.

320. Qurʾān 26:36–37.

321. *Makanahu.* See *Glossarium*, CDLX, s.v. *kwn: illico.*

The chiefs of the sorcerers whom Pharaoh had assembled for Moses were Sābūr,[322] ʿĀdūr,[323] Ḥaṭḥaṭ,[324] and Muṣfā[325]—four in number. They were the ones who believed when they saw what they did of God's power. All the sorcerers believed, and they said to Pharaoh, when he threatened them with death and crucifixion, *"We will not choose you above the clear proofs that have come unto us and above Him Who created us. So decree what you will decree."*[326] So Pharaoh sent to Moses to *"appoint a meeting between you and me that neither of us will fail to keep, at a place convenient to both."* [Moses] *said: "Your meeting will be the day of the feast"*—a feast day on which Pharaoh would go forth— *"let the people assemble when the sun is high*[327] to attend my affair and yours." Pharaoh assembled the people for that gathering. Then he ordered the sorcerers, saying: *"Come in ranks. Whoever is uppermost this day will be indeed successful"*[328]—that is, the successful one will be he who is greater than his companion. [473]

Fifteen thousand sorcerers, each with his cords[329] and staves, arranged themselves in ranks. Moses went forth, his brother with him, leaning on his staff, until he reached the assembly, while Pharaoh was in his assembly with the noblest people of his domain. The people crowded around Pharaoh. Moses said to the sorcerers when he came to them: *"Woe unto you! Do not invent a lie against God, lest He wipe you out by some punishment. He who lies fails miserably."*[330] The sorcerers disputed among themselves, and one said to the other in secret, *"Lo! These are two sorcerers who would drive you out of your country by their magic and destroy your best traditions."*[331] Then they said, *"O Moses! Either throw first, or let us be the first to throw." He said: "Nay, but you throw!" Then lo! Their*

---

322. Also Shānūr, Sālūr, Schâboun. See al-Ṭabarī, I, 472 n. *e*; Sātūr in Ibrāhīm, *op. cit.*, I, 408.

323. Also Ghādhūr, Gâboun. See al-Ṭabarī, I, 472 n. *f*; ʿĀdūr, Ibrāhīm, *op. cit.*, I, 408.

324. Also Ḥaṭḥaṭah, Hatîl, al-Ṭabarī I, 472 n. *g*.

325. Also Muḍʿā, al-Ṭabarī I, 472 n. *h*. *Addenda* I, DLXXXIV, lists five persons: Sābūr, Ghādūr, Ḥafẓ, Khaṭaṭ, and Muṣfā.

326. Qurʾān 20:72.

327. Qurʾān 20:58–59.

328. Qurʾān 20:64.

329. Cords of rope were used in divination and imprecation, e.g., blowing on knots, as in Qurʾān 113:4.

330. Qurʾān 20:61.

331. Qurʾān 20:63.

cords and their staves, by their magic, appeared to him as though they ran.[332]

The first people they dazzled by their sorcery were Moses and Pharaoh, and then the people afterward. Then each man among them threw whatever cord or staff he had in his hand, each becoming a serpent as big as a mountain, which filled the valley, one mounted on the other. *Moses conceived a fear in his soul,*[333] and he said, "By God! Verily they were staves in their hands, and they became serpents. [But] this staff of mine will not run" or so he had a presentiment. Therefore God inspired him, *"Throw what is in your right hand! It will eat up what they have made. Lo! What they have made is but a sorcerer's artifice, and a sorcerer shall not succeed in whatever he may attain."*[334] Moses was comforted and threw his
[474] staff from his hand. It faced their cords and staves that they had thrown—which were running serpents to the eyes of Pharaoh and the people—and began to overtake and swallow them, serpent by serpent, until there were neither few nor many of what they had thrown remaining in the valley. Then Moses grabbed it, and it became his staff in his hand, as it had been previously. *Then the sorcerers were cast down prostrating, saying: "We believe in the Lord of Aaron and Moses.*[335] If this were sorcery, it would not have overcome us." Pharaoh said to them, regretfully, having seen the clear victory: *"Have you put faith in him before I give you leave? Verily he is your chief who taught you magic. Now surely I shall cut off your hands and your feet alternately [and crucify you on the trunks of palm trees, and you will know for certain which of us has sterner and more lasting punishment." They said: "We do not choose you above the clear proofs that have come to us, and above Him Who created us], so decree what you will decree"*—namely, do what seems best to you—*"you will only end for us the life of this world*—over which alone you have power, but you have no power thereafter. *Verily, we believe in our Lord, that He may forgive our sins and the sorcery into which you forced us. God is better and more last-*

332. Qur'ān 20:65–66.
333. Qur'ān 20:67.
334. Qur'ān 20:69.
335. Qur'ān 20:70.

ing!"[336]—meaning, better than you as to reward and more lasting as to punishment.

God's enemy turned away defeated and cursed, but he refused to do anything but persist in disbelief and persevere in evildoing. God carried out signs against him and seized him with famine[337] and sent upon him the flood.

The account returns to that of al-Suddī. As for al-Suddī, he said in his account: It is mentioned that the signs by which God tested the people of Pharaoh came before the meeting of Moses with the sorcerers. When the arrow returned to him stained with blood, Pharaoh said, "We have slain the God of Moses," whereupon God sent upon them the flood,[338] which was heavy rain; everything they possessed [475] drowned. They cried out, "O Moses! Pray to your Lord to relieve us, and we will believe in you, and we will send the Israelites with you." God relieved them of the flood, and their seeds sprouted. They said, "But now it does not please us that we are not rained upon!" Then God sent locusts upon them that ate their produce. So they asked Moses again to pray to his Lord that He relieve them of the locusts, saying they would then believe in Him. Moses prayed, and He relieved them while a remnant was left of their standing grain. So they said, "We shall not believe, for a remnant is left of our grain." Then God sent upon them tiny locusts that are vermin, and they devoured the land entirely and entered between the clothing and skin of a person, biting him. A person would be eating food when it would become filled with vermin. [It got to the point where] one of them would build a pillar of bricks and plaster and make it slippery, so that nothing could climb on top of it, and he would put the food on top; but, when he climbed up to eat it, he found it full of vermin. No misfortune had ever befallen them that was worse than the vermin. And this is the *rijz*[339] or terror that God mentions in the Qur'ān as having stricken them. They asked Moses to pray to his Lord to remove this terror from them, saying they would then have faith in Him. Yet, when He removed it from them, they refused to believe. So God sent upon them blood. An Israelite and an Egyptian would drink from the

336. Qur'ān 20:71–73. Words in brackets omitted in text.
337. Based on Qur'ān 7:130.
338. Based on Qur'ān 7:134.
339. See Qur'ān 7:134.

same water, but the water of the Egyptian would become blood, while that of the Israelite would remain water.

When this became too difficult for them, they asked Moses to remove it and they would have faith in Him. Yet when he removed it from them, they refused to have faith. That is when God said: *"But when We eased them of the torment, behold! They broke their word"*[340]—about what they had pledged. That is when He said: *"We*
[476] *straitened Pharaoh's people with famine"*—that is, hunger—*"and the dearth of fruits, that perhaps they might heed."*[341] Then God inspired the two of them: *"Speak to him a gentle word, that perhaps he may heed or fear."*[342] They came to him, and Moses said to him: "O Pharaoh! Do you desire that I should grant that your youth will not fade to senility, that your dominion will never be removed from you, and that the pleasure of women, of drinking, and of riding be restored to you? And that when you die, you will enter the Garden? Trust me." These words made an impression on him—that is "the gentle word"—and he said, "Stay where you are until Haman comes." When Haman came, he said to him, "This man came to me." He said, "Who is he?" He said that, although previously [Pharaoh] had only called Moses "the sorcerer," when that day came he did not call him "the sorcerer." Pharaoh said, "Moses." Haman asked, "What did he say to you?" He replied, "He said to me such-and-such." Haman asked, "And what did you reply to him?" He said, "I said, '[Wait] until Haman comes and I take counsel of him.' " Haman found him weak and said: "My opinion of you was better than that. You will become a slave who serves, after having been a master who is served."

That was when Pharaoh went out and addressed his people, assembling them before him, and said: *"I am your Lord the Highest!"*[343] Between his saying *"I do not know that you have a god other than me"*[344] and his words *"I am your Lord the Highest,"*[345] forty years had passed. Then he said to his people: *"Lo! Verily this is a knowing sorcerer who would drive you out of your land with his*

340. Qur'ān 43:50.

341. Qur'ān 7:130. Qur'ān has *yadhdhakarūna* "they might heed," but text and MSS have *yarji'ūna* "turn back." Ibrāhīm, *op. cit.*, I, 411, uses Qur'ānic text.

342. Qur'ān 20:44.

343. Qur'ān 79:24.

344. Qur'ān 28:38.

345. Qur'ān 79:24.

magic. Now what do you counsel?" They said, "Put him off, him and his brother, and send into the cities summoners, who will bring unto you every knowing sorcerer."[346] Pharaoh said, *"Have you come to us to drive us from our land [with your magic], O Moses? But surely we can produce magic like it. So appoint a meeting between us and you, which neither we nor you will fail to keep, at a place equally convenient"* — meaning, equitable. Moses said: *"Your meeting shall be on the day of the feast, and let the people assemble when the sun has risen high."* That was a feast day for them. *Pharaoh went and gathered his strength, then returned.*[347] He sent out summoners in the cities, who assembled the sorcerers to him and assembled the people to watch. *It was said: "Are you [also] gathering?"* [They said:] *"So we shall be able to follow the sorcerers" [if they are the winners. And when the sorcerers came they said to Pharaoh:] "Will there surely be a reward for us if we are the winners?"* — meaning, a gift that you will give us. *He said: "Yes, you will surely then be one of those brought near me."*[348] *Moses said to them: "Woe to you! Do not invent a lie against God, lest He extirpate you by some punishment"* — meaning, destroy you by a punishment. *They debated with one another what they must do, and they kept their counsel secret* from Moses and Aaron. They said in their counsel: *"Lo! These are two sorcerers who would drive you out of your land with their sorcery and destroy your best traditions"*[349] — meaning, destroy the noblest of your people. Moses and the chief of the sorcerers met, and Moses said to him: "Tell me, if I overcome you, will you believe in me and bear witness that what I have brought is true?" He said: "Yes." The sorcerer then said: "Verily, tomorrow I shall bring magic that no magic can overcome. By God! If you overcome me, I shall believe in you and bear witness that what you say is true." Pharaoh was observing them, for this is Pharaoh's speech: *"This is a plot that you plotted in the city* ... when you two met to support each other ... *in order to drive its people from it."*[350] They said, *"O Moses! Either throw first, or let us be the first to throw."*[351] Moses said to them, "Throw," and they threw their

[477] [478]

346. Qur'ān 26:34–37.
347. Qur'ān 20:57–60. Words in brackets omitted in text.
348. Qur'ān 26:40–42. Words in brackets omitted in text.
349. Qur'ān 20:61–63.
350. Qur'ān 7:123.
351. Qur'ān 7:115.

cords and staves. They were thirty-odd thousand men,[352] not one of them without a cord and staff. *When they had thrown, they cast a spell upon the eyes of the people and frightened them,*[353] meaning, they terrified them. *Moses conceived a fear in his mind,* but God inspired him: *"Do not fear! ... Throw what is in your right hand. It will eat up what they have created."*[354] So Moses threw his staff, and it ate every one of their serpents. When they saw that, they prostrated themselves and said: *"We believe in the Lord of the Worlds, the Lord of Moses and Aaron!"*[355] Pharaoh said: *"Verily, I shall cut off your hands and feet on alternate sides and shall indeed crucify you on trunks of palm trees."*[356] He massacred them and cut them up, as ʿAbdallāh b. ʿAbbās related, when they said: *"Our Lord! Grant unto us steadfastness and make us die as those who have surrendered unto You."*[357] It is said that in the morning they were sorcerers and by the end of the day they were martyrs.

Then Pharaoh came out to the Israelites, and his people said to him: *"Will you let Moses and his people make mischief in the land and flout you and your gods?"*[358] His gods, according to what Ibn ʿAbbās asserts, were cattle. Whenever they saw a beautiful cow, he would order them to worship it. Therefore *"he produced for them a calf. . . ."*[359]

Then God commanded Moses to lead out the Israelites. He said: *"Take away My servants by night, for you will be pursued."*[360] Moses ordered the Israelites to go out and to borrow jewelry from the Egyptians. He also ordered that no man call out to another and that they should leave the lamps lit in their houses until morning;[361] whoever went out would cause damage.[362]

---

352. MS Tn has "they were thirty"; al-Thaʿlabī, ms. cited in al-Ṭabarī, I, 478 n. b, f. 129 b, has "and al-Suddī said: 'They were thirty (*thalāthūn* [sic!])-odd thousand'" (corrected to *thalāthīn* in al-Thaʿlabī, *op. cit.*, 164).

353. Qurʾān 7:116.

354. Qurʾān 20:67.

355. Qurʾān 7:121–22, 26:47–48.

356. Qurʾān 20:71; cf. 7:124.

357. Qurʾān 7:126.

358. Qurʾān 7:127.

359. Qurʾān 20:88.

360. Qurʾān 26:52.

361. *Yusrijū,* lit. "Kindle light." Not calling out and leaving the lamps lit seem to be intended to avoid arousing the suspicions of the Egyptians.

362. The Arabic has *wa-anna man kharaja adhan*: meaning unclear, probably connected with the previous phrase. Ibrāhīm, *op. cit.*, I, 414, has *idhā* instead of *adhan.*

Mūsā [b. Hārūn] — ʿAmr [b. Ḥammād[363] — Asbāṭ — al-Suddī][364] says: "That whoever went out" — but Mūsā says ʿAmr says: "I think it should read 'and he who went out ... ' said," "He ordered whoever went out to smear his door with his palm covered with blood to show that he had left. Also God would send out every child of adultery among the Egyptians from the Israelites to the Israelites and would send out every child of adultery among the Israelites from the Egyptians to the Egyptians, so that they would go to their fathers." [479]

Then Moses went out with the Israelites by night, while the Egyptians were unaware. Before that, they had prayed to God against the Egyptians when Moses said: *"Our Lord! You have given Pharaoh and his chiefs splendor and riches in the life of this world. [Our Lord! That they may lead men astray from Your way. Our Lord! Destroy their riches and harden their hearts so that they will not believe] till they see the painful doom."* God said: *"Your prayer is heard."*[365] Al-Suddī claimed that it was Moses who prayed and Aaron said "Amen." That was when God said: *"Your* [dual] *prayer is heard."*[366] Regarding his saying: *"Our Lord! Destroy their riches,"* it is said that the destruction of riches was that He turned their dirhams and dinars into stones. Then He said to the two of them: *"You two keep to the straight path."*[367] Then Moses and Aaron went out with their people. Death was cast down upon the Egyptians; every man's firstborn died. They buried them at dawn and were too busy to seek the Israelites until the sun arose. That is when God said: *"And they overtook them at sunrise."*[368]

Moses was at the rear of the Israelites, while Aaron was in the front, leading them. The believer said to Moses: "Where did you command us [to go]?" He said: "To the sea." He wanted to rush blindly, but Moses prevented him. Moses went out with six hundred

---

363. ʿAmr b. Ḥammād b. Ṭalḥah al-Qannād, Abū Muḥammad, d. 223/836. A transmitter of the commentary of Asbāṭ from al-Suddī. Died in al-Kūfah. Ibn Saʿd, *op. cit.*, VI, 285; *GAS*, I, 33 n. 3.

364. According to al-Ṭabarī, I, 479 n. *a.*, MS Tn omits *adhan* and says "That whoever went out"—but Mūsā says ʿAmr says: "I think it should read 'he who went out.... '"

365. Qurʾān 10:89–90.

366. Qurʾān 10:89–90.

367. Qurʾān 10:90.

368. Qurʾān 26:60.

and twenty thousand fighting men — those twenty years old were not counted because of their youth, nor those of sixty because of
[480] their age; only those in between were counted — in addition to the women and children. Pharaoh followed them with Haman at the forefront with a million and seven hundred thousand horses, and among them was not a single mare. That was when God said: *"Then Pharaoh sent into the cities summoners* [who said:] *'Lo! These indeed are but a little troop, and lo! They are offenders against us'*— meaning the Israelites — *'and lo! We are a ready host'"*[369] — meaning thereby that we have readied ourselves and have resolved on our affair. *And, when the two armies saw each other* and the Israelites looked at Pharaoh who was following them, they said: *"Lo! we are indeed caught!"*[370] And they said: "O Moses! *We suffered hurt before you came to us* — they slaughtered our sons and spared our women — *and since you have come to us.*[371] Today Pharaoh is overtaking us, and he will kill us. *Lo! We are indeed caught!* The sea is in front of us, and Pharaoh is behind us." Moses said: *"No, verily! For lo! My Lord is with me. He will guide me"*[372]—meaning, He will protect me. He continued: *"Perhaps your Lord will destroy your enemy and make you viceroys on earth, so that He may see how you behave."*[373]

Aaron approached and struck the sea, but the sea refused to open up, saying: "Who is this tyrant who is striking me?" Then Moses came and called the sea "Abū Khālid,"[374] striking it. *And it parted, and each part was as a lofty mountain*[375]—meaning, like a mighty mountain. Then the Israelites entered the sea. In the sea there were twelve paths, a path for each tribe. It was as though the paths then were separated by walls, and each tribe said: "Our companions have
[481] been slain!" When Moses saw that, he prayed to God, Who made them into bridges for them in the form of arches. Then the last of them could see the first, until all of them had gone out.

Then Pharaoh and his companions drew near, and when he looked

369. Qur'ān 26:53–56.
370. Qur'ān 26:61.
371. Qur'ān 7:129.
372. Qur'ān 26:61–62.
373. Qur'ān 7:129.
374. Abū Khālid, lit. "father of eternal (life), everlasting one."
375. Qur'ān 26:63.

at the sea that was split he said: "Do you not see how the sea split because of me and opened up for me, so that I may overtake my enemies and kill them?" For that was what God said: *"Then We brought near the others in that place*[376] — meaning, We made the people of Pharaoh draw near to there. When Pharaoh stood at the entrances to the paths, his horses refused to advance. Gabriel descended on a mare,[377] and the stallions smelled her odor and rushed blindly after her, until when the first of them was about to leave the sea and the last of them had entered, He commanded the sea to seize them, and it crashed together over them. Gabriel meanwhile busied himself with Pharaoh, by thrusting some of the sea pebbles into his mouth. When drowning overtook him, he said: *"I believe that there is no God save Him in Whom the Children of Israel believe, and I am one of those who surrender."* Then God sent Michael to him to upbraid him, and he said: *"What! Now! When until now you have rebelled and been one of the evildoers?"*[378]

Gabriel said: "O Muḥammad! I have not loathed any creature as I have loathed two men: One of them was a jinnī, namely Iblīs, when he refused to bow down to Adam; and the other is Pharaoh, when he said: *'I am your highest lord.'*[379] I wish that you had seen me — O Muḥammad! — when I took some sea pebbles and put them into Pharaoh's mouth, fearing that he would say some word for which God would have mercy upon him."

The Israelites said: "Pharaoh did not drown. Now he will overtake and kill us." Moses prayed to God, and He brought forth Pharaoh with six hundred and twenty thousand men covered with iron.[380] The Israelites took him as a sign, for that is the word of God to Pharaoh: *"But this day We save you in your body that you may be a sign for those after you"*[381] — meaning, a sign for the Israelites. [482]

When they wanted to journey onward, He set a trackless wilderness before them that confused them in their direction. Moses called upon the Israelite elders and asked them: "What is happening

376. Qur'ān 26:64.
377. See p. 64, above, where it is noted that Pharaoh's horses were only stallions.
378. Qur'ān 10:91–92.
379. Qur'ān 79:24.
380. Meaning unclear. The iron proves either that they were mighty warriors or that they were thus preserved to serve as a sign.
381. Qur'ān 10:93.

to us?" They said to him: "When Joseph died in Egypt, he exacted a promise from his brothers that they would not leave Egypt 'unless you take me out with you.' And that is the reason for this matter." He asked them where Joseph's burial place was located, but they did not know. Then Moses arose and proclaimed: "I beseech you, by God, that whoever knows the burial place of Joseph will tell it to me. But whoever does not know, let his ears be deaf to my words." He kept passing between men on both sides proclaiming this, and they did not hear his voice, until an old woman among them heard it and said: "Tell me, if I guide you to his grave, will you give me whatever I ask of you?" But he refused and said, "Not until I ask my Lord." Then God commanded him to grant this to her. Moses granted it to her, and she said: "What I want is that you will not inhabit a room in Paradise without inhabiting it with me." He said: "Very well." She said: "I am a very old woman, and I cannot walk, so carry me." He carried her, and, when they came near the Nile, she said: "He is
[483] in the midst of the water, so pray to God to uncover the water from him." So he prayed to God, and He removed the water from the grave. She said, "Dig him up." Moses did so and carried his bones. Then He opened the way for them, and they continued their journey. *They came to a people who were devoted to their idols. They said: "O Moses! Make for us a god even as they have gods." He said: "Lo! You are a people who are ignorant. Lo! As for these, their way will be ruined"*—meaning, what they are doing will be destroyed—*"and all that they are doing is in vain."*[382]

Ibn Isḥāq said—Ibn Ḥumayd—Salamah: And God brought the signs upon him in succession—meaning, on Pharaoh—and seized him with the drought when he refused to believe after all that had happened to him and the sorcerers. So He sent upon him the deluge, then the locusts, then the vermin, then the frogs, then blood, *all successive signs.*[383] He sent the deluge, and it overflowed the face of the earth; then it became still, so they could not plow or do anything until they suffered from hunger. When that overcame them, they said: "O Moses! *Pray for us to your Lord, . . . and if you remove this punishment from us, we will believe you and we will send out the Israelites with you."*[384] Moses prayed to his Lord, and He removed

382. Qurʾān 7:138–39.
383. Based on Qurʾān 7:130, 133.
384. Qurʾān 7:134.

the punishment from them. However, they did not fulfill anything that they had promised. Then God sent the locusts against them, and they ate the trees—according to what I have heard—to the extent that they would even eat the iron nails of doors, until their houses and dwellings collapsed. Then they asked of Moses what they had asked before. Moses again prayed to his Lord, and He removed it from them. But they did not fulfill anything they had said.

Then God sent vermin against them. I was told that Moses was commanded to go to a sand hill and strike it with his staff. So he [484] went to a mighty hill of poured sand and struck it with his staff. It covered the people of Egypt with vermin until their houses and food were covered over and they were prevented from sleeping or resting. When they became exhausted, they asked of Moses the same as they had asked previously. So he prayed to his Lord, and He relieved them, but they did not fulfill anything they had said they would.

Then God sent frogs against them, and they filled the houses, food supply, and vessels. No one could uncover any clothing, food, or vessel without finding frogs filling it. When that exhausted them, they asked of Moses the same as they had asked previously. So he prayed to his Lord, Who relieved them, but they did not fulfill anything they had said.

Then God sent blood upon them, and the water of Pharaoh's people became blood. They could not draw water from a well or a river, or ladle out water from a vessel, without its becoming fresh blood.

Muḥammad b. Ḥumayd related to us—Salamah—Muḥammad b. Isḥāq related to me—Muḥammad b. Kaʿb al-Quraẓī,[385] who related that, when thirst had exhausted them, a woman of Pharaoh's people would come to an Israelite woman and would say: "Let me drink from your water." She would ladle some for her from her jug or pour it for her from her waterskin, and it would become blood in the vessel. She would say: "Put the water in your mouth, then spit it into my mouth." She would take water into her mouth, but, when she spat it into the other woman's mouth, it became blood. They continued like this for seven days, when they said: *"Pray for us to your Lord, as He has promised you. Verily, if you relieve us of this punishment, we will surely believe in you and will indeed send the Chil-*

385. Muḥammad b. Kaʿb b. Sulaym al-Quraẓī, d. 118/736. Considered one of the most learned sources of tradition among the early scholars, he wrote a Qurʾān commentary and a historical work. *GAS*, I, 32; Ibn Ḥajar, *op. cit.*, IX, 420–22.

dren of Israel with you."[386] But, when the punishment was removed from them, they reneged and did not keep any promise they had made. So God commanded Moses to set out and informed him that
[485] He would deliver him and those with him and would also destroy Pharaoh and his armies. Moses had already prayed for their obliteration and had said: *"Our Lord! You have given Pharaoh and his chiefs splendor and riches in the life of this world, O Lord, that they may lead men astray from Your way"* ... to where He says ... *"and follow not the road of those who have no knowledge."*[387] So God turned their property into stone: the palm trees, the slaves, and their food. This was one of the signs that God showed Pharaoh.

Ibn Ḥumayd related to us — Salamah — Ibn Isḥāq — Buraydah b. Sufyān b. Farwah al-Aslamī[388] — Muḥammad b. Kaʿb al-Quraẓī, who said: ʿUmar b. ʿAbd al-ʿAzīz[389] asked me about the nine signs that God showed Pharaoh,[390] and I said: "The deluge, the locusts, the vermin, the frogs, the blood, his staff, his hand, the obliteration, and the sea." And ʿUmar said: "How do you know that obliteration is one of them?" I said: "Moses prayed against them, and Aaron said 'Amen,' and God turned their property into stone." So he said: "That is what can be called understanding (*fiqh*)!" Then he sent for a leather bag in which were things that ʿAbd al-ʿAzīz b. Marwān[391] had obtained in Egypt, when he was in charge of it, some of the remnants of the property of the pharaonites. He took out a peeled egg in two halves, and lo! It was stone (i.e., petrified), and a shelled nut, and it was stone, and a chick-pea, and a lentil.

Ibn Ḥumayd related to us — Salamah — Muḥammad — a man from Syria who had been in Egypt, who said: I saw a felled palm tree, and

---

386. Qurʾān 7:134.

387. Qurʾān 10:89–90. The omitted portion is: *O Lord! Destroy their riches and harden their hearts so they do not believe until they see the painful doom. He said: Your prayer is heard. Do you two keep to the straight path....*

388. Buraydah b. Sufyān b. Farwah al-Aslamī. *Index,* 66. Not further identified.

389. D. 102/720. Known also as ʿUmar II. He succeeded his uncle ʿAbd al-Malik in 96/714 and tried, during his brief reign, to reform the governmental system to strengthen Islam.

390. Ten plagues in the biblical account, which differs in the identification of some of the "signs."

391. D. 137/754. Son of the Umayyad caliph Marwān I and father of ʿUmar II, above, he was appointed governor of Egypt by his father and served for twenty years. *EI²*, s.v. "ʿAbd al-ʿAzīz b. Marwān."

it was stone,[392] and I saw a man—about whom I had no doubt that he was a man—and he was stone, one of their slaves. And God says: *"Verily We gave Moses nine signs, clear proofs"* ... up to ... *"accursed,"*[393] meaning wretched. [486]

Ibn Ḥumayd related to us—Salamah—Muḥammad b. Isḥāq—Yaḥyā b. ʿUrwah b. al-Zubayr[394]—his father,[395] that, when God commanded Moses to journey with the Children of Israel, He ordered him to carry Joseph with him in order to bury him in the Holy Land. So Moses asked about anyone who might know the place of Joseph's grave but found only an old Israelite woman who said: "O Prophet of God! I know his place. If you take me out with you and do not leave me behind in the land of Egypt, I will lead you to it." Moses said: "I will do so." He had promised the Israelites that he would set out with them when dawn broke, but he prayed to his Lord to delay his departure so that he might finish the matter of Joseph. He did so, and the old woman went out with Moses until she showed it to him, in a section of the Nile, within the water. Moses drew him out in a coffin of marble and carried him with him. ʿUrwah said: "Since then, the Jews transport their dead from every land to the Holy Land."[396]

Ibn Ḥumayd—Salamah—Ibn Isḥāq, who said: According to what I have heard, Moses said to the Israelites concerning what God had commanded him, "Borrow from them goods, jewelry, and clothing, and I will give their possessions as booty to you together with their destruction." When Pharaoh summoned [his] forces, one of the ways

---

392. This may refer to the remnants of petrified trees near Cairo, beyond the Muqaṭṭam hills. These are mentioned in nineteenth-century guidebooks. See Wilkinson, *Handbook*, 159, 195, 231, and Cook's *A Tourist's Handbook*, 164: "A desert space covered with fragments of sycamore and palm apparently turned to stone."

393. Qurʾān 17:101–2. The omitted portions of the verses read: *Do but ask the Children of Israel how he came to them; then Pharaoh said to him: Lo! I consider you one bewitched, O Moses. He said: In truth you know that none sent down these signs except the Lord of the heavens and the earth as proofs, and lo! I consider you.... Mathbūr* is here translated "lost" by Pickthall, and "cursed" by Arberry.

394. Yaḥyā b. ʿUrwah b. al-Zubayr, Abū ʿUrwah, d. ca. 114/732. He was a prominent Medinan and a nephew of ʿAbdallāh b. al-Zubayr. Ibn Ḥajar, *op. cit.*, XI, 258; al-Ziriklī, *op. cit.*, IX, 195.

395. ʿUrwah b. al-Zubayr, b. al-ʿAwwām al-Asadī, 24–94/643–712. He was one of the great legal scholars of Medina and a noted transmitter of traditions. Ibn Saʿd, *op. cit.*, V, 132–35; Ibn Ḥajar, *op. cit.*, VII, 180–85; *GAS*, I, 278; al-Ziriklī, *op. cit.*, V, 17.

396. See the account in Ginzberg, *op. cit.*, II, 181–83, for the Jewish version of the story of the finding and transport of Joseph's body.

he incited them against the Israelites was that he said as they set out: "They were not content to go forth by themselves but also took your wealth with them."

Ibn Ḥumayd — Salamah — Ibn Isḥāq — Muḥammad b. Kaʿb al-Quraẓī — ʿAbdallāh b. Shaddād b. Alhād:[397] I was told that Pharaoh
[487] went out in search of Moses with seventy thousand black horses, aside from the gray ones among his troops. Moses went out until the sea was before him and there was no way out. Pharaoh came up with his troops behind them. *When the two groups saw each other, Moses' companions said: "Verily we are indeed caught."* He replied: *"Not at all! Verily my Lord is with me. He will guide me"*[398] — meaning, to salvation — "He has promised that to me, and there is no duplicity in His promising."

Ibn Ḥumayd related to us — Salamah — Muḥammad b. Isḥāq: God, according to what I have been told, inspired the sea, saying: "When Moses strikes you with his staff, split yourself in two for him." The sea then spent the night, one part striking the other, out of fear of God and awaiting His command. Then God inspired Moses: *"Strike the sea with your staff,"*[399] and he struck it. Within the staff was God's power, which He had given to Moses. *The sea parted, and each part was as a mountain vast*[400] — that is, like the mountain on an elevated part of the earth. God was saying to Moses: *"Strike for them a dry path in the sea, fear not being overtaken, neither be afraid."*[401] When the sea came to rest for him with a straight dry path, Moses set out upon it with the Israelites, while Pharaoh followed him with his troops.

Ibn Ḥumayd related to us — Salamah — Muḥammad b. Isḥāq — Muḥammad b. Kaʿb al-Quraẓī — ʿAbdallāh b. Shaddād b. Alhād al-Laythī: It was transmitted to me that, when the Israelites entered the sea and none remained behind, Pharaoh approached. He was on a stallion of his horses and came closer until he was at the edge of
[488] the sea, unflinching about his situation while the horse feared to ad-

---

397. ʿAbdallāh b. Shaddād b. Alhād al-Laythī, d. ca. 82/701. A reliable transmitter of Shiʿite tendency, he transmitted traditions of ʿUmar and ʿAlī and was killed with other scholars who joined the rebellion of Ibn al-Ashʿath against al-Ḥajjāj. Ibn Saʿd, *op. cit.*, VI, 86–87.

398. Qurʾān 26:61–62.

399. Qurʾān 26:63.

400. Qurʾān 26:63.

401. Qurʾān 20:77.

vance. Then Gabriel appeared to him on a female horse in heat. He brought her near Pharaoh's stallion, and he smelled her. When he smelled her, Gabriel made her advance, and the stallion advanced with Pharaoh on his back. When Pharaoh's troops saw that Pharaoh had entered the sea, they entered with him, while Gabriel went ahead of them all. They were following Pharaoh, and Michael[402] was on a horse behind the people, urging them on, saying: "Catch up with your companion!" When Gabriel went out of the sea, with no one ahead of him and Michael remained standing on the other side with no one behind him, the sea closed over them. Pharaoh cried out when he saw what he did of God's power and authority and recognized his humiliation. His soul forsook him, and he called out: *"There is no god but the God in Whom the Children of Israel believe, and I am one of those who surrenders."*[403]

Ibn Ḥumayd related to us—Abū Dāwūd al-Baṣrī[404]—Ḥammād b. Salamah—ʿAlī b. Zayd[405]—Yūsuf b. Mihrān[406]—Ibn ʿAbbās: Gabriel came to the Prophet and said: "O Muḥammad! I wish that you had seen me when I was stuffing slimy mud into Pharaoh's mouth for fear that mercy would come over him."[407] God said: *"Now! When hitherto have you rebelled and have been one of the wrongdoers? But this day We save you in your body"*—that is, complete, nothing of you will be gone—*"so that you may be a sign for those after you"*[408]—that is, a warning and testimony. It used to be said that, if God had not brought him out with his body so that they recognized him, some of the people would have doubted Him.

[Ibn Isḥāq said]:[409] When he took the Children of Israel across the [489]

---

402. Arabic: Mikāʾīl, i.e., the archangel.

403. Qurʾān 10:91.

404. Abū Dāwūd al-Ṭayālisī al-Baṣrī, Sulaymān b. Dāwūd b. al-Jārūd, 133–ca. 203/750–ca. 818. He transmitted traditions from a number of sources, and Aḥmad b. Ḥanbal, among others, transmitted from him. Ibn Ḥajar, *op. cit.*, IV, 186; Ibn Saʿd, *op. cit.*, VII, 2, 51; al-Ziriklī, *op. cit.*, III, 187.

405. ʿAlī b. Zayd b. ʿAbdallāh b. Judʿān Abū al-Ḥasan, al-Taymī al-Baṣrī, d. 127/744 or 130/747. Blind from birth, he was considered a transmitter of weak traditions. *GAS*, I, 71; Ibn Saʿd, *op. cit.*, VII/2, 18; al-Ziriklī, *op. cit.*, V, 101.

406. Yūsuf b. Mihrān. Transmitted from Ibn ʿAbbās and was considered reliable. Ibn Saʿd, *op. cit.*, VI, 1, 161.

407. For this theme, see p. 65, above, where the term *maqlah, maql* "pebbles, earth in a well" is used. Here the word is *ḥamāʾ* "slimy mud."

408. Qurʾān 10:93.

409. So in MS Tn. See al-Ṭabarī, I, 488 n. *g*.

sea, *they came upon a people who were devoted to idols they had. They said: "O Moses! Make for us a god [such] as they have gods." He said: "Lo! You are a people who do not know... Lo! As for these, their way will be destroyed, and all that they are doing is in vain." He said: "Shall I seek for you a god other than God, when He has favored you above all creatures?"*[410] When God destroyed Pharaoh and his people, saving Moses and his people, He appointed for Moses thirty nights.

The account returns to that of al-Suddī. Then Gabriel came to take Moses to God. He approached on a horse, and al-Sāmirī[411] saw him but did not know him. It is said that it was the horse of life. [Al-Sāmirī] said when he saw him, "Verily this is something momentous!" So he took some of the dust from the hoof of the horse. Then Moses set out, making Aaron his vice-regent over the Children of Israel, and promised to meet them in thirty nights, but God added to them ten.[412] Aaron said to them: "O Children of Israel! Spoils are not permitted to you, and the ornaments of the Egyptians are spoils, so gather all of them together and dig a pit for them, burying all of them in it. When Moses returns, if he permits them for you, then you may take them. Otherwise, they are things you may not consume." They assembled all the ornaments in that pit, and al-Sāmirī brought the handful of dust. He threw it [upon the pit], and God brought forth from the ornaments *a corporeal calf of saffron color, and it gave forth a lowing sound.*[413]

The Israelites had counted the appointed time of Moses; they counted each night a day, and each day a day. When it was the twentieth day, the calf came forth. When they saw it, al-Sāmirī said to them: *"This is your God and the God of Moses, but he has forgotten."*[414] He said: "Moses left his God here and went looking for Him." So they clung to the calf and worshiped it, for it could bellow
[490] and walk. Aaron said to them: "O Children of Israel! *You are only*

410. Qur'ān 7:138–40.

411. This name, which means "the Samaritan," occurs several times in the Qur'ān in connection with the story of the calf of gold. See Qur'ān 20:85, 87–88, 95. Al-Ṭabarī, in his *Tafsīr* on these verses, sees in al-Sāmirī a prominent Israelite of the Samaritan tribe. As punishment for his sin, Moses forbade the Israelites to have contact with him, hence providing an explanation for the separation of the Samaritans from other Israelites. See *Shorter Encyclopaedia of Islam,* 501–2, s.v. *"al-Sāmirī."*

412. See Qur'ān 7:142.

413. Qur'ān 7:148, 20:88.

414. Qur'ān 20:88.

being seduced with it"—meaning, you are only being tested with it, that is, the calf—*"For lo! Your Lord is the Beneficent."*[415] Aaron and those Israelites who were with him continued not to fight them, while Moses was off speaking with his God. When He spoke with him, He said: *"What made you hasten from your people, O Moses?" He said: "They follow close upon my track. I hastened to You, my Lord, that You might be pleased." He said: "Lo! We have tested your people in your absence, and al-Sāmirī has misled them."*[416]

When He had related their tale to him, Moses said, "O Lord! This al-Sāmirī ordered them to adopt the calf. Tell me, who breathed the soul into it?" The Lord said: "I did." Moses said: "Then, my Lord, You misled them."

Moses, after his Lord had spoken to him, desired to see Him and said: *"My Lord! Show me Yourself that I may gaze upon You." He replied: "You will not see Me. But gaze upon the mountain, and, if it stands still in its place, then you will see Me."*[417] Angels surrounded the mountain, and the angels were surrounded by fire, and angels surrounded the fire, and those angels were surrounded by fire. Then his Lord revealed Himself to the mountain.

Mūsā b. Hārūn related to me—ʿAmr b. Ḥammād—Asbāṭ—al-Suddī—ʿIkrimah—Ibn ʿAbbās: He revealed of Himself no more than the equivalent of the tip of the little finger, and He sent the mountain crashing down,[418] while Moses fell down in a faint. He remained in a faint as long as God wished, and then he recovered his senses, saying: *"Glory unto You! I turn to You repentant, and I am the first of the believers"*—among the Israelites. *He said: "O Moses! I have chosen you above mankind through My messages and My speaking to you. So hold what I have given you, and be among* [491]
the thankful." And He[419] *wrote for him, upon the tablets, the lesson to be learned from all things and its explanation*—regarding what is permissible and what is forbidden—*"So take fast hold of it"*—meaning, with seriousness and striving—*"and command your people to take hold of the best in it"*[420]—namely, the best of what they find in it. After that, no one was able to look at Moses in his

415. Qurʾān 20:90.
416. Qurʾān 20:83–85.
417. Qurʾān 7:143.
418. Qurʾān 7:143.
419. So in text. Qurʾān has here: "We."
420. Qurʾān 7:143–45.

face, so he would cover his face with a piece of silk cloth. He took the tablets *and returned to his people angry and sorry*—meaning saddened. *He said: "O my people! Has not your Lord promised you a good promise"* (to where it says)... *"We did not break your appointed time of our own will"*—meaning, through our own ability—*"but we were laden with burdens of ornaments of the people"*—meaning, the jewelry of the Egyptians—*"so we cast them [into the fire] as al-Sāmirī proposed."*[421] That was when Aaron said to them, "Dig a pit for these jewels, and cast them into it," and they cast them in. Then al-Sāmirī threw his dust.

Then Moses threw down the tablets, *and he seized his brother by the head, dragging him toward him.*[422] *Aaron said: "O son of my mother! Do not clutch my beard or my head! I feared that you would say, 'You have caused division among the Children of Israel and have not waited for my word.'"*[423] So Moses left Aaron and turned to al-Sāmirī, saying: *"And what have you to say, O Sāmirī?"* Al-Sāmirī said: *"I perceived what they do not perceive [so I seized a handful from the footsteps of the messenger, and then threw it in. Thus my soul commended to me." (Moses) said: "Then go! And lo! In this life, it is for you to say: 'Touch me not!' And lo! There is for you an appointment you cannot break. Now look upon your god, of which you have remained a worshiper. Verily we will burn it] and scatter its dust over the sea."*[424] Thereupon, he seized the calf and killed it, then filed it down and scattered it into the sea. There was no flowing sea into which it did not fall. Then Moses said to them, "Drink some of the water." They drank, and whoever drank it, the gold in the water would show itself on those who had loved [the calf].
[492] That was when He said: *"And the calf was made to sink into their hearts because of their unbelief."*[425] When the Israelites repented after Moses came *and they saw that they had gone astray, they said: "Unless our Lord has mercy upon us and forgives us, we verily are of the lost."*[426] God refused to accept the repentance of the Israelites, except for the circumstance that they had disliked fighting among

421. Qur'ān 20:86–87; cf. 7:150.
422. Qur'ān 7:150.
423. Qur'ān 20:94.
424. Qur'ān 20:95–97.
425. Qur'ān 2:93.
426. Qur'ān 7:149.

themselves when they worshiped the calf.[427] Moses said to them: *"O my people! You have wronged yourselves by your choosing the calf, so turn in penitence to your Creator, and kill the guilty yourselves."*[428] So those who had worshiped the calf and those who did not worship it struck one another with swords. Whoever was killed of the two parties was a martyr. The slaying increased until they were almost destroyed; until seventy thousand were killed among them; and until Moses and Aaron prayed: "Our Lord! The Children of Israel are destroyed! Our Lord! The remnant! The remnant!" He therefore commanded them to put down their weapons, and He forgave them, so that those who were slain were martyrs, and those who remained were forgiven, for this is His word: *"He relented toward you. Lo! He is the Relenting, the Merciful."*[429]

Ibn Ḥumayd related to us — Salamah — Muḥammad b. Isḥāq — Ḥakīm b. Jubayr — Saʿīd b. Jubayr — Ibn ʿAbbās: Al-Sāmirī was a man of Bājarmā,[430] of a people who worshiped cows. The love of worshiping cows was in his soul, but he had professed Islam [submission] among the Children of Israel. When Aaron judged among the Israelites and Moses departed from them to go to his Lord, Aaron said to them: "You were laden with burdens of ornaments, goods, and jewelry of the people of Pharaoh's family,[431] so purify yourselves [493]
of all that, for it is uncleanliness." He kindled a fire for them and said: "Cast into it whatever you have with you [of those items]." They said "Yes," and began to bring whatever jewelry and goods they had with them, casting them into the fire until, when the jewels became broken in it, al-Sāmirī saw the trace of Gabriel's horse and took some dust from its hoofprint. Then he drew near to the pit and said to Aaron, "O prophet of God! Shall I throw in what is in my hand?" He agreed, thinking that it was like the goods and jewels the others had brought, and [al-Sāmirī] cast it into it, saying: "Be a saffron-colored calf, which bellows."[432] And it became a trial and se-

427. Meaning, presumably, that they had worshiped the calf out of reluctance to cause internecine warfare over the issue. Only on that basis could they be forgiven.

428. Qurʾān 2:54.

429. Qurʾān 2:54.

430. A village in the Jazīrah (northern Mesopotamia) near al-Raqqah. Yāqūt, *op. cit.*, I, 454.

431. See Qurʾān 20:87.

432. See Qurʾān 20:88.

duction, and he said: *"This is your God and the God of Moses."*[433] They devoted themselves to it and loved it with a love unlike anything they had ever felt. God said: *"But he has forgotten"*—meaning, he, al-Sāmirī, abandoned the state of Islam [submission] he had been in—*"Do they not see, then, that it returns no words to them and possesses for them neither harm nor use?"*[434]

Ibn ʿAbbās continues: Al-Sāmirī's name was Mūsā b. Ẓafar. He happened to be in the land of Egypt and entered among the Israelites. When Aaron saw the state into which they had fallen, he said: *"O my people! You are only being seduced therewith. [For lo! Your Lord is the Beneficent, so follow me and obey my order!" They said: "We shall by no means be its worshipers] until Moses returns to us."*[435] Aaron stayed with those Muslims who were not seduced, while those who worshiped the calf continued their worship. Aaron feared that, if he traveled on with those Muslims who were with him, Moses would say to him: *"You have caused division among the Children of Israel and have not waited for my word,"*[436] for he was reverential, obedient to Moses.

Moses traveled on with the Israelites to the mountain,[437] for God had set a meeting with them when He rescued them and destroyed their enemy at the right side of the mountain. When Moses jour-
[494] neyed from the sea with the Children of Israel and they needed water, he prayed to God to give His people water. God commanded Moses to strike the rock with his staff,[438] and twelve springs burst forth from it, a spring from which each tribe would drink and that they would recognize.

When God spoke to Moses, he desired to see Him and asked his Lord if he might look at Him. But God said to Moses: *"You will not see me, but gaze upon the mountain! [If it stands still in its place, then you will see Me." And, when his Lord revealed [His] glory to the mountain, He sent it crashing down, and Moses fell down senseless. When he awoke, he said: "Glory be to You! I turn to You repen-*

---

433. Qurʾān 20:88.
434. Qurʾān 20:89.
435. Qurʾān 20:90–91.
436. Qurʾān 20:94.
437. *Al-Ṭūr,* the name by which Mt. Sinai is known in the Qurʾān. See Qurʾān 52:1, 95:2, and several other references.
438. See Qurʾān 7:160.

tant,] and I am the first of the believers." Then God said to Moses: *"I have chosen you above mankind by My message and by My speaking. So hold what I have given you [and be among the thankful. And We wrote for him, upon the tablets, the lesson to be drawn from all things, then told him: 'Hold it fast; and command your people, (saying:) "Take the better (course) therein.] I shall show you the abode of the evildoers."'"*[439] And He said to him: *"What has made you hasten to leave your folk, O Moses?"* ... to where He says ... *"Then Moses went back to his people, angry and sad,"*[440] and with him was God's covenant on his tablets. When Moses reached his people and saw that they were worshiping the calf, he threw the tablets down from his hand. They were, according to what has been said, of green chrysolite. Then he seized the head and beard of his brother, saying: *"What held you back, when you saw they had gone astray, that you did not follow me? [Have you then disobeyed my order?" He said: "O son of my mother! Clutch not my beard or my head! I feared lest you should say: 'You have caused division among the Children of Israel'".]*[441] And he said: *"O son of my mother! The people have judged me to be weak and almost killed me. Oh, do not make my enemies rejoice over me, and do not place me among the evildoers."*[442] Moses relented and said: *"My Lord! Have mercy on me and my brother; bring us into Your mercy; You the most Merciful of those who show mercy."*[443] He approached his people and said: *"O my people! Has not your Lord promised you a fair promise? [Did the time appointed appear too long for you, or did you wish that wrath from your Lord should come upon you, that you broke your appointment with Me?" They said: "We did not break our appointment with You of our own will, but we were laden with burdens of ornaments of the people, then cast them (in the fire), for thus al-Sāmirī proposed. Then he produced for them] a saffron-colored calf that bellows."*[444]

---

439. Qur'ān 7:143–45.

440. Qur'ān 20:83–86. The omitted portions of the verses read: *He said: They are on my track. I hastened to You that You might be well pleased. He said: Lo! We have tried your people in your absence, and al-Sāmirī has misled them.*

441. Qur'ān 20:92–94.

442. Qur'ān 7:150.

443. Qur'ān 7:151.

444. Qur'ān 20:86–88.

He drew near to al-Sāmirī and said: *"And what have you to say, O Sāmirī?" He said: "I perceived what they did not"* ... to where it says ... *"He embraces all things in His knowledge."*[445] Then he took the tablets. God says: *"He took up the tablets, and in their inscrip-*
[495] *tion there is guidance and mercy for all those who fear their Lord."*[446]

Ibn Ḥumayd related to us — Salamah — Ibn Isḥāq — Ṣadaqah b. Yasār[447] — Saʿīd b. Jubayr — Ibn ʿAbbās: God had written for Moses on the tablets exhortation and details of everything, as well as guidance and mercy. And, when he threw them down, God removed six-sevenths of them and left one-seventh, saying: *"And in their inscription, there is guidance and mercy for all those who fear their Lord."*[448]

Then Moses gave orders that the calf should be burned to ashes, then strewn over the sea. Ibn Isḥāq said, "I heard some scholars say that burning it (*iḥrāq*) was really filing it (*saḥl*); then he scattered it on the sea." And God knows best.

Then Moses chose among seventy good men of the best[449] of them and said, "Go to God, and repent to Him for what you have done. Ask Him for forgiveness for those of your people you have left behind. Fast; purify yourselves and your garments." Then he took them to Mount Sinai at the set time that God had appointed for him, because he could not come to Him except with His permission and knowledge. The seventy said to him — from what has been told to me — after they had done what he had ordered them to do and had gone out with him to meet his Lord, "Ask if we may hear the speech of our Lord." And he said, "I shall do it." When Moses neared the mountain, the pillar of cloud fell upon it until the mountain was completely obscured. Moses drew near and entered into it, saying to the people, "Draw near!" Now, when He had spoken to Moses, a radiant light had descended on his forehead. Because no human being could look at him, a veil was placed in front of him. The people drew near
[496] so that, when they entered the cloud, they fell down, prostrating

---

445. Qurʾān 20:95–98. For the full text, see p. 74, above.

446. Qurʾān 7:154.

447. Ṣadaqah b. Yasār. A client of some Meccans, he transmitted few traditions but was considered reliable. Ibn Saʿd, *op. cit.*, V, 357.

448. Qurʾān 7:154.

449. *Al-khayra fa-al-khayra.* Repeated at n. 454, below. Ibn al-Athīr, *op. cit.*, I, 191, has *min akhyārihim* "from the best of them."

themselves. They heard Him as He was speaking to Moses, commanding him and forbidding him, what to do and not to do.

When God had finished commanding Moses, the cloud was removed from Moses, and he approached the people, who said to him: *"We will not believe in you until we see God plainly."*[450] Then *the trembling came upon them*[451] — that was the *lightning*.[452] Their souls were taken by surprise, and they all died. Then Moses arose, adjuring his Lord and praying to Him, asking Him humbly, saying: *"My Lord! If You had wanted, You would have destroyed them long before, and me as well.*[453] They were foolish, and those of the Children of Israel who were behind me are now destroyed owing to what the foolish ones among us have done. This is indeed destruction for them. I chose seventy good men among them, the best![454] I shall return to them, and not one man will be with me. Why should they believe me?" Moses continued adjuring his Lord and asking Him until He returned their souls to the [seventy]. [He also asked Him] to forgive the Israelites for their worship of the calf, but God responded, "No! Not until they kill themselves."

Ibn ʿAbbās continued: I was informed that they said to Moses, "We will be steadfast in God's command." Moses commanded that those who had not worshiped the calf should kill those who had. They sat in their enclosures, while the people unsheathed their swords and began to kill them. Moses wept, and the young boys and women hurried to him, begging pardon for them. He forgave and pardoned them, and then Moses ordered them to hold back their swords.

As for al-Suddī, he mentioned in his account, the chain of authorities of which I have given previously, that the journey of Moses to his Lord, with the seventy men he had chosen from his people, was [after God had forgiven the worshipers of the calf among his people. [497]
This was that he mentioned,][455] after the tale I have already related from him, that, after his saying that *He is the Relenting, the Merci-*

450. Qurʾān 2:55; 4:153.
451. Qurʾān 7:155.
452. Qurʾān 2:55; 4:153.
453. Qurʾān 7:155.
454. *Fa-al-khayr*. See n. 449, above.
455. The section within brackets is partially or totally omitted in two manuscripts. From "after God had forgiven ... to ... that he mentioned" in MS BM and from "among his people ... to ... that he mentioned" in MS Tn. See al-Ṭabarī, I, 497, n. *a*.

ful,[456] God commanded Moses to come to Him with some Israelites to apologize for worshiping the calf. He set an appointed time for them, and *Moses chose seventy men from his people*[457] whom he regarded highly. Then he brought them to make apologies. When they came to the place, they said: *"We will not believe in you until we see God plainly*[458] ... for you have already spoken to Him, so show Him to us." ... Then the lightning seized[459] them, and they died. Moses arose, weeping and praying to God, and said: "My Lord! What shall I say to the Children of Israel when I come to them after You have slain the best of them? *My Lord! If You had wanted, You would have destroyed them long before, and me as well. Will You destroy us for what the foolish among us did?"*[460] God inspired Moses that "these seventy were from those who accepted the calf," whereupon Moses says: *"It is only Your trial of us. You send astray thereby whom You will and guide whom You will"* ... to where he says ... *"Lo! We have repented to You"*[461] ... meaning, we have turned back to You ... and that is His word: "Then you said, *'O Moses! We will not believe in you until we see God plainly'; [even while you gazed] and the lightning seized you"*[462] ... and the lightning is fire. Then God revived them. Each man rose up and lived, looking at the others and at how they were revived. They said: "O Moses! You pray to God, and anything you ask of Him, He gives you. So pray to Him to make us prophets." So he prayed to Him, and He
[498] made them prophets, for that is His word: *"Then We revived you after your death"*[463]—but He made one letter precede and another go behind.[464]

Then He commanded them to journey on to Jericho, which is the land of Jerusalem.[465] They journeyed until they were near it.[466]

---

456. Qur'ān 2:54.

457. Qur'ān 7:155.

458. Qur'ān 2:55; cf. also 4:153.

459. Based on Qur'ān 2:55.

460. Qur'ān 7:155.

461. Qur'ān 7:155. The section omitted is *You are our Protecting Friend, therefore forgive us and have mercy on us, You, the best of all who show forgiveness and ordain for us in this world what is good as well as in the Hereafter.*

462. Qur'ān 2:55.

463. Qur'ān 2:56.

464. *Baʿathnākum min baʿdi mawtikum* "we revived [or "we sent"] you [as prophets] after your death."

465. Or Palestine: *Wa-hiya 'arḍ bayt al-maqdis.* See n. 180, above, on this usage.

Moses sent out twelve chiefs, [one] from each of the Israelite tribes, who set out to bring him an account of the giants.[467] One of the giants, who was called Og,[468] met them. He seized the twelve and placed them in his waistband, while on his head was a load of firewood. He took them off to his wife and said to her, "Look at these people who claim that they want to fight us." He flung them down in front of her, saying, "Shouldn't I grind them under my foot?" But his wife said, "No, rather let them go, so they will tell their people what they have seen." He did that, and after the twelve were released one said to the other, "O people! If you tell the Children of Israel the account of this people, they will forsake the prophet of God. So conceal it, and tell only the two prophets of God, and let them come to their own conclusion." They all made a pact with each other about concealing it, and then they returned. But then ten of them immediately broke the pact, each one of them telling his brother and father what they had seen of Og. However, two men concealed the event but went to Moses and Aaron and told them the account, whereupon God said: *"God made a covenant with the Children of Israel, and we sent among them twelve chiefs."*[469] Moses said to them: *"O my people! Remember God's favor to you, how He placed prophets among you, and He made you kings* ... each man among you ruling himself, his family, and his wealth ... *O my people! Go into the Holy Land that God has inscribed for you"* ... meaning, that God [499]
has ordained for you ... *"Turn not back in flight [for surely you turn back] as losers." They said*—from what they had heard from the ten —*"Lo! A giant people are there, and lo! We shall not enter it until they leave from there; only then will we enter." Then two men of those who were God-fearing and to whom God had been gracious, spoke: "Enter in upon them by the gate."*[470]

Those two were the men who had concealed the report. They were Joshua b. Nun, the servant of Moses, and Caleb b. Jephunneh—some

---

466. Text has *minhum* "near them," but MS BM has *minhā* "near it." Al-Ṭabarī, I, 498 n. *a.*; Ibrāhīm, *op. cit.*, I, 429, reads *minhā*.

467. *Al-jabbārīn,* for the biblical *bnei ʿanaq,* who were "men of great stature ... 'we were in our own sight as grasshoppers, and so we were in their sight.'" See Numbers 13:32–33.

468. Arabic: *ʿĀj*. See Numbers 21:33, where Og, king of Bashan, went out against the Israelites.

469. Qurʾān 5:12.

470. Qurʾān 5:20–23.

say Kilāb b. Jephunneh — the brother-in-law of Moses.[471] When Moses said: "O people! *Enter in upon them by the gate,*" they said, "*O Moses! We will never enter the land as long as they are in it. So you go with your Lord, and the two of you fight. We will be sitting home.*" Moses became angry and prayed against them, saying: "*My Lord! I have control of none but myself and my brother, so distinguish between us and the wrongdoing people.*" This was a hasty act that Moses had done rashly, for God then said: "*This land will be forbidden to them for forty years that they will wander on the earth bewildered.*"[472] When this bewildered wandering was cast upon them, Moses regretted what he had said. Those people who were obedient to him went to him and said, "What have you done to us, O Moses?" When he regretted, God revealed to him, "*Do not grieve*" that is, do not be sad — "*about the people* — you have named — *the wrongdoers.*"[473] So he was not sad. Then they said: "O Moses! How
[500] can we find water for ourselves here? Where is there food?" So God sent down to them manna and quails.[474] Manna[475] and quails would fall down on the trees; the quail (*salwā*) is a bird resembling the *sumānā*.[476] A person would look at the bird, and if it was fat he would slaughter it; otherwise, he would let it go. When it became fat, he would return to it.

Then they said, "This is the food, but where is the drink?" So Moses was commanded, and he struck the rock with his staff, and there broke forth from it twelve springs, each tribe drinking from one spring. Then they said, "This is the food and drink, but where is the shade?" So God shaded them with clouds, and they said, "This

---

471. Or "was allied by marriage to Moses." According to MS C, Caleb "was the husband of Miriam bt. Amram, the sister of Moses and Aaron." Al-Ṭabarī, I, 499 n. *d.* Jewish legend says that Caleb married Bithiah, the daughter of Pharaoh. See Ginzberg, *op. cit.*, II, 270.

472. Qurʾān 5:23–26.

473. Qurʾān 5:23–26.

474. See Qurʾān 2:57.

475. *Taranjubīn*, also *taranjabīn*, *turanjabīn*, from Persian. A kind of manna. See Lane, *op. cit.*, 306, s.v. *taranjubīn* "Persian manna." Al-Bayḍāwī, *Anwār al-tanzīl*, I, 155, glosses *mann wa-salwā* by *al-taranjubīn wa-al-sumānā*. Al-Ṭabarī, I, 500 n. *a.*, has variant readings: *zanjabīl*, *zanjīl*, i.e., "ginger."

476. *Salwā*, *sumānā* both refer in English to quail. See Lane, *op. cit.*, s.vv. *slw*, *smn*. Biblical Hebrew has *s*ᵉ*law*, Exodus 16:13, Numbers 11:32. But the plural *salwīm* in Numbers 11:31 seems to derive from a form *salwah*.

is the shade, but where is the clothing?" So their garments grew on them, as young boys grow,[477] and did not become ragged on them, for that is His word: *"We caused the cloud to shade them, and sent down for them the manna and the quails"*[478] ... and His words: *"And when Moses asked for water for his people, We said: 'Smite the rock with your staff.' And there gushed out from it twelve springs, so that each tribe knew their drinking place.* They settled that, and then they said, *'O Moses! We are weary of one kind of food; so call upon your Lord for us that He bring forth that which the earth produces—of its herbs, and its cucumbers, its grain'* ... that is, its wheat ... *'its lentils and its onions.' He said: 'Would you exchange that which is meaner for that which is better? Go down to Egypt'*—meaning, one of various countries[479]—*'there you will get what you ask for.'"*[480] When they left the wilderness, the manna and quail were removed from them, and they ate vegetables.

When Moses met Og, he leaped ten cubits into the heavens. His [501] staff was ten cubits, and his height was ten cubits. His staff struck Og's anklebone, killing him.

Ibn Bashshār[481] related to us — Mu'ammal[482] — Sufyān — Abū Isḥāq[483]—Nawf: The base of Og's head[484] was eight hundred cubits high, while Moses' height was ten cubits and his staff ten cubits. Then he jumped into the air ten cubits and struck Og, hitting his anklebone. Og fell down dead, becoming a bridge for the people to cross over.

---

477. *Taṭūlu ʿalayhim kamā taṭūlu al-ṣubyān,* meaning unclear. Ibrāhīm, *op. cit.,* I, 431, has *maʿahum* "grew with them."

478. Qur'ān 7:160; see 2:57.

479. *Miṣran min al-amṣār,* taking *miṣr* as "country," rather than as "Egypt."

480. Qur'ān 2:60–61.

481. Muḥammad b. Bashshār b. ʿUthmān b. Dāwūd al-ʿAbdī al-Baṣrī Bundār, Abū Bakr, 167–252/783–866. Considered a reliable transmitter, he was cited by al-Bukhārī, Muslim, Abū Dāwūd, and others. Ibn Ḥajar, *op. cit.,* IX, 70–71; *GAS,* I, 113–14; al-Ziriklī, *op. cit.,* VI, 277.

482. Mu'ammal b. Ismāʿīl al-ʿAdawī, Abū ʿAbd al-Raḥmān, d. 207/822. He was a trustworthy transmitter, though with many errors because he recited from memory. Ibn Saʿd, *op. cit.,* V, 367; Ibn Ḥajar, *op. cit.,* X, 380; al-Ziriklī, *op. cit.,* VIII, 290–91.

483. Abū Isḥāq al-Hamdānī al-Sabīʿī, ʿAmr b. ʿAbdallāh, 33–129/653–745. A Kūfan, he transmitted from numerous sources and was an expert on the *maghāzī. GAS,* I, 283; Ibn Saʿd, *op. cit.,* VI, 123; Ibn Ḥajar, *op. cit.,* VIII, 63–67; al-Ziriklī, *op. cit.,* V, 251.

484. *Sarīr.* See Lane, *op. cit.,* s.v.: "the part where the head rests upon the neck."

Abū Kurayb related to us—Ibn ʿAṭīyah[485]—Qays[486]—Abū Isḥāq—Saʿīd b. Jubayr—Ibn ʿAbbās: Moses' staff, his leap, and his height were each ten cubits. He struck the anklebone of Og, killing him. Og then became a bridge for the people of the Nile. It is said that Og lived for three thousand years.

---

485. Al-Ḥasan b. ʿAṭīyah al-ʿAwfī, d. 181/797. Ibn Ḥajar, *op. cit.*, II, 294; *GAS*, I, 30.

486. Qays b. al-Rabīʿ al-Asadī, Abū Muḥammad, d. 168/784. He was noted for his extensive travel to hear traditions and his learning. Ibn Saʿd, *op. cit.*, VI, 262–63.

The Deaths of Moses and of Aaron, the Sons of Amram

Mūsā b. Hārūn al-Hamdānī related to us—ʿAmr b. Ḥammād—Asbāṭ—al-Suddī, in an account that he mentioned—Abū Mālik and Abū Ṣāliḥ—Ibn ʿAbbās; also Murrah al-Hamdānī—ʿAbdallāh b. [502]
Masʿūd; as well as—some of the companions of the Prophet: Then God inspired Moses, saying: "I am going to take Aaron to me,[487] so bring him to such and such a mountain." Moses and Aaron went toward that mountain and lo! There was a tree, unlike any that had ever been seen, and lo! There was a dwelling, and within it a bedstead on which were cushions, and a pleasant smell all about. When Aaron saw the mountain and the house and what was in it, it pleased him, and he said: "O Moses! I would like to sleep on this bed." Moses said to him: "Then go to sleep on it." He said: "But I am afraid that the master of this house will return and be angry with me." Moses said to him: "Do not be afraid! I will protect you from the master of this house, so sleep!" Aaron said: "O Moses! Rather sleep with me, so, if the master of this house comes, he will be angry with both of us." When they fell asleep, death took Aaron. When he felt its touch, he said: "O Moses! You have deceived me!" When he was dead, the house was taken away, the tree disappeared, and the bed was raised to heaven.

---

487. Lit. *mutawaff* "cause [him] to die." For other legends about the death of Aaron, see Schwarzbaum, "Jewish, Christian, Moslem and Falasha Legends of the Death of Aaron, the High Priest."

When Moses returned to the Children of Israel without Aaron, they said that Moses had killed Aaron, because he had envied their love for him, for Aaron was more forbearing and more lenient with them, while Moses had a certain harshness toward them. When this reached Moses, he said to them: "Woe unto you! He was my brother.
[503] Do you think that I would kill him?" And when they spoke against him more, he arose and performed two *rakʿah*s,[488] and then prayed to God, Who made the bed descend so that they could see it between heaven and earth; and then they believed Moses.

Then, while Moses was walking with his servant Joshua, a black wind suddenly approached. When Joshua saw it, he thought that the Hour[489] was at hand. He clung to Moses and said, "The Hour is appearing while I cling to Moses, the prophet of God." But Moses withdrew himself gently from under his shirt, leaving it in Joshua's hand. When Joshua returned with the shirt, the Israelites seized him, saying, "You have killed the prophet of God!" He said, "No, by God! I have not killed him. He pulled himself away from me." But they did not believe him and wanted to kill him. He said, "If you do not believe me, give me a delay of three days." Then he prayed to God, and every man who was guarding him was approached in a dream and informed that Joshua had not killed Moses; rather, "We have raised him up to Us," and they left him alone. Not one of those who had refused to enter the village of the giants with Moses remained, but they [had] died without witnessing the victory.

Ibn Ḥumayd related to us — Salamah — Ibn Isḥāq: The sincere friend of God (i.e., Moses) hated death and found it distressing.[490] Because he hated it, God wanted him to love death and to hate life. So prophecy was transferred to Joshua b. Nun, and he would walk with Moses morning and evening. Moses would say to him: "O prophet of God! what has God caused to happen to you?" Joshua b. Nun would respond: "O Prophet of God! Did I not accompany you so-and-so many years? Did I ever ask you about anything God did with you until you mentioned it first?" Joshua would not mention any-

488. Two *rakʿah*s are two sections of the Muslim prayer ceremonial, going through certain ritual postures and recitations. See *Shorter Encyclopaedia of Islam*, s.v. *Ṣalāt*.

489. *I.e.*, the hour of final judgment.

490. Compare the following account of the death of Moses with the Jewish *midrash* in Ginzberg, *op. cit.*, III, 463–79.

thing to him, and when Moses saw that he hated life and loved death. [504]

Ibn Ḥumayd said — Salamah — Ibn Isḥāq: The Chosen One of God, according to what Wahb b. Munabbih told me, used to seek shade under a trellis, eating and drinking from a stone trough. When he wanted to drink after he had eaten, he would put his mouth into that trough as an animal would, humbling himself to God when God honored him as He did with His speech.

Wahb said, and it was mentioned to me in regard to his death, that the Chosen One of God went out from that trellis of his one day for some need, and not one of God's creatures was aware of him. He passed by a small group of angels digging a grave. He recognized them and approached them, until he was standing next to them. He saw then that they were digging a grave more beautiful than he had ever seen, nor had he seen the like of the greenness, lushness, and beauty that was in it. He said to them, "O angels of God! For whom are you digging this grave?" They replied, "We are digging it for a servant who is esteemed by his Lord." He said, "This servant is surely in a lodging from God[491] that I have never seen the like of [before] today as a place to lie down or to enter." That was when there was about to occur from God what occurred regarding his being taken. The angel said to him, "O Chosen One of God, would you want it to be yours?" He said, "I should like that." They said, "Go down and lie down in it, turn your face to your Lord, and breathe the lightest breath you have ever breathed." He descended, lay down in it, and turned to his Lord. Then he breathed, and God took his soul, whereupon the angels covered him over. The Chosen One of God had been abstemious in this world, desiring what was with God. [505]

Abū Kurayb—Muṣʿab b. al-Miqdām[492]—Ḥammād b. Salamah—ʿAmmār b. Abī ʿAmmār, a *mawlā* of the Banū Hāshim[493] — Abū Hurayrah:[494] The Messenger of God said that the Angel of Death

491. *La-bi-manzalin,* perhaps for *la-bi-manzalatin* "is surely esteemed by God." Ibn al-Athīr, *op. cit.*, I, 198, has *"lahu manzalun karīmun."*

492. Muṣʿab b. al-Miqdām. *Index,* 553. Not further identified.

493. ʿAmmār b. Abī ʿAmmār, *mawlā* of the Banū Hāshim. Probably the son of Yāsir b. ʿĀmir al-Kanānī, Abū ʿAmmār, d. ca. 615, an early convert to Islam. Al-Ziriklī, *op. cit.*, IX, 153.

494. Abū Hurayrah, ʿAbd al-Raḥmān b. Ṣakhr al-Dawsī, b. 602, d. 61/679. This Companion of the Prophet was noted for the large number of traditions, that he transmitted, many of them were used by al-Bukhārī and Muslim. *EI*², s.v. "Abū Hurayra," al-Ziriklī, *op. cit.*, IX, 80–81; Ibn Ḥajar, *op. cit.*, XII, 262–67.

used to come to people in clear view until he came to Moses, who slapped him and put out his eye. He continued: He returned and said, "O Lord! Your servant Moses put out my eye. Were it not for his regard with You, I would have caused him distress." God said to him, "Go to My servant Moses, and tell him to place the palm of his hand on the back of an ox; for each hair his hand covers, he has a year. Give him a choice between that and dying now." So the Angel of Death went to him and gave him the choice. Moses said to him, "What will happen after that?"[495] He replied, "Death," so he said, "Then let it be now!" He inhaled him with a breath that took away his soul. After that [death] came to people secretly.

Ibn Ḥumayd related to us—[Salamah]—Abū Sinān al-Shaybānī[496]—Abū Isḥāq—ʿAmr b. Maymūn:[497] Moses and Aaron both died in the wilderness, Aaron dying before Moses. They had both gone out in the wilderness to a certain cave where Aaron died and Moses buried him. Then Moses returned to the Children of Israel, who said, "What has Aaron done?" Moses replied, "He has died." They said, "You lie! You have killed him because of our love for him"—because he was beloved by the Children of Israel. Moses beseeched his Lord, complaining of what he had encountered from the Children of Israel. God revealed to him, "Take them to his burial place, and I shall revive him so that he may inform them that he died a natural death and that you did not kill him." He took them to the grave of Aaron and called out, "O Aaron!" and he emerged from his grave, shaking the dust off his head. Then Moses said, "Did I kill you?" and Aaron replied. "No, by God! I died a natural death." Moses said,
[506] "Then return to your bed," and they departed.

The entire span of the life of Moses was one hundred and twenty years — twenty of them during the reign of Afrīdhūn and one hundred during the reign of Manūshihr. The beginning of God's sending him as a prophet, until He took Moses to Himself, was during the reign of Manūshihr.

Then, after Moses, God sent Joshua b. Nun b. Ephraim b. Joseph b. Jacob b. Isaac b. Abraham as a prophet and commanded him to journey toward Jericho and do battle with the giants who were there.

---

495. I.e., after the span of years equal to the number of hairs covered by his hand.

496. Abū Sinān Ḍirār b. Murrah al-Shaybānī. A reliable transmitter of tradition in al-Kūfah. Ibn Saʿd, *op. cit.*, VI, 236.

497. ʿAmr b. Maymūn al-Awdī, d. 74 or 75/693 or 694. Related traditions from ʿUmar. Ibn Saʿd, *op. cit.*, VI, 80.

Earlier scholars have disagreed about who committed this act and when Joshua journeyed there: Was the journey there during the lifetime of Moses b. Amram or after his death? Some of them said that Joshua did not journey, and was not commanded to journey, to Jericho, except after Moses and all those who refused to journey there with Moses b. Amram, when God commanded them to fight the giants there, had died. They said: Moses and Aaron both died before leaving the wilderness.

Mention of Those Who Said That: ʿAbd al-Karīm b. al-Haytham,[498] related to me—Ibrāhīm b. Bashshār[499]—Sufyān, who said: Abū Saʿīd[500] — ʿIkrimah — Ibn ʿAbbās: When Moses prayed: *"My Lord! I have control of none but myself and my brother, so distinguish between us and the wrongdoing people," God said: "This land will be forbidden to them for forty years during which they will wander bewildered in the earth."*[501] Ibn ʿAbbās continued: Then they entered the wilderness, and whoever entered the wilderness and was over twenty years old died there. Moses died in the wil- [507]
derness, and Aaron died before him. They continued their aimless wandering for forty years. Joshua and those who remained with him struggled against the city of the giants, and Joshua eventually conquered them.

Bishr[502] related to us — Yazīd b. Zurayʿ — Saʿīd — Qatādah: God said, *"This land will be forbidden to them for forty years"* . . . to the end of the verse.[503] The towns were forbidden to them, and they could not settle in a town for forty years. It has been mentioned to us that Moses died during these forty years, and none of them entered the Holy Land[504] except their sons and the two men who said what they did.[505]

---

498. ʿAbd al-Karīm b. al-Haytham b. Ziyād al-Qaṭṭān, d. 278/891. He visited major centers of learning in Iraq, Damascus, and Egypt and was considered a trustworthy transmitter. *GAS*, I, 153–54.

499. Ibrāhīm b. Bashshār al-Ramādī, Abū Isḥāq. A companion of Ibn ʿUyaynah (n. 33, above), he died in al-Baṣrah. Ibn Saʿd, *op. cit.*, VII/2, 58.

500. Possibly Saʿīd b. Abī Saʿīd al-Miqbarī, Abū Saʿd. *Index*, 230, 232. Not further identified.

501. Qurʾān 5:25–26.

502. *I.e.*, Bishr b. Muʿādh. See n. 98, above.

503. Qurʾān 5:25–26. *[during which they will wander in the earth bewildered. So do not grieve over the wrongdoing people.]*

504. *I.e.*, *bayt al-maqdis*.

505. Namely, Joshua and Caleb, who were true to the agreement not to reveal what they had seen when spying out the land.

Mūsā b. Hārūn al-Hamdānī related to me saying—ʿAmr[506]—Asbāṭ—al-Suddī, in an account the chain of authorities of which I have mentioned previously: None of those who had refused to enter the city of the giants with Moses remained, but all died without participating in the conquest. After the forty years had passed, God sent Joshua b. Nun as a prophet, and he told the Children of Israel that he was a prophet and that God had commanded him to fight the giants. They gave him their allegiance and believed him, so he attacked the giants. They attacked and rushed at the giants, slaying them all. A band of Israelites would gather around the neck of one of the giants and strike it. Yet they were unable to cut through it.

Ibn Bashshār related to us—Sulaymān b. Ḥarb[507]—Abū Hilāl[508]—Qatādah, regarding God's word, *"This land will be forbidden to them,"*[509] he said, "[that means] forever."

Al-Muthannā[510] related to me, saying—Muslim b. Ibrāhīm[511]—Hārūn al-Naḥwī[512]—al-Zubayr b. al-Khirrīt[513]—ʿIkrimah, regarding His word, *"This will be forbidden to them for forty years during which they will wander in the earth,"*[514] he said, "What is forbidden to them is the wandering."

[508] Others have said that it was Moses who conquered Jericho but Joshua was in command of the vanguard of Moses when he journeyed forth against them.

Mention of those who said that: Ibn Ḥumayd related to us—Salamah—Ibn Isḥāq: Moses journeyed with them, after the youngsters from among the offspring of those who had refused to fight the giants

506. ʿAmr b. Muḥammad al-ʿAnqarī (?). See Ibn Saʿd, *op. cit.*, VI, 281–82.

507. Sulaymān b. Ḥarb al-Azdī al-Wāshijī, Abū Ayyūb, 140–235/757–849. A trustworthy transmitter of many traditions, he served as *qāḍī* in Mecca, then returned to al-Baṣrah, where he died. Ibn Saʿd, *op. cit.*, VII/2, 52; al-Ziriklī, *op. cit.*, III, 183; Ibn Ḥajar, *op. cit.*, IV, 178.

508. Abū Hilāl Muḥammad b. Sulaym, Abū ʿAbdallāh, al-ʿAbdī. He lived during the reign of al-Maʾmūn, when he served as *qāḍī*. Ibn Saʿd, *op. cit.*, VII/2, 93.

509. Qurʾān 5:26.

510. Al-Muthannā b. Ibrāhīm al-Āmulī, d. 224/837. *Index*, 497; *GAS*, I, 20, 27, 35, 41.

511. Muslim b. Ibrāhīm al-Azdī al-Farāhidī, Abū ʿAmr, d. 223/836. A Baṣran who transmitted from several authorities and was cited by al-Bukhārī, Abū Dāwūd, and others. A trustworthy transmitter. Ibn Saʿd, *op. cit.*, VII, 2, 55; *GAS*, I, 103; Ibn Ḥajar, *op. cit.*, X, 121–23.

512. Hārūn al-Naḥwī. *Index*, 605. Not further identified.

513. Al-Zubayr b. al-Khirrīt. *Index*, 203. Not further identified.

514. Qurʾān 5:26.

with Moses grew up, after their fathers had perished, and after the forty years had passed during which time they were made to wander aimlessly. With him were Joshua b. Nun and Caleb b. Jephunneh. The latter was, as they claim, married to[515] Miriam bt. Amram, the sister of Moses and Aaron, and was thus the brother-in-law of the latter.[516] When they reached the land of Canaan Balaam b. Beʿor, the diviner,[517] was there, a man to whom God had granted knowledge. Among the lore that God had given him was the mighty name of God,[518] according to reports, to which, when God was prayed to by means of it, He responded; and when something was requested by means of it, He granted it.

Ibn Ḥumayd related to us — Salamah — Muḥammad b. Isḥāq — Sālim Abū al-Naḍr,[519] who related that when Moses came into the land of the Children of Canaan in the land of Syria, Balaam was in Bāliʿah, one of the towns of al-Balqāʾ.[520] When Moses, together with the Israelites, settled in this dwelling place, Balaam's people came to him, saying, "O Balaam! Moses b. Amram, with the Israelites, has come to remove us from our land, to kill us, and to settle the Israelites in it and make it their dwelling place. We are your people who have no dwelling place, but you are a man whose prayer is answered. So go forth and pray to God against them." He replied, "Woe unto you! He is a Prophet of God, who has angels and believers with [509]

515. *ʿAlā maryam;* see *Glossarium,* CCCLXXV, s.v. *ʿlʾ*.

516. See above, n. 471.

517. Balʿam b. Baʿūr, *al-maʿrūf.* But *Glossarium,* CCCLVIII, suggests the possible reading *al-ʿarūf* (used by Ibrahim, *op. cit.,* I, 437), equivalent to *ʿālim,* the term used to describe Balaam on p. 94, below. See Lane, *op. cit.,* s.v. *ʿārif:* like *ʿālim* "signifying knowing . . . particularly [skilled in divine things] possessing knowledge of God, and of His kingdom . . . see also *maʿrūf.*" For a full discussion of the Arabic stories connected with Balʿam, see H. Schützinger, "Die arabische Bileam-Erzählung." See also al-Thaʿlabī, *op. cit.,* 209–12.

518. Possibly reflecting the Jewish concept of *shem ha-m^eforash,* the ineffable name of God, Muslim tradition speaks of *al-ism al-aʿẓam,* Muḥammad having said that whoever calls upon God by this name shall obtain all his desires. See Khaṭīb al-Tibrīzī *Mishkāt al-masābīḥ* X, 1.

519. Sālim Abū al-Naḍr. *Index,* 220. Not further identified.

520. Yāqūt, *op. cit.,* I, 479, cited by Le Strange, *op. cit.,* 416, says only that Bāliʿah is in al-Balqāʾ and is the place of origin of Balaam. Al-Balqāʾ was a district of the province of Damascus, east of the Jordan, between the districts of Damascus and Karak. Le Strange, *op. cit.,* 36, following Yaʿqūbī, states that its capital was ʿAmmān; on p. 456, following Abū al-Fidāʾ, he states that its capital was Ḥusbān (see below), which seems to have been true during the Mamluk period. See al-Thaʿlabī, *op. cit.,* 209, on al-Balqāʾ.

him. How can I go and pray against them when whatever I know is from God?" They said, "But, we have no dwelling place." They continued cajoling him and pleading with him until they beguiled him, and he was won over. He mounted his she-ass and headed for the mountain where he could observe the Israelite army, Mount Heshbon.[521] He had not journeyed very far[522] on the she-ass when she lay down with him on her back. He got off and struck her. When he was sharp with her she arose, and he mounted her again. But she did not travel far until she lay down with him again, and he did what he had previously done. She got up, and he mounted her. She did not travel far until she lay down with him, and he beat her until, when he was sharp with her, God permitted her to speak, and she argued with him, saying, "Woe to you, O Balaam! Where are you going? Don't you see the angels in front of me, turning me back? Will you go to the Prophet of God and the believers to pray against them?" Balaam did not stop beating her, so God opened the path to her when he did that to her.

They traveled together until, from Mount Heshbon, they overlooked the Israelite army. Balaam began to pray against them. However, he could not utter a prayer against the Israelites without God's turning his tongue instead against his own people, nor could he pray for his people without God's turning his tongue instead toward the Israelites. So his people said to him, "Do you know what you are doing, O Balaam? You are praying for them and against us." He said, "I have no control over this matter. This is a matter over which God
[510] has power." As his tongue lolled and he fell down upon his chest, he said to them, "Both this world and the next have departed from me, and nothing remains but stratagems and deceptions. So I will plan a stratagem for you, using deceit. Adorn your women and give them some goods. Then send them to the Israelite army to sell them. Command each to give herself to any man who desires her, because, if even one of the men commits fornication, then you will be protected against them."

---

521. Mount Heshbon is Arabic Ḥusbān, Ḥasbān. Cf. Le Strange, *op. cit.*, 456. See also Popper, *Egypt and Syria under the Circassian Sultans*, XV, 15 (Ḥasban), 51 (Ḥusbān).

522. *Fa-mā sāra ʿalayhā ghayra qalīlin*, here, but al-Thaʿlabī, *op. cit.*, 210, has *falamma sāra ʿalayhā ghayra baʿīdin;* Ibn al-Athīr, *op. cit.*, I, 201, has *fa-mā sāra ʿalayhā illā qalīlan.*

They did as they were instructed. When the women reached the Israelite army, one of the Canaanite women, named Cozbi, daughter of Zur, who was head of his people and of the sons of his father, those of them who had been in Midian, he being the eldest of them, passed by one of the most powerful Israelite men, named Zimri b. Salu, chief of the tribe of Simeon b. Jacob b. Isaac b. Abraham.[523] Because he was pleased by her beauty, he arose and took her by the hand. They approached Moses, and Zimri said, "I believe that you will say that 'This is forbidden to you.'" Moses replied, "Certainly, she is forbidden to you. Do not draw near her." Zimri responded, "By God! We will not obey you in this matter." Then they entered his tent and had intercourse. As a result, God sent the plague among the Israelites.

Phineas b. Eleazar b. Aaron, a man who possessed strength and great courage, managed affairs for Moses. He had been absent when Zimri b. Salu did what he did. When he returned, the plague was raging among the Israelites. After he was informed of Zimri's affair, he seized his spear, which was made entirely of iron, entered the tent where the two were lying beside one another, and pierced them with his spear. Taking the spear in his forearm, propping his elbow on his waist, and leaning the spear against his jaw, Phineas left the tent [511]
with both of them raised to the heavens. The firstborn of Eleazar, Phineas, began to call out, "My God! We will do this to those who disobey You," and the plague was lifted. A count was taken of the Israelites who had perished in the plague from the time Zimri had accosted the woman until Phineas killed him; they found that seventy thousand Israelites had perished. Even those who gave the lowest figures said twenty thousand during one hour alone. Since then, from every animal the Israelites sacrificed, they would give the descendants of Phineas b. Eleazar b. Aaron the stomach, the foreleg, and the jaw, because he propped his spear on his waist, held it by his forearm, and leaned it against his jaw. Because Phineas was Eleazar's firstborn son, they gave their firstborn and the firstborn of all their possessions as well.[524]

---

523. Based on the biblical account in Numbers 25, here the man's name is Zimrī b. Shalūm, and the name of the Midianite woman is Kasbā bt. Ṣūr.

524. A reflection of the biblical rules regarding the portions of sacrificial animals given to the priests (Leviticus 7:14, 30, 36; Numbers 18:10–11), as well as the commandment regarding the redemption of the firstborn son (Exodus 13:15; 34:19; Deuteronomy 15:19). See *EJ*, VI, 1306–7.

Regarding Balaam b. Be'or, God revealed to Muḥammad, *"Recite to them the tale of him to whom We gave Our revelations, but he sloughed them off"*—meaning Balaam b. Be'or—*"so Satan overtook him [and he became one who leads astray. Had We willed We could have raised him by their means, but he clung to the earth and followed his own lust. Therefore his likeness is as that of a dog: If you attack him, he pants with his tongue out, and if you leave him, he pants with his tongue out. Such is the likeness of the people who deny Our revelations. Narrate to them the history (of the men of old), that] perhaps they may take thought"*[525]—namely, the Children of Israel. "I have brought them the history of what occurred among them but that they concealed from you. Perhaps they would then consider and realize that only a prophet could bring them this history of what happened to them in the past, a prophet whose account comes from heaven."

Then Moses sent Joshua b. Nun ahead to Jericho with the Israelites. [Joshua] entered with them and slew the giants who lived there. He smote those he smote among them, and there remained of them only a remnant on the day on which he smote them. Night approached, and [Joshua] feared that, if the night covered them, the giants would elude him. So he asked the sun to stand still and prayed to God to detain it. He did so until [Joshua] extirpated them. Then
[512] Moses entered Jericho with the Israelites and remained there as long as God wished. Then God took Moses to Himself; the whereabouts of his grave are unknown.

On the other hand, al-Suddī related in his account, the chain of transmission of which I have mentioned previously, that Joshua b. Nun fought the giants after the death of Moses and Aaron. He related about him and them what I am mentioning, recounting therein that God sent Joshua as a prophet after the forty years had ended. Joshua summoned the Children of Israel and told them that he was a prophet whom God had commanded to fight the giants. They gave him their allegiance and believed him. A man of the Israelites named Balaam went forth. He was a learned man, one who knew the great ineffable name [of God]. But he became an unbeliever and went over to the giants, saying, "Do not be afraid of the Israelites. When you go to fight them, I will utter a prayer against them, and they will

525. Qur'ān 7:175–76.

perish." He obtained all the worldly goods that he had wanted from them, but he could not approach their women, because of their enormous size. Therefore, he resorted to intercourse with one of his she-asses. God was speaking about Balaam when He said, *"Recite to them the tale of him to whom We gave Our revelations"* ... that is, he saw ... *"yet he sloughed them off, so Satan overtook him, and he became one who leads astray"* ... to where he said ... *"but he clung to the earth and followed his own lust. Therefore his likeness is as that of a dog: If you attack him, he pants with his tongue out; if you leave him, he pants with his tongue out."*[526] And Balaam used to pant with his tongue out just as a dog does.

Joshua, along with the people, went to battle against the giants, while Balaam accompanied the giants on his she-ass. He intended to curse the Israelites, yet, whenever he wished to pray against them, the prayer went against the giants instead. The giants said, "Verily, you are only praying against us." Balaam replied, "But I only intended to affect the Children of Israel." When he reached the gate of the city, an angel took hold of the tail of his she-ass and held it tight. [Balaam] began to goad her, but she would not move. When he continued to beat her, she spoke, saying, "You have intercourse with me by night and ride me by day. Woe is me from you! If I could go farther, I would, but this angel is stopping me." [513]

Joshua fought a fierce battle against the giants on Friday, lasting until the evening when the sun set and the sabbath began. He prayed to God and said to the sun, "Verily, you and I are both obedient to God. O my God! Turn the sun back for me." The sun was turned back for him, and the daylight lengthened by an hour on that day. He put the giants to flight and the Israelites stormed after them, slaying them. A group of the Israelites would gather around the neck of one [giant], striking but not cutting it. They collected their spoils, which Joshua commanded them to sacrifice. The spoils were sacrificed, but fire did not descend to consume them. So Joshua said, "O Children of Israel! God has a request of you. Come now and swear allegiance to me." So they swore allegiance to him. But the hand of one man stuck to Joshua's hand. Joshua said, "Bring me what you have." The man brought him the head of an ox made of gold crowned with

526. Qurʾān 7:175–76. For complete text of verses, see preceding occurrence, n. 525, above.

sapphires and gems that he had retained fraudulently for himself. Joshua placed it, as well as the man, in the sacrifice. Fire came, consuming both the man and the sacrifice.

As for the people of the Torah, they say that Aaron and Moses per-
[514] ished in the wilderness and that God inspired Joshua after Moses, commanding him to cross the Jordan to the land He had promised and given to the Israelites. Joshua exerted himself in obeying God's command and sent [spies] toward Jericho to reconnoiter it. Then he journeyed on, with the Ark of the Covenant, until he crossed the Jordan, within which a road appeared for him and his companions. He then surrounded the city of Jericho for six months. During the seventh month, the Israelites blew their horns, gave a single great shout, and the walls of the city proceeded to fall. They sacked the city, setting it and all that was in it on fire, except for the gold, silver, and vessels of copper and iron, for these they put into the treasury. Then, however, one of the Israelites took something fraudulently, which made God angry with them. They were put to flight, and Joshua became greatly grieved until God revealed that he should draw lots from among the tribes. He did so, and the lot fell upon the man who had taken items fraudulently. His stolen loot was removed from his house. Then Joshua stoned him and burned everything that belonged to him. They named that place after the one who possessed the loot, who was ʿĀḥir. The place is known, until this day, as the valley of ʿĀḥir.[527]

Then Joshua rallied them against the king of Ai[528] and his people, with God guiding them to battle. God commanded Joshua to lay an ambush for them. He did so, and conquered Ai, crucifying its king on a piece of wood and setting fire to the city. He slew twelve thousand men and women of its inhabitants. The people of the valley of Gibeon[529] deceived Joshua so that he pledged their safety. But, when he became aware of their deceit, he prayed to God against them—that they should become hewers of wood and drawers of water; they
[515] became so. He also wanted Bāziq,[530] the king of Jerusalem, to be re-

527. Ghawr ʿĀḥir, Hebrew *ʿemeq ʿakhor*, Joshua 7:24, 26; 15:7. In this biblical account, the man who stole from the booty was named Achan (ʿAkhan), and no link is made between his name and that of the valley.

528. Arabic: ʿĀyī. See Joshua 8 for the biblical account.

529. Arabic: ʿImaq Jabʿūn. See Joshua 9–10 for the account of the trick played by the Gibeonites and their later relations with Joshua.

530. A misreading of the biblical Adoni-Zedek (*ṣedeq*), king of Jerusalem, Joshua

duced to beggary.[531] Then the kings of the Amorites,[532] who were five in number, sent one to the other, and all of them assembled against Gibeon, the people of which asked Joshua for assistance. Joshua gave it to them, and they routed the kings, driving them down into the gorge of Ḥawrān.[533] God then cast down hailstones upon them, and there were more people killed by the hail than were slain by the swords of the Israelites.

Joshua asked the sun to stand still and the moon to rise until he could avenge his enemies before the beginning of the sabbath. Both [luminaries] did so while the five kings fled and hid in a cave. Joshua gave orders to close off the entrance to the cave until he finished avenging himself on his foes. Then he gave orders for them to be brought forth, whereupon he killed and crucified them. He then took them down from the pieces of wood and threw them into the cave in which they had been hiding. He then attacked the remaining kings one by one in Syria, wiping out thirty-one among them; and he divided up the land he had conquered.

Then Joshua died and was buried on Mount Ephraim. After his death, the tribes of Judah and Simeon battled against the Canaanites. The Israelites ravaged their women, and they slew ten thousand of them in Bāziq.[534] They seized the king of Bāziq, cutting off his thumbs and great toes. The king of Bāziq replied, "Seventy kings, with cut-off thumbs and great toes, used to pick up bread from under my table. Now God has paid me back for my actions." The king of Bāziq was then taken to Jerusalem, where he died. The sons of Judah continued to fight the remaining Canaanites and took control of their land.

The span of Joshua's life was one hundred and twenty-six years, and his authority over the Israelites, from the time of death of Moses until his death, lasted twenty-seven years. [516]

10:1, or confusion with Adoni-Bezek, king of Bezek, Judges 1:5. See n. 534, below. Septuagint Joshua 10:1 has Adonibezek, a possible source for this reading. Text has Ūrshalīm; MS BM has Urasalam.

531. *Yataṣaddaqu.* See *Glossarium,* CCCXXIII, *sensu mendicavit.*

532. Here *al-armāniyīn,* but Joshua 10:5 speaks of the "five kings of the Amorites" —Hebrew *emorī.*

533. Classical Auranitis, one of the southeastern portions of the province of Damascus, north of the Balqā'. See n. 520, above. Its capital was Buṣrā. See Le Strange, *op. cit.,* 32–34; Yāqūt, *op. cit.,* II, 357–58.

534. Bezek, a city of the Canaanites and Perizzites. See Judges 1:4–7, where the words of Adoni-Bezek (*i.e.,* lord of Bezek) are given in almost the same form as here.

It is said that the first man to rule as king among the kings of Yemen was from Ḥimyar, during the age of Moses b. Amram. He was named Shamīr b. al-Amlūl,[535] and he built the city of Ẓafār[536] in Yemen, driving out the Amalekites who were there. At that time, this Shamīr b. al-Amlūl al-Ḥimyarī, had been selected as a governor over Yemen and its vicinity by the king of Persia.

Hishām b. Muḥammad al-Kalbī asserted that a remnant of Canaanites remained after Joshua slew those of them he had slain. He also asserted that Ifrīqīs[537] b. Qays b. Ṣayfī b. Saba᾿ b. Kaʿb b. Zayd b. Ḥimyar b. Saba᾿ b. Yashjub b. Yaʿrub b. Joktan (Qaḥṭān) passed by them on his way toward Ifrīqiyah. He carried them from the coasts of Syria and brought them to Ifrīqiyah. Then he conquered it, killing its king, Jirjīr,[538] and settled it with the remnant of the Canaanites whom he had taken with him from the coasts of Syria.[539] [Al-Kalbī] said the Berbers are so named because Ifrīqīs said to them, "How much noise *(barbara)* you make!" Therefore they were called Berbers. It is also mentioned that Ifrīqīs said, in a poem, regarding their noise:

Canaan made noise when I drove them
from lands of destruction[540] to a life of wonder.[541]

Among the Berbers from Ḥimyar were the Ṣinhājah and Kutāmah, who are still among them today.[542]

---

535. Probably the same as Shamr b. al-Umlūk al-Ḥimyarī, supposedly contemporary with Moses, who built Ẓafar and drove the Amalekites out of Yemen. See al-Ziriklī, *op. cit.*, III, 253.

536. An ancient city in Yemen, south of Ṣanʿā᾿, and a capital of the Himyarite kings. See Yāqūt, *op. cit.*, III, 576–77.

537. The same as Afrīqūs b. Qays b. Ṣayfī, whose exploits in North Africa were doubted by Ibn Khaldūn. See *al-Muqaddimah,* trans. Rosenthal, I, 21–25, on errors concerning Yemenite history. Also written Ifrīqīsh, in MS Tn. See n. 125, above, where Ifrīqīs is listed as a descendant of Isaac. See also n. 154, above, and n. 797, below, for similar genealogies.

538. According to Ibn Khaldūn, ʿAbdallāh b. al-Zubayr, during the Muslim conquest of North Africa in 27/647/48, killed Gregory (Jirjīr), the Byzantine governor of the province. See Ibn Khaldūn, *op. cit.,* trans. Rosenthal, III, 474 n. 1939. There was undoubtedly confusion between those two events. MS C has Jirjīs, but other MSS have Jirjīr.

539. Perhaps reflecting the Phoenician establishment of Carthage.

540. MS Tn has *al-mulk* "dominion," instead of *al-hulk* "destruction." Ibn Khaldūn, *Histoire,* I, 111, has *al-ḍank* "straitness."

541. Ibn Khaldūn, *Histoire,* I, 111, has *al-khaṣab* "fruitfulness," instead of *al-ʿajab* "wonder."

542. Two great Berber groups. See Ibn Khaldūn, *al-Muqaddimah,* trans. Rosenthal, I, 22, for a specific refutation of this claim of Himyarite origin.

The Affair of Korah b. Izhar b. Kohath[543] [517]

Korah was the cousin of Moses. Al-Qāsim[544] said—al-Ḥusayn[545]—Ḥajjāj[546]—Ibn Jurayj: [Regarding] His word: *Korah was of the people of Moses,*[547] he said: "This means the son of his uncle, the brother of his father." He said: "Korah was the son of Izhar"—thus said al-Qāsim—"[He was] the son of Kohath, and Moses was the son of ʿArmar b. Kohath, and *ʿArmar* in Arabic is *ʿImrān*." Thus said al-Qāsim, but in fact it is *Amram,* [not *ʿArmar*].

As for Ibn Isḥāq, he said what Ibn Ḥumayd related to us—Salamah—[Ibn Isḥāq]: Izhar b. Kohath married Shummayth bt. Tabāwīb[548] b. Barakiyā[549] b. Yaqsān b. Abraham, who bore him Amram b. Izhar and Korah b. Izhar. Thus Korah, according to Ibn Isḥāq, was the uncle of Moses, the brother of his father by both his father and his mother. As for the learned men of the forebears of our people and of the people of the two scriptures,[550] they agree with what Ibn Jurayj said.

---

543. *Qārūn* in Arabic. The biblical story of Korah is found in Numbers 16; the Jewish legends about him are in Ginzberg, *op. cit.*, III, 286–303. See also *EJ*, X, 1190–94; EI^2, s.v. "Ḳārūn"; al-Thaʿlabī, *op. cit.*, 188–92.

544. *I.e.*, al-Qāsim b. al-Ḥasan al-Hamadānī. See n. 243, above.

545. Al-Ḥusayn b. Dāwūd al-Maṣṣīṣī. See n. 244, above.

546. Al-Ḥajjāj b. Muḥammad. See n. 245, above.

547. Qurʾān 28:76.

548. Unpointed in text. Pointing comes from MS Tn.

549. MS Tn has Baraknā. The editor suggests it is Hebrew Berachya.

550. *I.e.*, the Torah and the Gospels, the Jews and the Christians.

The Mention of Those among Our Past Scholars Whose Reports about That Have Reached Us

Abū Kurayb related to us—Jābir b. Nūḥ[551]—Ismāʿīl b. Abī Khālid[552]—Ibrāhīm,[553] concerning [God's] saying that *Korah was of the people of Moses:* He was the paternal cousin of Moses.

Ibn Bashshār[554] related to us—ʿAbd al-Raḥmān[555]—Sufyān—Simāk b. Ḥarb[556]—Ibrāhīm: Korah was the paternal cousin of Moses.

[518] Ibn Wakīʿ related to us—my father—Sufyān—Simāk—Ibrāhīm said [concerning the statement] that *Korah was of the people of Moses;* he was his paternal cousin and he treated [Moses] unjustly.

Ibn Wakīʿ related to us—Yaḥyā b. Saʿīd al-Qaṭṭān[557]—[Sufyān][558] Simāk b. Ḥarb—Ibrāhīm: Korah was the paternal cousin of Moses.

Ibn Wakīʿ related to us—Abū Muʿāwiyah[559]—Ibn Abī Khālid—Ibrahim: *Korah was of the people of Moses* means that he was his paternal cousin.

Bishr b. Muʿādh related to us—Yazīd—Saʿīd—Qatādah: Concerning His saying that *Korah was of the people of Moses,* it has been related to us that he was his paternal cousin, [son of] his father's brother; he was called "al-Munawwir" because of the beauty of his description in the Torah.[560] But the enemy of God played the hypocrite, just like al-Sāmirī,[561] and injustice destroyed him.

---

551. Jābir b. Nūḥ al-Ḥamānī, Abū Bashīr. *Index,* 93. Not further identified.

552. Ismāʿīl b. Abī Khālid, *mawlā* of al-Bujaylah, al-Aḥmasī, d. 146/763. *GAS,* I, 821.

553. Ibrāhīm b. Yazīd b. Qays al-Nakhaʿī, Abū ʿImrān, 50–97/670–715, a leading jurist and transmitter of traditions from al-Kūfah. Ibn Saʿd, *op. cit.,* VI, 188–99; Ibn Ḥajar, *op. cit.,* 177–79; al-Ziriklī, *op. cit.,* I, 76; *GAS,* I, 403–4.

554. Muḥammad b. Bashshār. See n. 481, above.

555. ʿAbd al-Raḥmān b. Mahdī b. Ḥassān al-ʿAnbarī al-Luʾluʾī al-Baṣrī, 135–98/752–814. One of the leading memorizers of traditions. *GAS,* I, 781; al-Ziriklī, *op. cit.,* IV, 115.

556. Simāk b. Ḥarb b. Aws b. Khālid al-Dhahilī al-Bakrī, Abū al-Mughīrah, d. 123/741, a Kūfan transmitter of traditions. Ibn Ḥajar, *op. cit.,* IV, 222; al-Ziriklī, *op. cit.,* III, 202.

557. Yaḥyā b. Saʿīd al-Qaṭṭān al-Taymī, Abū Saʿīd, 120–98/737–813. A Baṣran memorizer of traditions, he rendered legal opinions according to Abū Ḥanīfah. Ibn Saʿd, *op. cit.,* VII, 2, 47; *GAS,* I, 852; al-Ziriklī, *op. cit.,* IX, 181.

558. MS Tn inserts—Sufyān—, missing in other MSS.

559. Abū Muʿāwiyah al-Ḍarīr. See n. 251, above.

560. There seems to be no basis for this in the Torah. The genealogy of Korah is given as b. Izhar b. Kohath (Numbers 16:1), as here.

561. Korah, al-Sāmirī, Haman, and Pharaoh (Firʿawn) are all the prototypes of evil tyrants in the Qurʾān and are often compared with one another. See n. 302, above.

Bishr b. Hilāl al-Ṣawwāf[562] — Jaʿfar b. Sulaymān al-Ḍubaʿī[563] — Mālik b. Dīnār:[564] I was told that Moses b. Amram was the paternal cousin of Korah, whom God had given great wealth; as God described it, *We gave him so much treasure that the very keys thereof would have been a burden for a troop of mighty men*[565] ... by His saying *burden,* He meant something oppressive.

It is said that the keys of his storehouses were, we were told by Ibn Ḥumayd — Jarīr[566] — Manṣūr[567] — Khaythamah,[568] regarding His statement that *the very keys thereof would have been a burden for a troop of mighty men,*[569] as we find written in the Gospels:[570] [519]
The keys of Korah [equal] the burden of sixty mules with white blazes on their foreheads and white legs. No key was greater than a finger in length, and each one was connected to a treasure.

Abū Kurayb related to me — Hushaym[571] — Ismāʿīl b. Sālim[572] — Abū Ṣāliḥ: The very keys thereof would have been a burden for a troop. He said. "The keys of his storehouses were carried by forty mules."

---

562. Bishr b. Hilāl al-Ṇawwāf. *Index,* 70. Not further identified.

563. Jaʿfar b. Sulaymān al-Ḍubaʿī, Abū Sulaymān, *mawlā* of Banū al-Ḥarīsh, d. 178/794, a reliable transmitter, tending toward Shiʿism. Ibn Saʿd, *op. cit.,* VII, 2, 44.

564. Mālik b. Dīnār al-Sāmī al-Nājī, Abū Yaḥyā, d. 131/748, from al-Baṣrah. He was noted as an ascetic and transmitted traditions from Anas b. Mālik, among others. Ibn Ḥajar, *op. cit.,* X, 14–15; Ibn Saʿd, *op. cit.,* VII, 2, 243; al-Ziriklī, *op. cit.,* VI, 134; *GAS,* I, 634.

565. Qurʾān 28:76.

566. Jarīr b. ʿAbd al-Ḥamīd al-Rāzī al-Ḍabbī, 110–188/728–804. A Kūfan who lived and died in al-Rayy, he was much sought after for his extensive knowledge of tradition (Ibn Saʿd, *op. cit.,* VII, 2, 110; al-Ziriklī, *op. cit.,* II, 111), according to *Index,* 99. But *GAS,* I, 404, seems to indicate that Jarīr b. Ḥāzim was the next in transmission from Manṣūr b. al-Muʿtamir, below.

567. Manṣūr b. al-Muʿtamir b. ʿAbdallāh al-Sulamī, Abū ʿAttāb, d. 132/749 or 750. A very famous Kūfan transmitter, than whom no one had memorized more traditions, he was considered very reliable. Ibn Ḥajar, *op. cit.,* I, 312; Ibn Saʿd, *op. cit.,* VI, 235; al-Ziriklī, *op. cit.,* VIII, 245.

568. Khaythamah b. ʿAbd al-Raḥmān. He was a reliable traditionist, born in Medina, who lived in al-Kūfah. Ibn Saʿd, *op. cit.,* VI, 200–1.

569. Qurʾān 28:76.

570. No mention of this is found in the Gospels.

571. Hishām in text. Reading with Ibrahim, I, *op. cit.,* 444 n. 2, who identifies him as Hushaym b. Bashīr b. al-Qāsim al-Sulamī, Abū Muʿāwiyah, 104–83/722–99. A transmitter of *ḥadīth* from Ismāʿīl b. Sālim, according to Ibn Ḥajar, *op. cit.,* XI, 59–63; Ibn Saʿd, *op. cit.,* VII/2, 61; *GAS,* I, 38; al-Ziriklī, *op. cit.,* IX, 89.

572. Ismāʿīl b. Sālim al-Asadī. A Kūfan who lived in Baghdad before it became the ʿAbbāsid capital, he was considered a reliable authority and was much quoted by Hushaym above. Ibn Saʿd, *op. cit.,* VII/2, 67.

Abū Kurayb related to us—Jābir b. Nūḥ—al-Aʿmash[573]—Khaythamah: The keys of Korah were carried by sixty mules, and each key, resembling a finger (and made) of leather, was for the door of a specific treasure.

Ibn Wakīʿ related to us—my father—al-Aʿmash—Khaythamah, who said: "The keys of Korah were made of leather, each like a finger, and each for a separate storehouse. When Korah traveled, his keys were carried on sixty mules with white blazes and white legs. The enemy of God rebelled because of the ill luck and trial God desired to inflict through him on His people due to the greatness of his wealth."

It is said that his oppression of them consisted of his having surpassed them in luxurious garments. The like of this was related to me by ʿAlī b. Saʿīd al-Kindī,[574] Abū al-Sāʾib[575] and Ibn Wakīʿ—Ḥafṣ b. Ghiyāth[576]—Layth[577]—Shahr b. Ḥawshab.[578] The people warned Korah about his oppression, forbade him to do it, and commanded him to expend what God had given him for His sake and to make use of it in obedience to Him, as God has reported regarding them, that they said to [Korah], as He said: *When his own people said to him, "Do not exult; lo! God does not love the exultant. But seek the abode of the Hereafter with what God has given you. Do not neglect*
[520] *your portion of this world, and be generous as God has been generous to you. Do not seek corruption in the earth; lo! God does not love corrupters."*[579] He meant by saying "do not neglect your portion of this world" that, while you are in this world, you should not neglect to take your portion in it for your hereafter.

Korah's response showed his ignorance and his heedlessness of God's forbearance toward him, which He mentioned in His book,

---

573. Al-Aʿmash. See n. 219, above.

574. ʿAlī b. Saʿīd al-Kindī. *Index*, 396. Not further identified.

575. Abū al-Sāʾib. See n. 250, above.

576. Ḥafṣ b. Ghiyāth b. Ṭalq al-Nakhaʿī al-Azdī, Abū ʿUmar, 117–94/735–810. He was a *qāḍī* of al-Kūfah, a reliable memorizer of tradition, and a companion of Abū Ḥanīfah. Ibn Saʿd, *op. cit.*, VI, 271–72; al-Ziriklī, *op. cit.*, II, 291–92.

577. (Al)-Layth b. Saʿd b. ʿAbd al-Raḥmān, Abū al-Ḥārith, al-Miṣrī, 95–175/713–91. He was a leading traditionist and legal scholar of Egypt in his day. Ibn Ḥajar, *op. cit.*, VIII, 459; Ibn Saʿd, *op. cit.*, VII/2, 517; *GAS*, I, 520.

578. Shahr b. Ḥawshab al-Ashʿarī, 20–100/641–718. A Syrian who settled in Iraq, he served as a government official and was considered a rather weak transmitter. Ibn Saʿd, *op. cit.*, VII/2, 158; Ibn Ḥajar, *op. cit.*, IV, 369; al-Ziriklī, *op. cit.*, III, 259.

579. Qurʾān 28:76–77.

where [Korah] said to them: *"I have been given what I have been given of* this world *only on account of knowledge I possess."*[580] It is said that the meaning of that was "because of good I possess." Thus it was related from Qatādah. Someone else said that he meant, "If God were not pleased with me and did He not know my excellence, He would not have given me this." But God, giving the lie to his meaning,[581] said, *"Did he not know that God had already destroyed of generations before him men who were mightier than he in strength and greater in respect to gathering,"*[582] i.e., of wealth. If God gives wealth and this world only to those who please Him and possess excellence with Him, then He would not have destroyed those who possessed great wealth before him whom He did not destroy, despite the quantity of it that He had given them. Neither the warnings of those who warned him, nor the reminders of him who reminded of God and His good counsel, turned Korah back from his ignorance and oppression of his people through the use of his great wealth. Instead, he persisted in his wrong course and in going astray. He would go out among his people in his finery, mounted on a white work horse with a purple saddle, and dressed in yellow-dyed garments. He took along with him three hundred slave girls in similar garb on similarly adorned nags, as well as four thousand of his companions. Someone has said that his companions, whom he took along in the same garb and adornment, numbered [521] seventy thousand.

Ibn Wakīʿ related to us — Abū Khālid al-Aḥmar[583] — ʿUthmān b. al-Aswad[584] — Mujāhid:[585] Regarding *Then he went out before his people in his pomp,*[586] he said, [means] on white work horses with purple saddles, [their riders] wearing yellow-dyed [garments]. The people who had gone astray, among those before whom Korah went forth in his pomp, wanted the like of what had been given him and said: *"Ah, would that we had been given the like of what has been*

580. Qurʾān 28:78.

581. *Qīla* seems used here as a noun, "meaning." See also n. 590, below. Other versions have *qabla* "before."

582. Qurʾān 28:78.

583. Sulaymān b. Ḥayyān Abū Khālid al-Aḥmar. *Index,* 248. Not further identified.

584. ʿUthmān b. al-Aswad. *Index,* 374. Not further identified.

585. Mujāhid. See n. 172, above.

586. Qurʾān 28:79.

given to Korah! Lo! He is the possessor of great good fortune!"[587] But people knowledgeable of God disapproved of them for saying this, and they responded, *"Woe unto you!*[588] O You who desire what has been given to Korah! Rely on God. Do what God has commanded you, and desist from what He has forbidden. For verily God's reward and recompense to those who obey Him are better for those who believe in Him and His messengers and those who perform pious deeds, according to what He has commanded. God says, *And none but the steadfast will obtain it."*[589] He says [interpreting]: "No one will not obtain the meaning[590] of this statement except those who are steadfast in avoiding the pomp of the life of this world and who prefer God's great reward for pious deeds over the pleasures of this world and its passions and who act [to obtain it] as that requires."

When the evildoer became arrogant and continued his wrong course, undervaluing God's favor, God tried [Korah], from His precept regarding his wealth and the right He obliged from him regarding it with what his avarice brought upon him, namely, the most painful of His punishments, by which he became a warning to those who have passed away[591] and an exhortation to those remaining behind.

Abū Kurayb related to us—Jābir b. Nūḥ—al-Aʿmash—al-Minhāl
[522] b. ʿAmr—ʿAbdallāh b. al-Ḥārith[592]—Ibn ʿAbbās: When the [duty of] alsmgiving was revealed, Korah came to Moses and agreed with him [on giving] one dinar for every thousand dinars, and for every thousand dirhams one dirham, and one article (*shayʾ*) for every thousand—or he said, "for every thousand sheep (*shāh*), a sheep." Abū Jaʿfar al-Ṭabarī said: "I am uncertain [about the proper wording]."

Then Korah returned to his house, made an account of his possessions and found that his tax would be very high. So he gathered the Israelites and said, "O Children of Israel! Moses has given you com-

---

587. Qurʾān 28:79.

588. Qurʾān 28:80.

589. Qurʾān 28:80.

590. *Qīla,* as in n. 581, above. Or "what is meant by."

591. Here *li-al-ghābirīn*. MS C has *li-al-ʿābirīn* with similar meaning, but MS Tn has *li-al-muʿtabirīn* "to those who take heed, or learn a lesson."

592. ʿAbdallāh b. Ḥārith b. Nawfal al-Hāshimī, 9–84/630–703. One of the noblest of Quraysh and a nephew of Muʿāwiyah, he supported Ibn Zubayr and had to flee to Oman, where he died. See Ibn Saʿd, *op. cit.*, V, 15–16; al-Ziriklī, *op. cit.*, IV, 205.

mandments about everything, and you have obeyed him. Now he wants to take your possessions." They replied, "You are our elder and master, so command us as you wish." He said, "I command you to bring so-and-so, the prostitute, and offer her an agreed price. Then let her accuse [Moses of committing adultery] with her." So they called her and set a price, on the condition that she accuse him [of adultery with her]. Then Korah went to Moses and said, "Your people have gathered together for you to give them commandments and prohibitions." So Moses went out to them while they were on a plain of the land and said, "O Children of Israel! Whoever steals, we will cut off his hand; whoever forges a lie against someone, we will flog him eighty stripes; whoever fornicates and has a wife, we will flog him until he dies or stone him until he dies." Abū Jaʿfar [al-Ṭabarī] said, "I am uncertain about this."[593]

Then Korah said to him, "Even if it were you?" Moses replied, "Even if it were I." Korah said, "The Israelites claim that you committed adultery with so-and-so." [Moses] said, "Call her, and if she says so, then it is as she says." When she arrived, Moses said to her, "O so-and-so!" She said, "Here I am!" He said, "Did I do to you what these people say?" She replied, "No! They lie. They set a price with
me on the condition that I accuse you of [committing adultery] with [523]
me." Then he stood up and bowed down, while he was still among them, and God inspired him, saying, "Command the earth to do whatever you want." Moses said, "O earth! Seize [these people]!" And it took hold of them up to their ankles. Then he said, "O earth! Seize them!" And it took hold of them up to their knees. Then he said, "O earth! Seize them!" And it took hold of them up to their necks. The narrator continued: They began saying, "O Moses! O Moses!" and pleading with him. He said, "O earth! Seize them!" And it covered them up. Then God inspired him, "My servants said to you 'O Moses! O Moses!' but you did not have mercy. But, if it had been I, they would have found Me *Nigh, Responsive.*"[594]

---

593. This statement reflects the long-standing dispute in Islamic law over punishment for sexual misconduct, deriving from certain differences between the Qurʾān and *Ḥadīth* on the subject. Imprisonment at home (Qurʾān 4:15) or flogging (Qurʾān 24:2) are the punishments specified in the Qurʾān. In the prophetic *Ḥadīth* stoning is added (with considerable discussion about its having been included in a Qurʾānic verse, later abrogated, the provisions of which remained in effect). This also reflects the difference in punishment of a virgin (*bikr*) and a married person (*muḥṣan*). See *Shorter Encyclopaedia of Islam,* s.v. "Zināʾ."

594. Qurʾān 11:61.

And these were His words: *"Then Korah exhibited his pomp before his people."*[595] His "pomp" was when he went out on sorrel mares with purple saddles, [their riders] wearing garments dyed yellow. *"Those who desire life of this world said, 'Ah, we wish that we had been given the like of what has been given to Korah [Lo! He is lord of rare good fortune.' But those who had been given knowledge said: 'Woe unto you! The reward of God for him who believes and does right is better, and only the steadfast will attain it.' So We caused the earth to swallow him and his dwelling place. Then he had no host to help him against God. Nor was he one of those who can save themselves. And morning found those who had coveted this place only yesterday crying: 'Ah, God enlarges provision for whom He will of His servants and straitens it. If God had not been gracious to us, He would have caused it to swallow us.] Disbelievers never prosper.'* O Muḥammad! *That is the Abode of the Hereafter. We assign it to those who do not seek oppression on the earth, nor corruption. The ultimate issue is to the godfearing."*[596]

Abū Kurayb related to us—Yaḥyā b. ʿĪsā[597]—al-Aʿmash—al-Minhāl—a man—Ibn ʿAbbās, more or less the same version, but he added to my version. He said that after that the Israelites endured distress and great famine; they went to Moses and said, "Pray to your Lord for us." He continued: So he prayed for them, and God inspired him, "O Moses! Do you speak to Me about a people because of whose sins what is between Me and them has become dark? They called out to you, and you did not respond to them—if it had been I, I would have answered them."

[524] Al-Qāsim[598] related to me—al-Ḥusayn[599]—ʿAlī b. Hāshim b. al-Barīd[600]—al-Aʿmash—al-Minhāl—Saʿīd b. Jubayr—Ibn ʿAbbās, regarding His saying that *Korah was of the family of Moses:* He was his paternal cousin, and, while Moses judged in one area of the Israelites, Korah did in another. He continued: Korah called on a harlot among the Israelites and offered her a price if she would accuse

---

595. Qurʾān 28:79.
596. Qurʾān 28:79–83.
597. Yaḥyā b. ʿĪsā. *Index,* 637. Not further identified.
598. *I.e.,* al-Qāsim b. al-Ḥasan. See n. 243, above.
599. *I.e.,* al-Ḥusayn b. Dāwūd. See n. 244, above.
600. ʿAlī b. Hāshim b. al-Barīd, d. 181/797. A traditionist of al-Kūfah, he was considered a reliable transmitter. Ibn Saʿd, *op. cit.,* VI, 273.

Moses [of committing adultery] with her. Then he left him alone, until a day came on which the Israelites assembled with Moses. Korah went to him saying, "O Moses! What is the punishment if someone steals?" Moses replied that his hand should be cut off. He said: "And if it were you?" Moses said: "Yes." Then Korah said: "And what is the punishment if someone commits fornication?" And Moses replied that he should be stoned. Korah said, "Even if it were you?" He replied, "Yes." Korah said, "Verily, you have done that." Moses said, "Woe to you! With whom?" He replied, "With so-and-so." Moses called her and said, "I adjure you by Him Who revealed the Torah, did Korah tell the truth?" She said, "My God! Since you have adjured me, then I bear witness that you are innocent, that you are the messenger of God, and that God's enemy, Korah, offered me a price to accuse you [of adultery] with me."

Ibn ʿAbbās continued: Moses sprang up, then prostrated himself. God inspired him: "Lift up your head, for I have commanded the earth to obey you." So Moses said to the earth, "Seize them!" And it seized them until they sank to their loins. Korah called out, "O Moses!" But he said, "Seize them!" And it seized them until they sank to their chests. He called out again, "O Moses!" But he said, "Seize them!" He continued: And they disappeared. God said to him, "O Moses! Korah called out to you for help, and you did not help him. But, if he had called to Me for help, I would have responded and would have come to his aid."

Bishr b. Hilāl al-Ṣawwāf[601] related to us—Jaʿfar b. Sulaymān al-Ḍubaʿī[602]—ʿAlī b. Zayd b. Judʿān:[603] ʿAbdallāh b. al-Ḥārith[604] left his house and entered the prayer enclosure. When he came out again, [525]
he sat down and leaned back on it, as we sat around him. He mentioned Solomon b. David. *He said, "O Chiefs! Which of you will bring me her throne before they come to me, surrendering?"* to where He said: *"For lo! My Lord is Absolute in independence, Bountiful."*[605] The narrator continued: Then he was silent about the

601. Bishr b. Hilāl al-Ṣawwāf. See n. 562, above.

602. Jaʿfar b. Sulaymān al-Ḍubaʿī. See n. 563, above.

603. ʿAlī b. Zayd b. Judʿān. See n. 405, above.

604. ʿAbdallāh b. Ḥārith b. Nawfal. See n. 592, above.

605. Qurʾān 27:38–40. The following is omitted in al-Ṭabarī: *A stalwart of the jinn said: I will bring it to you before you can rise from your place. Lo! I verily am strong and trusty for such work. One who possessed knowledge of scripture said: I will bring it to you before your gaze returns to you. When he saw it set in his presence,*

account of Solomon and said that *Korah was of Moses' people, but he oppressed them.*[606] He was given so much treasure, as God mentioned in His book, *that its keys would have been a burden for a troop of mighty men.*[607] Korah said: *"I have been given it only on account of knowledge I possess."*[608]

Korah treated Moses as an enemy and harmed him, while Moses would forgive and pardon Korah because of their kinship. [This relationship persisted] until Korah built a house, making its door of gold and placing on the walls sheets of gold. The chiefs of the Israelites would visit him in the morning and evening, and he would offer them food, and they would converse with him and make him laugh. [God] did not send down upon Korah his distress and misfortune until he sent for an Israelite woman known for obscene speech and famous for insult. She came, and he said to her: "Would you like me to make you wealthy, to give you [gifts], and to let you consort with my wives? It is on the condition that you come to me while the chiefs of the Israelites are here and say, 'O Korah! will you not keep Moses from me?'" She said, "Of course." So when Korah sat with the chiefs of the Israelites, he sent for the woman. She came and stood before him, but God turned her heart, causing her to repent. She said to her-
[526] self, "I will not find today any repentance better than not harming the messenger of God and chastising the enemy of God."

Then she said, "Verily Korah said to me, 'Would you like me to make you wealthy, to give you [gifts], and to let you consort with my wives? It is on condition that you come to me while the chiefs of the Israelites are here and say, "O Korah! will you not keep Moses from me?"' But I found no repentance better than not harming the Messenger of God and chastising the enemy of God." When she spoke these words, Korah was abashed, lowered his head, and fell silent among the chiefs of the Israelites, realizing that he had fallen into his damnation. Her speech spread among the people until it reached Moses. When Moses heard the news, his anger grew strong. He

---

(Solomon) said: This is of the bounty of my Lord, that He may test me whether I give Him thanks or am ungrateful. Whoever gives thanks only gives thanks for (the good of) his soul; and whoever is ungrateful (is so only to his soul's hurt).

606. Qur'ān 28:76. The change of subject is probably intended to contrast the different attitudes of Solomon and Korah to God's bounty.

607. Qur'ān 28:76.

608. Qur'ān 28:78.

cleansed himself in water, then prayed and wept, saying: "O Lord! Your enemy is causing me harm; he seeks my disgrace and shame. O Lord! Give me power over him!" God inspired him: "Command the earth to do whatever you want; it will obey you."

Moses went to Korah, and when he met him Korah detected evil in Moses' face toward him, and he said, "O Moses! Have mercy on me!" Moses said, "O earth! Seize them!" The narrator continued: The house began to move and sank with Korah and his companions up to their ankles. Korah began begging, "O Moses! Have mercy on me!" But Moses said, "O earth! Seize them!" And his house moved and sank, swallowing Korah and his companions up to their knees, while he was pleading with Moses, "O Moses! Have mercy on me!" Moses continued, "O earth! Seize them!" And his house moved and sank, and Korah and his companions were swallowed up to their navels while he was pleading with Moses, "O Moses! Have mercy on me!" Moses continued, "O earth! Seize them!" And he, his house, and his friends were all consumed by the earth.

[God] said to Moses, "O Moses! How harsh you are! But—by My glory—if only [he had called to] Me, I would have responded to him."

Bishr b. Hilāl related to me—Jaʿfar b. Sulaymān—Abū ʿImrān al-Jawnī:[609] I have heard that it was said to Moses, "I shall never again [527] subject the earth to anyone, after you."[610]

Bishr related to us — Yazīd[611] — Saʿīd — Qatādah: *So We caused the earth to engulf him and his dwelling place.*[612] It was mentioned to us that he is [further] engulfed the length of a man's stature every day, and he continues to sink into [the earth], but he will not reach its bottom until the Day of Resurrection.

When[613] God's vengeance descended upon Korah, the believers who had exhorted and warned Korah advised him to acknowledge His truth and act in obedience to Him, praised God for His favor to them, whereas those who desired the wealth and comfort in life that Korah possessed were filled with regret, and they became aware of their error in desiring it. They said what God related about them in

---

609. Abū ʿImrān al-Jawnī. *Index,* 411. Not further identified.

610. Ibn al-Athīr, *op. cit.,* I, 206, has here: "I shall not again make the earth obey anyone." Al-Ṭabarī, I, 527 n. *a.*

611. *I.e.,* Yazīd b. Zurayʿ. See n. 305, above.

612. Qurʾān 28:81.

613. This is preceded by "Abū Jaʿfar said" in Ibrāhīm, *op. cit.,* I, 451.

His book: *"Alas! God makes provision abundant for those worshipers whom He will and straitens it [for whom He will]. If God had not been gracious to us*—and averted from us what Korah and his companions suffered for what we had ourselves sought yesterday — *He would have caused the earth to swallow us too*[614] — as He caused it to swallow him and them. But God rescued from every dread and trial His prophet Moses, those believers who held fast to His covenant with the Children of Israel, His servant Joshua b. Nun, and those who followed him in obedience to their Lord. Meanwhile He destroyed His enemies and theirs, Pharaoh, Haman, Korah, and the Canaanites, for their disbelief and rebellion against Him, and for their insolence, by drowning some of them, engulfing some of them in the earth, and [slaying] some of them by the sword. He made them examples for those who take warning from them and exhortation for those who are admonished by them, despite the abundance of their
[528] possessions, the number of their troops, the strength of their power, and the enormity of their physiques and bodies. But their possessions, bodies, power, armies, and helpers were of no use to them against God's will, because they disavowed God's signs and spread corruption on the earth, and they took God's servants for themselves as property: so there encompassed them what they were secure from. We seek God's help from a deed that will bring His anger near, and we pray to Him for success in what will bring His love near and draw close to His mercy."

It is related from the Prophet what Aḥmad b. ʿAbd al-Raḥmān b. Wahb[615] told us—my paternal uncle—al-Māḍī b. Muḥammad[616]—Abū Sulaymān[617] — al-Qāsim b. Muḥammad[618] — Abū Idrīs al-Khawlānī[619]—Abū Dharr:[620] "The Messenger of God said to me that

614. Qurʾān 28:82.

615. Aḥmad b. ʿAbd al-Raḥmān b. Wahb al-Qurashī, Abū ʿAbdallāh, Baḥshal, d. 264/877. He was used by Muslim as a reliable transmitter, but later he was considered a weak source. Ibn Ḥajar, *op. cit.*, I, 54; al-Ziriklī, *op. cit.*, I, 141.

616. Al-Māḍī b. Muḥammad. *Index*, 491. Not further identified.

617. Abū Sulaymān ʿAlī b. Sulaymān. *Index*, 247. Not further identified.

618. Al-Qāsim b. Muḥammad b. Abī Bakr, Abū Muḥammad, 37–107/657–725. A grandson of the caliph Abū Bakr, in his time he was considered one of the greatest scholars. Ibn Ḥajar, *op. cit.*, VIII, 333–35; al-Ziriklī, *op. cit.*, VI, 15.

619. Abū Idrīs al-Khawlānī ʿĀʾidh Allāh b. ʿAbdallāh b. ʿUmar 8–80/630–700. A Damascene scholar and jurist under ʿAbd al-Malik. Ibn Ḥajar, *op. cit.*, V, 85; al-Ziriklī, *op. cit.*, IV, 4.

620. Abū Dharr al-Ghifārī, Jundab b. Junādah b. Sufyān b. ʿUbayd, d. 32/652. One

'the first of the prophets of the Israelites was Moses and the last was Jesus.' I said, 'O Messenger of God! What was in the pages of Moses' revelation?' He replied, 'It was all examples: I wondered at one who was sure of hellfire but laughed, I wondered at one who was sure of death but rejoiced, and I wondered at one who was sure of the reckoning tomorrow but did not act.'"

Joshua's administration of the Israelites' affairs, from the time of the death of Moses until Joshua's death, was altogether twenty years during the time of Manūshihr and seven years during the time of Afrāsyāb.[621]

We will return now to an account of those Persians who ruled in Babylon[622] after Manūshihr.

---

of the earliest Muslims, he was a Companion of the Prophet. Al-Ziriklī, *op. cit.*, II, 136–37.

621. Text has Afrāsyāt. The same as Frāsiāb. See n. 623, below.

622. Possibly referring to Mesopotamia in general, where the Sasanian Persian capital, Ctesiphon, was located on the Tigris river.

The Persians Who Ruled in Babylon after Manūshihr

An account of the Persians who ruled in Babylon after Manūshihr, since the chronology of history can be accurately determined only
[529] by the sequence of the length of lives of their kings.

When Manūshihr the king, b. Manshakhūnar b. Manshakhwārnāgh died, Frāsiyāb b. Fashanj b. Rustam b. Turk[623] conquered Khunyārith[624] and the kingdom of the Persians and betook himself, according to what is said, to Babylon. His stays in Babylon and in Mihrijān Qudhaq[625] became frequent, and he worked much corruption in the kingdom of the Persians. It is said that when he conquered their kingdom he said, "We are hurrying to destroy mankind,"[626] and that his oppression and tyranny were great, destroying whatever was built in the land of Khunārath. He stopped up the streams and water conduits,[627] so that the people were afflicted by drought in[628] the fifth year of his reign until he left Persia and was

---

623. Text has Frāsyāt (Afrāsyāb, Frāsyāb) b. Pesheng, king of Turān (*i.e.*, the Turks), hence a bitter enemy of the Iranians. See Justi, *op. cit.*, 103, s.v. "Franrasyan." See also *Enc. Ir.* I/6, s.v. "Afrāsīāb," and n. 143, above.

624. Khunyārith, Khunārath, Arabic forms of Khwanirath "center of the continents." Middle Persian Xwanirah, Avestan X^{v}aniraθa, in old Iranian cosmology the seventh and central continent, encircled by the six others. An ancient name used for the Iranian realm given to Īraj. See al-Ṭabarī, I, 229 (trans. Brinner, 26 n. 93).

625. Also Qadhaq, a region of Jibāl province in west-central Iran. See Yāqūt, *op. cit.*, IV, 498. Arabic forms of *Mihragān *Kōdak, lit. "smaller Mihragān."

626. Reading *al-bariyyah;* al-Ṭabarī has here *al-barriyah* "the wasteland."

627. Referring to surface canals and underground water channels (*qanāt*).

628. *Fī* here should probably be *min.*

driven back to the land of the Turks. Meanwhile, the waters sank into the earth, the fruit-bearing trees were barren, and the people remained in the greatest affliction because of his tyranny, until Zaw b. Ṭahmāsb appeared. The name Zaw(w) can also be pronounced other ways: some saying Zāb b. Ṭahmāsfān, one saying Zāgh, and another saying Rāsab b. Ṭahmāsb (Ṭahmāsp) b. Kānjū b. Zāb b. Arfas b. Harāsf b. Wīdanj b. Aranj b. Būdhajawasb (Nawadjawsh) b. Maysū b. Nawdhar (Nōdar) b. Manūshihr.[629] Zaw's mother was Mādūl[630] bt. Wāman b. Wādharjā b. Qawad (Kawād) b. Salm b. Afrīdhūn. [530]

It is said that during his reign, Manūshihr became angry at Ṭahmāsb, because of a crime he had committed while stationed on the Turks' borders to fight against Frāsiyāb. Manūshihr wanted to kill him, but the mighty men of his kingdom spoke to him about forgiving Ṭahmāsb. Manūshihr's justice, according to what has been mentioned, consisted of treating equally the noble and the humble, the near and the distant, in punishment when one of his subjects merited that for a crime he committed. But he refused to grant them what they requested and said to them, "This is, in religion, a weakness. [But since] you refuse to do what I want (i.e., execute him), [Ṭahmāsb] will never inhabit or stay in any part of my domain." So

629. The genealogical information given here by al-Ṭabarī may be compared with that from the *Bundahishn* (Anklesaria, *op. cit.*, 296–97, chap. 35.26, where some of the names are in Avestan letters; the manuscripts differ in some details):

Bundahishn	al-Ṭabarī
Manuščihr	Manūshihr
Nōdar	Nawdhar
Mašvāk	Maysū
Nōδaēā/Nōiṯ.agā	Būdhajawasb (Nawadjawsh)
Raγ	Aranj
Vaētaṇg	Wīdang
Hwāsp	Harāsf
Araβš	Arfas
Barzišt	Zāb
Kanak	Kānju
Tahmāsp	Ṭahmāsb +
Uzaw	Zaw (Zāb)

630. Māderek bt. Wāman. See Justi, *op. cit.*, 183, s.v. "Madērek," and 347, s.v. "Wāman (b. Wādherjā)." Mādūl, called Māderek in *Mujmal*, 28, is not mentioned by name in the *Bundahishn*, where she is merely referred to as "the daughter of Wāmūn/Nāmūn the sorcerer, "but Wādharjā may be identical with Middle Persian Nōδargā/Vaδargā (in Avestan letters; Anklesaria, *op. cit.*, 298–99, chap. 35.37, 41), a descendant of Manuščihr.

[531] he banished him from his kingdom, and Ṭahmāsb went to the land of the Turks, arriving at the region belonging to Wāman. He beguiled Wāman's daughter, who was imprisoned in a castle because the astrologers had mentioned to Wāman, her father, that she would bear a son who would kill him. He brought her out of the castle in which she was inprisoned, after she had become pregnant with Zaw by him. Then Manūshihr permitted Ṭahmāsb's return to Khunārath, the Persian kingdom, after he had completed the term of his punishment. He brought along Mādūl, the daughter of Wāman, the two of them having used deception to effect her escape from the castle, traveling from the land of the Turks to the Persian kingdom. She bore him Zaw after he returned to the land of Īrankard.[631]

Then, according to what has been mentioned, Zaw killed his grandfather Wāman in one of his raids against the Turks. He also expelled Frāsiyāb from the Persian kingdom until he drove him back to the Turks after wars and battles between them. The conquest of the Persians by Frāsiyāb in Babylon lasted twelve years, from the time Manūshihr died, until Zaw b. Ṭahmāsb drove him out and expelled him to Turkistan. It has been said that Zaw's expulsion of Frāsiyāb from what he controlled of the Persian kingdom took place on the day of Ābān in the month of Ābānmāh.[632] The Persians adopted this day as a holiday because Frāsiyāb's evil and oppression were removed from them. They made it the third of their holidays, after Nawrūz and al-Mihrjān.[633] Zaw was praised for his rule and behaved well toward his subjects. He commanded the restoration of what
[532] Frāsiyāb had spoiled in Khunārath and Babylon and the rebuilding of the fortresses of that land that had been destroyed. He also cleaned out the streams and conduits that had been filled with earth and whose water had been made to disappear, and he dug out the watercourses that had been stopped up, so that he restored all, according to what has been mentioned, to the best possible condition. He remitted the land tax from the people for seven years, dispensing with

631. Īranshahr, according to al-Ṭabarī, I, 531 n. *d*. Yāqūt, *op. cit.*, I, 417, quotes Abū al-Rayḥān al-Khwārazmī (al-Bīrūnī), who says that Īranshahr includes Iraq, Fārs, Jibāl, and Khurāsān.

632. Abān is the tenth day of any month. Abānmāh is the eighth month of the Iranian calendar.

633. Nawrūz (Nawrōz) is the spring festival at the equinox; Mihrjān (Mihragān) is the autumn festival.

it. During his reign, Persia prospered, the waters increased, and the people's livelihoods were abundant. He dug out a canal in al-Sawād[634] and named it al-Zāb,[635] and gave orders to have a city built on its shores; this is the place [now] called "al-Madīna al-ʿAtīqa."[636] He surrounded it with a province called "al-Zawābī,"[637] which he divided into three districts: one of them, the district of the Upper Zāb; one, the district of the Middle Zāb; and the third, the district of the Lower Zāb. He ordered the seeds of mountain aromatic plants[638] as well as tree roots to be carried there and had sown and planted respectively those that are sown and those that are planted.

He was the first for whom were invented all kinds of cooked food, and who gave orders about them, and all varieties of edibles. He gave his troops horses and riding animals that had been plundered and chased to him from the Turks and others. On the day he became king and the crown was placed on his head, he said: "We are progressing in restoring what the deluder Frāsiyāb had destroyed."

He had [acting] as his vizier over the kingdom Karshāsb b. Athraṭ
(Thrit) b. Sahm (Sām)[639] b. Narīmān b. Ṭūrak b. Shayrāsb b. Arwa- [533]
shāsb (Aurušaspa) b. Ṭūj[640] b. Afrīdhūn the king, but one of the Per-

634. Generally synonymous with the alluvial plain of Iraq.

635. This indicates that we are dealing with the Zābī canals and not the Zāb rivers. See n. 637, below.

636. A part of al-Madāʾin, namely Ctesiphon on the east side of the river. See *EI*², s.v. "al-Madāʾin."

637. A district south of al-Madāʾin, named for the Zābī canals rather than the two Zāb or Zābī rivers of northern Iraq. See Rowson, *op. cit.*, 155 n. 565.

638. *Al-rayāḥīn.*

639. Karshāsb, also Persian Garshāsb, Middle Persian Karisāsp, Avestan Kərəsāspa, a legendary hero and dragon killer (see Justi, *op. cit.*, 161; Mayrhofer, *op. cit.*, 60 no. 216; *Enc. Ir.*, III/2, s.v. "Aždahā," esp. 196). Athraṭ, Middle Persian Aθrat (in Avestan letters; Anklesaria, *op. cit.*, 296–97, chap. 35.33), Avestan Θrita, was, according to *Yasna* 9.10, the third human to have pressed the Haoma (cf. n. 4, above), for which he received the fortune of fathering two sons, Kərəsāspa and Urvāxšaya (Mayrhofer, *op. cit.*, 82 no. 315). Sahm = Middle Persian Sām (Anklesaria, *op. cit.*, 296–97, chap. 35.33), Avestan Sāma (the name of a family; Mayrhofer, *op. cit.*, 74–75 no. 280).

640. Narīmān, in the Avesta *naire.manah*, "manly minded," an epithet of Kərəsāspa, but interpreted in the later tradition as a name and incorporated in the genealogy (for the confusion in the attribution of Narīmān, see Justi, *op. cit.*, 225); he is not listed in the *Bundahishn*, where Sām is said to be the son of Tūrag. Tūrak, Middle Persian Tūrag, father of Sām, is not mentioned in the Avesta (see Justi, *op. cit.*, 329, s.v. "Tūrak"). Shayrāsb is probably a mistake for *Shaydāsb, from Middle Persian *Šēdāsp "who possesses sorrel horses," and Arwashāsb is possibly from Middle Persian

sian genealogists gave him a different genealogy, saying that he was Karshāsb b. Asās b. Ṭahmūs b. Ashak b. Nars b. Raḥar b. Dursaru b. Manūshihr the king. Some say that Zaw and Karshāsb were partners in rule; but what is generally recognized about the two of them is that kingship belonged to Zaw b. Ṭahmāsb, and Karshāsb was his vizier and aide. Karshāsb held a powerful position among the Persians except that he did not rule. According to what has been said, all of Zaw's reign until he died lasted three years.

Then after Zaw, Kayqubādh (Kay Kawād) ruled. He was Kayqubādh b. Zāgh b. Nūḥiyāh b. Maysū b. Nawdhar b. Manūshihr.[641] He was married to Qartak bt. Tadarsiyā the Turk. Tadarsiyā was one of
[534] the Turkish chiefs and of their powerful men. [Qartak] bore him Kay Afinah (Afibah), Kay Kāus (Kā(w)ūs), Kay Arsh, Kaybah Arsh (Kay Biyarš), Kayfāshīn (Kay Pisina, Pisīn), and Kaybayh.[642] These were the most powerful kings and the fathers of the most powerful kings.

It is said that Kayqubādh, on the day he became king and the crown was placed on his head, said, "We are subduing the Turkish lands and exerting ourselves in improving and taking care of our
[535] land," and that he assigned the river and spring waters for irrigating the lands. He gave names to the lands, determined their boundaries, set up provinces, and clarified the divisions[643] of each province and

---

*Arušāsp, from Avestan *aurušāspa* "who possesses reddish horses," said of Miθra (Bartholomae, *op. cit.*, 191); in the *Bundahishn* these two are called Spaēnyasp, perhaps "who possesses white horses" (see Justi, *op. cit.*, 306–7, s.v. "Spaēnāsp") and Dūrōšāsp (see Justi, *op. cit.*, 87), respectively (Anklesaria, *op. cit.*, 296–97 chap. 35.33).

641. Avestan Kavi Kavāta, Pahlavi Kay Kawād, the first Kayanid king, son of Uzavua, according to older Iranian sources. He, however, married Farhang, not Qartak. See Justi, *op. cit.*, 159, s.v. "Kawāta." See also Christensen, *Les Kayanides*, passim.

642. The Avestan (*Yašts* 13.132, 19.71) and Middle Persian (Anklesaria, *op. cit.*, 296–97, chap. 35.29–30) names of the Kayanids (the order differs in the sources), compared with those given by al-Ṭabarī:

Avesta	Bundahishn	al-Ṭabarī
Kavi Kavāta	Kay Kawād	Kayqubādh
Kavi Aipvaŋhu	Kay Abiweh	Kay Afinah (Afibah)
Kavi Usaδan	Kay Arš	Kay Kāus
Kavi Aršan	Kay Pisinang	Kay Arsh
Kavi Pisina	Kay Byarš	Kaybah Arsh (Kay Biyarsh)
Kavi Byaršan	Kay Kayus	Kay Fāshīn
		Kay Bayh

643. *Ḥayyiz*, but perhaps used verbally *(wa)-ḥayyaza* "(and) divided." See *Glossarium*, CCVIII, s.v. *ḥwz*. Ibrāhīm, *op. cit.*, I, 456, has *ḥyr*, for *ḥayr*(?). See Lane, *op. cit.*, 685, "a garden," or "pasturage."

its territory.[644] He commanded the people to take the land, and collected a tithe from its produce to provision the army. According to what has been mentioned, Kayqubādh was compared to Pharaoh in his promotion of prosperity, his defense of the land from enemies, and his self-aggrandizement.

It is said that the Kayanid kings[645] and their sons were of his stock, and many wars took place between him and the Turks and others. He resided at the border between the Persian kingdom and the Turks, near the river of Balkh,[646] to prevent the Turks from making any incursions to the Persian border. His rule lasted one hundred years, but God knows best.

---

644. *Ḥarīm.* See *Glossarium*, CLXC (*i.e.*, for CLX), s.v. *ḥrm, territorium* = *ḥaram.*

645. Those mentioned above, usually known as the Kayanids. See Christensen, *Les Kayanides.*

646. The river of Balkh is the Jayḥūn, also called Oxus or Amu Darya. See n. 147, above.

The Israelites and the Chiefs Who Were Over Their Affairs after Joshua

Now let us return to mention of the Israelites and the chiefs who were over their affairs after Joshua b. Nun, and the events that occurred during the eras of Zaw and Kayqubādh.

There is no difference of opinion among scholars of the history of past generations and of the affairs of foregone peoples from our community and others that Caleb b. Jephunneh was the one in charge of the affairs of the Israelites after Joshua b. Nun, then Ezekiel b. Buzi after him;[647] he is the one who is called "Ibn al-ʿAjūz" (the son of the old woman).

Ibn Ḥumayd related to us—Salamah—Ibn Isḥāq: Ezekiel b. Buzi was named Ibn al-ʿAjūz because his mother asked God for a son even though she had grown old and barren. Then God gave him to her. For that reason he was called "son of the old woman." It was he who prayed for the people, whom God mentioned in the Book to
[536] Muḥammad, as it has reached us: *"Consider those who left their houses in their thousands, fearing death."*[648]

---

647. Ḥizqīl b. Būdhī (b. Būrī in Thaʿlabī, *op. cit.*, 221). There is no biblical source for this statement. Ezekiel was a prophet of the exilic period (sixth century B.C.E.) and lived in Babylonia. The basis for the mention of Caleb is Judges 1:12, but his younger brother Othniel seems to have been the first real leader. Compare the story here with the version of the valley of the dry bones in Ezekiel 37:1–14.

648. Qurʾān 2:243.

Muḥammad b. Sahl b. ʿAskar[649] related to me—Ismāʿīl b. ʿAbd al-Karīm[650]—ʿAbd al-Ṣamad b. Maʿqil,[651] who heard Wahb b. Munabbih say: Misfortune afflicted some of the Israelites, as did a calamity of the time. They complained of what had afflicted them saying, "Would that we had died! We would have rest from what we are now experiencing." God inspired Ezekiel: "Your people cried out from misfortune, claiming that they would have liked to die and have rest. But what rest is there for them in death? Do they think that I cannot raise them up after death? So set out for such and such a great plain, for there are four thousand there."

Wahb said: Those are the ones about whom God said: "*Consider those who left their houses in their thousands, fearing death.*[652] Arise and proclaim to them!" Now their bones were already scattered, the birds and beasts of prey having scattered them. But Ezekiel called to them, saying: "O you crumbling bones! God commands you to join together!" And the bones of each person joined together. Then Ezekiel called out a second time, saying "O you bones! God commands you to be covered with flesh!" They were then covered with flesh and, after the flesh, with skin, and became bodies. Then Ezekiel called a third time, saying: "O you souls! God commands you to return to your bodies!" Their souls arose with God's consent, and they magnified Him in unison.

Mūsā b. Hārūn related to me—ʿAmr b. Ḥammād—Asbāṭ—al-Suddī in a report he cited—Abū Mālik and Abū Ṣāliḥ—Ibn ʿAbbās; and Murrah al-Hamdānī—Ibn Masʿūd; and—people among the [537]
companions of the Prophet: "*Consider those who left their houses in their thousands fearing death. And God said to them: Die! and then He brought them back to life.*"[653] In a city called Dāwardān,[654] before Wāsiṭ, a plague occurred. Its common people fled and settled in one region; most of those who remained in the city perished, while the others escaped and not many of them died. When the

649. Muḥammad b. Sahl b. ʿAskar al-Bukhārī. *Index*, 515. Not further identified.

650. Ismāʿīl b. ʿAbd al-Karīm b. Maʿqil b. Munabbih, d. 210/825, a Yemenite scholar. Ibn Saʿd, *op. cit.*, V, 399.

651. ʿAbd al-Ṣamad b. Maʿqil b. Munabbih. He related traditions from Wahb b. Munabbih. Ibn Saʿd, *op. cit.*, V, 398.

652. Qurʾān 2:243.

653. Qurʾān 2:243.

654. A town one parasang east of al-Wāsiṭ, site of a monastery named for Ezekiel, in central Iraq. See Yāqūt, *op. cit.*, II, 541–42.

plague was lifted, they returned to the city in safety. Those who had remained said: "These friends of ours were more resolute than we. If we had done what they did, we would have remained alive. Verily, if the plague occurs a second time, we will go out with them." A plague recurred the next year, and they fled, being thirty thousand odd, settling in that place that was an extensive valley. In the valley, one angel called to them from the bottom and another from the top: "Die!" And they died, so that all of them perished and their bodies decayed.

A prophet named Ezekiel[655] passed by them. When he saw them, he stopped and began to think about them. He twisted his mouth and fingers, and God inspired him: "O Ezekiel! Do you want Me to show you how I shall revive them?" Ezekiel replied, "Yes," his only thought being that he would be astonished at God's power over them, so he said "Yes." He was told, "Call out!" So he called out: "O you bones! Verily God commands you to join together!" The bones began to fly one to another until they were bodies of bones. Then God inspired him: "Call out 'O you bones! Verily God commands you to be covered with flesh!'" And they became covered with flesh and blood, and the clothes in which they died covered their bodies again. Then it was said to him "Call out!" and he called out: "O you bodies! Verily God commands you to arise!" So they arose.

Mūsā related to me—ʿAmr—Asbāṭ, who said that Manṣūr b. al-
[538] Muʿtamir claimed—Mujāhid that these people said, after being revived: "Glory be to You, our Lord! We praise You! There is no god but You." Then they returned to their people alive, knowing that they had been dead, with the color of death on their faces. They wore not a garment that did not become dirty like a shroud. Then they died at their appointed times that had been decreed for them.

Ibn Ḥumayd related to us — Ḥakkām[656] — ʿAnbasah[657] — Ashʿath[658]—Sālim al-Naṣrī:[659] Once while ʿUmar b. al-Khaṭṭāb was praying, there were two Jews behind him. When ʿUmar wanted to

---

655. Text has Hizqīl, a variant of the usual Ḥizqīl.

656. Ḥakkām b. Salm. See n. 224, above.

657. ʿAnbasah b. Saʿīd. See n. 225, above.

658. Ashʿath b. Sawwār al-Thaqafī, d. ca. 137/754, considered weak in transmission of tradition. Ibn Saʿd, *op. cit.*, VI, 249.

659. Sālim Sabalān, *mawlā* of the Banū Naṣr, hence al-Naṣrī. He related traditions from Āʿishah, the wife of the Prophet. Ibn Saʿd, *op. cit.*, V, 222.

prostrate himself, he left a space,[660] whereupon one of the Jews said to his companion: "Is it he?" He continued: When ʿUmar turned away from his prayer, he said, "Tell me about what one of you said to his companion 'Is it he?'" They said, "We find mentioned in our book a horn of iron[661] that gives what was given to Ezekiel, who revived the dead with God's permission." ʿUmar said, "We do not find Ezekiel in our Book, and no one revived the dead by God's permission except Jesus b. Mary." The two of them said, "Do you not find in the Book of God '*and messengers We have not mentioned to you*'?"[662] ʿUmar said, "Of course." They said, "As for the revival of the dead, we will relate to you that a plague afflicted the Israelites. A group left and, when they were at the beginning of a mile, God killed them, and the people built a wall over them. When their bones had decayed, God sent Ezekiel, and he stood over them. He said whatever God desired, and God revived them for him. God revealed regarding that (event): '*Consider those who fled from their homes in their thousands, fearing death,*'" etc.[663]

Ibn Ḥumayd related to us — Salamah — Muḥammad b. Isḥāq — [539]
Wahb b. Munabbih, that, when God took Caleb b. Jephunneh, after Joshua's death, He appointed as a successor among the Israelites Ezekiel b. Buzi, who was the son of the old woman. It was he, we have been informed, who prayed for the people whom God mentioned in the Book to Muḥammad as: "*Consider those who went forth from their houses,*" etc.[664]

Ibn Ḥumayd — Salamah — Ibn Isḥāq: One of their accounts reached me according to which they fled a plague or epidemic or disease, which afflicted the people, fearful of death. They were thousands of people, and when they settled in an elevated part of the land God said to them, "Die!" and all of them died. The people of that land resolved to build an enclosure around them to protect them against wild animals. Then they left them there, because they were

660. *Khawwa,* the meaning of which is unclear here.

661. *Qarnan min ḥadīd,* possibly a reference to Micah 4:13: "I will make thy horn iron"; 1 Kings 22:11 and 2 Chronicles 18:10: "And Zedekiah ... made him horns of iron." It is not connected there with the story of Ezekiel, however.

662. Qurʾān 4:164.

663. Qurʾān 2:243. The verse continues: *[And God said to them: Die! And then He brought them back to life. Lo, God is a Lord of kindness to mankind, but most of mankind do not give thanks].*

664. Qurʾān 2:243.

too many to be covered up. Periods and ages passed over them until they had become decayed bones, when Ezekiel b. Buzi passed by them. He stopped where they were and wondered at them. He was filled with pity for them, and it was said to him: "Would you like God to revive them?" He said, "Yes." And it was said to him, "Call out to them and say, 'O you decayed bones that have rotted and decayed, let each bone return to its companion.'" And he called this out to them, and he looked at the bones rushing to each other, seizing each other. Then it was said to him, "Say: 'O you flesh and sinews and skin, cover the bones, with your Lord's permission.'" The narrator said: He looked at them, and the sinews took the bones, then
[540] the flesh, the skin, and the hair, until creatures were completed, who had no souls in them. Then he prayed for life for them, and something from heaven covered him, distressing him until he fainted from it. He then recovered, and the people were sitting, saying, "Glory be to God" for God had revived them.

The length of Ezekiel's sojourn among the Israelites has not been mentioned to us.

When God took Ezekiel, it is reported, misdeeds multiplied among the Children of Israel. They abandoned the covenant with God that had been made with them in the Torah and worshiped idols. Then God sent to them, as it is told, Elijah.

Elijah[665] *b. Yāsīn b. Phineas b. Eleazar b. Aaron b. Amram*

Ibn Ḥumayd related to us—Salamah—Muḥammad b. Isḥāq: When God took Ezekiel, misdeeds became great among the Israelites. They forgot what had been God's covenant with them, to the extent that they erected idols and worshiped them instead of God. Then God sent to them Elijah b. Yāsīn b. Phineas b. Eleazar b. Aaron b. Amram as a prophet. After Moses, the prophets of the Israelites were sent to them only with a renewal of what they had forgotten of the

665. Arabic: Ilyās, based on Greek Elias, for Hebrew Eliyahu, Eliah, obviously treated by al-Ṭabarī as a figure distinct from al-Khiḍr; see the discussion of this question in n. 1, above. The Bible gives no genealogical information; he is called simply Elijah the Tishbite. His story is found in 1 Kings 17–22 and 2 Kings 1–2. The Jewish legendary material is in Ginzberg, *op. cit.*, IV, 195–235. See also al-Thaʿlabī, *op. cit.*, 223–29.

Torah. Elijah was with one of the kings of the Israelites named Ahab, whose wife's name was Jezebel. He would listen to [Elijah] and believe him, and Elijah would keep his affairs in order, while the remainder of the Israelites had adopted an idol that they worshiped in- [541]
stead of God, called "Baal."

Ibn Isḥāq said: I have heard some sages say that Baal was only a woman whom they worshiped instead of God. God says to Muḥammad: *"And lo! Elijah was one of those sent, when he said to his people: 'Will you not ward off [evil] [will you cry to Baal and forsake the best of Creators?] God, your Lord, and the Lord of your forefathers?'"*[666] Elijah began to call them to God, but they would not listen to anything from him, only what came from the king. Now kings were scattered throughout Syria, each one exploiting one of its regions. One day, the king with whom Elijah was, keeping his affairs in order and considering him [alone] among his fellow [rulers] to be rightly guided, said: "O Elijah! By God I consider what you are urging as nothing but delusion. By God! I do not believe that so-and-so and so-and-so (enumerating some of the kings of the Israelites) who worshiped the idols instead of God, are faring any differently than we do, eating, drinking, enjoying life, given rule, not losing any of their temporal possessions, because of their stance, which you claim is delusion, while we do not see that we have any advantage or superiority over them."

They claim—but God knows best—that Elijah was taken aback and his hair and skin stood up. Then he abandoned Ahab and left. The king then performed the deeds of his peers, worshiping idols and doing what they did. Elijah said: "O my God! Verily the Israelites accept only disbelief in You and worship of another, so change Your favor toward them" or whatever he said.

Ibn Ḥumayd—Salamah—Muḥammad b. Isḥāq: It was mentioned to me that [Elijah] was inspired: "We have placed the matter of the sources of their sustenance in your hands, so that it will be you who will give orders regarding their lives."

So Elijah said: "My God! Hold back rain from them!" And it was [542]
withheld for three years, until the beasts of burden, cattle, insects, and trees were destroyed and people led miserable lives. According to what is said, after Elijah called down this order upon the Israel-

666. Qur'ān 37:123–26. Words in brackets are omitted in the text.

ites, he went into hiding, fearing for his life. Wherever he was, sustenance was sent down to him. Whenever people detected the smell of bread in a house, they would say: "Elijah must have entered that place!" They would search for him, and the people of that dwelling would suffer at their hands. One night, he sought shelter with an Israelite woman who had a son named Elisha b. Akhṭūb,[667] who suffered some injury. She gave Elijah shelter and hid him. So Elijah prayed for her son, and he was cured of his injury. Then Elisha followed Elijah, believing in him and holding him to be truthful. He clung to him and went with him wherever he went. Elijah had become aged and grown old, while Elisha was still a young lad.

They claim—but God knows best—that God inspired Elijah that: "You have destroyed many creatures, beside the Israelites, who did not rebel. Their destruction I would not have desired for the sins of the Israelites, among the beasts, cattle, birds, insects, and trees, by withholding rain from the Israelites." And they claim—but God knows best—that Elijah replied: "O Lord! Let me be the one who prays for them and brings them relief from the distress they are suffering. Perhaps they will return and abandon their present worship of other than You." He was told "So be it."

Then Elijah went to the Israelites and said: "Verily you have been
[543] destroyed by misfortune, and the beasts, cattle, birds, insects, and trees have been destroyed because of your sins. Verily you are following delusion and falsehood"—or whatever he said—"and if you would like to know this and to know that God is angry at what you are doing and to know that what I have been urging upon you is the truth, then bring out these idols that you worship, which you claim are better than what I urge upon you. If they respond to you, then it is as you say. But, if they do not act, then you will know that you are deluded and should abandon [them]. Then I will pray to God, and He will relieve you of the distress you are suffering." They said, "You are acting justly." So they brought out their idols and abominations with which they sought God's favor and which He did not accept. They prayed to them, but they were not answered, nor were they re-

---

667. There is no figure by this name in the Bible. The biblical story of the widow and her unnamed son, whom Elijiah restores to life (1 Kings 17:10–24), seems to be confused with the story of Elisha b. Shaphat, who followed Elijah (1 Kings 19:19–20) and who later helped the woman of Shunem bear a son and then restored him to life (2 Kings 4:8–37).

lieved of the distress in which they were, so they realized the extent of their error and falsehood.

Then they said to Elijah, "O Elijah! We are perishing. Pray to God for us." So Elijah prayed for their relief, that they be given rain. A cloud, like a shield, came forth over the surface of the sea, with God's permission, while they were watching. Then the clouds rushed toward him, and it became overcast, whereupon God sent the rain and watered them. Their land was revived, and He relieved them of the distress they were in. But they did not abandon [their idols] or repent, but continued in the worst of their deeds.

When Elijah saw this ingratitude of theirs, he prayed to his Lord to take him to Himself and to give him rest from them. It is claimed that he was told: "Await such-and-such a day. Then go to such-and-such a village. Whatever comes to you, mount it, and do not fear it." So Elijah went out, with Elisha b. Akhṭūb, until when Elijah was in the village that was mentioned to him at the place he was com- [544]
manded, a steed of fire approached, until it stopped in front of him. He jumped on it, and it took off with him, while Elisha was calling out, "O Elijah! O Elijah! What commands do you have for me?" That was the last they saw of him. God covered him with feathers, clothed him in fire, and stopped for him the pleasure of food and drink. He flew with the angels, becoming human-angelic, earthly-heavenly.

After Elijah, control over the affairs of the Israelites was taken by Elisha, according to what we have been told by Ibn Ḥumayd—Salamah—Ibn Isḥāq, who said: I was told by Wahb b. Munabbih that, after Elijah, Elisha was made a prophet among the Israelites.[668] He remained among them for as long as God wished him to be; then He took him to Himself. People followed each other in succession among them with sins increasing while the Ark was among them. Within it was the Sakīnah[669] and a remainder of what the people of

---

668. Elisha's story in the Bible is found from 1 Kings 19–22 to 2 Kings 13. Jewish legends are in Ginzberg, *op. cit.*, IV, 239–46; and see al-Thaʿlabī, *op. cit.*, 229–31. The chronology is quite confused here, jumping from the time of Joshua (ca. 1150 B.C.E.) to Elijah and Elisha (865–30 B.C.E.) and now back to the period of the Judges who ruled over Israel after the death of Joshua.

669. Hebrew: *shekhinah* "the presence (of God)." In the story of Abraham's building of the Kaʿbah, al-Ṭabarī, I, 274 (trans. Brinner, 69–71), the Sakīnah is pictured as a strong wind with the power of speech. See *Shorter Encyclopaedia of Islam*, 489. See also a different version in n. 708, below. Al-Thaʿlabī, *op. cit.*, 237, gives several different Muslim versions of the meaning of the term.

Moses and Aaron had left. It was handed down as an inheritance from one generation to another. God would rout any enemy who met the Israelites while they were advancing and marching with the Ark. The Sakīnah, according to what Ibn Isḥāq mentioned — Wahb b. Munabbih—some of the Israelites' sages, was the head of a dead cat, and, when it cried out within the Ark with the howling of a cat, the Israelites were assured of victory and conquered.[670]

Then a ruler succeeded among them, called Īlāf.[671] God had blessed them in their mountain from Jerusalem.[672] No enemy could enter the city against them; and with it they needed nothing else. One Israelite, as it is reported, would gather dust on a stone, then
[545] throw grain on it; and God would bring forth for him and his family [enough grain] that he could eat for a year. He might have an olive and from it he would press enough for him and his family to eat for a year. But when their misdeeds became great and they abandoned their covenant with God, an enemy came down upon them, and they went out against him, taking along the Ark, as usual. They marched out with it and were fought against until it was torn from their hands.

Their king Īlāf came [to them] and was informed that the Ark had been taken forcibly. When he heard the news, he bowed down his neck and died of grief. Their affairs became disordered and changed,[673] and their enemy plundered them and trod upon them, until their children and women were stricken. They remained in turmoil about their affairs and in disagreement about their situation. At times they persevered in their trespass and error, whereupon God would give power over them to one by means of whom He took vengeance on them. Then, at times, they would resort to repentance, and God would protect them against the evil of whoever desired evil for them. This took place until God sent Saul[674] as king and returned

670. MS C inserts here "Mention of those kings who ruled the Israelites after that."

671. Īlāf or Aylāf. Not identifiable with any biblical figure except perhaps Eli the priest, who judged Israel just before Samuel. He, however, is mentioned by name later. The story of the death of Īlāf/Aylāf is similar to that of Eli. See p. 134, below. For the Jewish legends about the judges, see Ginzberg, *op. cit.*, IV, 21–54.

672. *Fī jabalihim min iliyā*. Iliyā is Arabic Aelia, the Latin name given to Jerusalem by Hadrian.

673. Text has *wa-ikhtalafa*, but al-Thaʿlabī, *op. cit.*, 234, has *wa-ikhtalla* "became entangled, disordered." See al-Ṭabarī, I, 545 n. *d*.

674. Arabic: *Ṭālūt*. See *Shorter Encyclopaedia of Islam*, 571–72, for an explanation of the deviation of the name from the Hebrew Shaʾūl.

the Ark of the Covenant to them. A period of four hundred and sixty years passed, from the death of Joshua b. Nun, during which time command of the Israelites belonged in part to the judges and leaders among them, and in part to others who overcame them so that they were ruled over by others, until rule was established among them and prophecy returned to them through Samuel b. Bālī.[675]

According to what is said, the first to be given power over the Israelites was a man descended from Lot named Cushan.[676] He oppressed and humbled them for eight years. Then a younger brother of [546]
Caleb, named Othniel b. Kenaz,[677] delivered them from Cushan's hand and held power among them, it is said, for forty years. Then power over them was given to a king named Eglon,[678] who ruled for eighteen years, and from whom, it is said, a man of the tribe of Benjamin named Ehud b. Gera, with a withered right hand,[679] delivered them. Ehud held sway over them for eighty years. Then a king from the Canaanites named Jabin[680] held power over them and ruled for twenty years.

It is said that then a woman prophet named Deborah delivered them, and also that a man named Barak ruled their affairs on her behalf for forty years.[681] Power over them was then given to a group of Lot's descendants whose dwellings were on the borders of the Ḥijāz; they ruled for seven years.[682] Then a man of the children of Naphtali b. Jacob delivered them from Lot's descendants. His name was Gideon b. Joash,[683] and he ruled their affairs for forty years. After Gideon, his son Abimelech b. Gideon[684] managed their affairs for three years. After Abimelech, Tola b. Puah,[685] a son of Abimelech's maternal un-

675. See al-Ṭabarī, I, 545 n. *i*, for variants of his name. In the Bible his father is named Elkanah. See p. 129, where he is b. Bālī b. Alqamah.

676. Cushan-rishathaim, king of Aram-naharaim (Mesopotamia). Judges 3:8.

677. See Judges 3:8.

678. ʿAjlūn, king of Moab. See Judges 3:12–25.

679. Ahūd. The English Bible simply says that he was left-handed. The Hebrew is *asher iṭṭer yad yemino* "who bound up his left hand"; *iṭṭer*, in later Hebrew, means "withered." See Judges 3:15–30.

680. Text: Yāfīn, biblical Jabin, king of Canaan, the captain of whose army was Sisera. Judges 4:2.

681. Text: Dabūrā. Deborah was a prophet and called Barak (Baraq) to lead the Israelites in battle against Sisera's army. Judges 4:4–24.

682. The Bible speaks of them as Midianites. See Judges 6:1ff.

683. Jadʿūn b. Yuwāsh. See Judges 6:11–8:35.

684. Abīmalik. See Judges 9:1–57.

685. Tūlagh b. Fuwā. See Judges 10:1–2.

cle—some say his paternal uncle—managed them for twenty-three years. Then after Tola an Israelite named Jair[686] managed their affairs for twenty-two years. Then the Ammonites,[687] a tribe among the Palestinian people, ruled over them for the next eighteen years.

[547] Then a man among them named Jephthah[688] held control over them for six years. After him, Ibzan,[689] an Israelite, ruled them for seven years. Next, Elon[690] ruled them for ten years; and then Kayrūn—whom some call "ʿAkrūn" [Ekron?][691]—for eight years. Then the people of Palestine and their kings oppressed them for forty years.[692] Samson, an Israelite, governed them for the next twenty years.[693] After Samson, the Israelites remained without a king or [other] leader of their affairs, it is said, for ten years.[694] Eli[695] the priest ruled their affairs following this period, and in his days the people of Gaza and Ascalon took the Ark of the Covenant by force. When he had managed their affairs for forty years, Samuel was sent as a prophet. He had ruled, it is recounted, for ten years when the Israelites asked him—when their enemies humiliated and shamed them for their rebellion against their Lord—to send them a king with whom they might strive together on behalf of God. Samuel said to them what God has related in His glorious Book.[696]

---

686. Yāʾir. See Judges 10:3–5.

687. Banū ʿAmūn. See Judges 10:7–18.

688. Yaftaḥ. See Judges 11:1–12:7.

689. Text has Bajshūn/Bajsūn. Ibrāhīm, *op. cit.*, I, 466 has Yajshūn. See Judges 12:8–10.

690. Alūn. See Judges 12:11–12.

691. Judges 12:13–15. Bible has Abdon.

692. *I.e.*, the Philistines. Judges 13:1.

693. Shamsūn. Judges 13:2–16:31.

694. "In those days there was no king in Israel." Judges 18:1, 21:25.

695. Here ʿAlī, but later ʿAylī/ʿAylā. See n. 722, below. Al-Thaʿlabī has ʿAylī throughout.

696. A reference to Qurʾān 2:246–47, where the prophet is not named but is clearly Samuel.

The History of Samuel b. Bālī b. Elkanah b. Jeroham b. Elihu b. Tohu b. Zuph[697] and of Saul and Goliath

In the account of Samuel b. Bālī, we find that after the Israelites suffered prolonged distress and after foreign kings humiliated them, op- [548]
pressed their land, killed their men, took their women and children captive, and seized by force the Ark in which were the Sakīnah and the rest of what the family of Moses and Aaron had left behind, and by which they were helped to victory when they confronted the enemy, they prayed humbly to God to send them a prophet who would put their affairs in order.

Mūsā b. Hārūn al-Hamdānī related to me—ʿAmr b. Ḥammād—Asbāṭ—al-Suddī in an account he reported—Abū Mālik and Abū Ṣāliḥ—Ibn ʿAbbās; and—Murrah—Ibn Masʿūd; and—men among the companions of the Prophet: The Israelites battled the Amalekites, whose king was Goliath.[698] The [Amalekites] gained control over the Israelites, imposing a head tax[699] upon them and taking

---

697. Text has Shamwīl b. Bālī b. ʿAlqamah b. Yarūkham b. Alīhū b. Tāhu b. Ṣūf. See n. 674, above. For the biblical story of Samuel, see 1 Samuel 1–28. For the Jewish legends, see Ginzberg, *op. cit.*, IV, 57–70. See also al-Thaʿlabī, *op. cit.*, 232–40, who explains the name Shamwīl as the Hebrew equivalent of Ismāʿīl (232).

698. Goliath in the Bible is the hero of the Philistines, not the Amalekites.

699. *Jizya*, in traditional Islamic law, is the poll tax collected from non-Muslims in Muslim states; hence the term is used anomalously here. See *EI*², s.v. "djizya."

their Torah. The Israelites asked God to send them a prophet with whom they could fight. The tribe of the prophets had perished, and only one pregnant woman of them remained. The [Israelites] confined her to a house, fearing that she would bear a girl, then substitute for her a boy, seeing the Israelites' desire for her child. The woman prayed earnestly to God to grant her a son, and she gave birth to a boy whom she named Shamʿūn,[700] saying: "God heard my prayers."

When the boy grew older, his mother handed him over to learn the Torah in the Temple. An elder sage assumed responsibility for him and adopted him. When the boy matured so that God could send him as a prophet, Gabriel came to him while the boy was sleeping
[549] near the old man, who would entrust him to no one else, and Gabriel called out, in the old man's tone of voice: "O Samuel!"[701] and the boy got up, frightened, and said to the old man: "O my father! Did you call me?" The old man did not want to say "No" and alarm the boy, so he said, "O my son! Go back to sleep." The boy returned and fell asleep; then [Gabriel] called him a second time. The boy returned again saying, "Did you call me?" He replied, "Go back to sleep. If I call you a third time, do not answer me." On the third time, Gabriel appeared to him and said, "Go to your people and bring them your Lord's message. For God has sent you among them as a prophet."

But, when [Samuel] presented himself to [the Israelites], they considered him a liar, saying, "You have been hasty regarding prophecy. We will pay no attention to you." They said, "If you are a speaker of truth, then *send us a king to fight for the sake of God,*[702] as a sign of your prophecy." Samuel[703] said, *"Would you then refrain from fighting, if fighting were prescribed for you?" They said, "Why should we not fight for God's sake when we have been driven from our*

---

700. Shamʿūn (Ibrāhīm, *op. cit.*, I, 467, has Samʿūn) is from the Hebrew root *sh-m-ʿ* (cognate to Arabic *s-m-ʿ*), meaning "to hear," but is not connected with Samuel's name in Hebrew—it is equivalent to the Hebrew for Simeon (Shimʿon). MSS BM and C have here Samʿūn, probably to fit the etymological connection with "Allāhu *samiʿa* duʿāʾī"—"God has heard my prayer." In the section that follows, it alternates with two other forms of Samuel's name, Shamwīl and Ashamwīl.

701. Shamwīl is a closer equivalent to Hebrew Shᵉmuʾel for Samuel. In the Bible, 1 Samuel 1:20, the name is given a very weak etymology: *ki me-YHWH sheʾiltiw* "for *I have asked him* from YHWH." Al-Thaʿlabī, *op. cit.*, has Shamwīl throughout.

702. Qurʾān 2:246.

703. Here Shamʿūn.

dwellings with our children[704]—by tax payment?" So he prayed to God and was given a staff, the size of which was the height of the man who would be sent as the king. Samuel said: "Your companion's height should reach that of this staff." They measured themselves by it, but they did not match it. Saul was a water carrier, carrying water on a donkey of his; his donkey went astray, so he went out on the road to search for it. When they saw [Saul], they called him over and measured him with [the staff], and he matched it. *Their prophet said to them: "Lo! God has raised up Saul to be a king for you."*[705] But the people said: "You have never been more untruthful than you are now. We belong to the tribe of kingship. He is not from that tribe, and *'he has not been given wealth enough'*[706] that we should follow him." The prophet said: *"Lo! God has chosen him above you, and has increased him abundantly in wisdom and stature."*[707] They said, "If you are truthful, bring us a sign that this [550]
man is a king." He said: *"Lo! The token of his kingship is that the Ark, in which there is the Sakīnah, and a remnant of that which the family of Moses and the family of Aaron left behind, will come to you from your Lord."*[708] ... The Sakīnah is a basin of gold in which the hearts of the prophets are washed. God gave it to Moses, and he placed the tablets in it.[709] The tablets, according to what we have been told, were of pearls, sapphire, and chrysolite. As for the "remnant," it is the staff of Moses and fragments of the [broken] tablets. The Ark, and all that was in it, came to be in the house of Saul. The Israelites believed in the prophecy of Samuel[710] and handed kingship over to Saul.

Al-Qāsim informed us—al-Ḥusayn—Ḥajjāj—Ibn Jurayj—Ibn ʿAbbās: The angels brought the Ark, carrying it between heaven and earth, while the people watched it, until they placed it with Saul.

Yūnus[711] related to me—Ibn Wahb[712]—Ibn Zayd:[713] "The angels

---

704. Qurʾān 2:246 bis.

705. Qurʾān 2:247. For the biblical story of Saul, see 1 Samuel 9–31 and 2 Samuel 1. For the Jewish legends, see Ginzberg, *op. cit.*, IV, 65–91. See also al-Thaʿlabī, *op. cit.*, 235–56, 239–44.

706. Qurʾān 2:247 *bis*.

707. Qurʾān 2:247 *bis*.

708. Qurʾān 2:248.

709. Another interpretation of the concept of Sakīnah. See n. 669, above.

710. Shamʿūn.

711. Yūnus b. ʿAbd al-Aʿlā b. Mūsā b. Maysarah al-Ṣadafī, Abū Mūsā, 170–264/787–877. One of the great legalists of Egypt, he was noted for his traditions. *GAS*, I,

brought the Ark down by day while [the people] watched with their own eyes, until they placed it in their midst." He continued, "They acknowledged it reluctantly, and then they left angry."

The account returns to al-Suddī's: Eighty thousand men went out with Saul. Now Goliath was one of the strongest of men and the most courageous. He went forth ahead of the troops, and his companions would not join him until he himself put to flight whomever he met. When [the Israelites] went forth, Saul said to them: *"Lo! God will test you by a river. Whoever [therefore] drinks of it, he is not of me, and whoever does not taste of it is of me."*[714] This was the river of Palestine.[715] They drank from it out of fear of Goliath; only four thousand of them crossed with Saul, while seventy-six thousand turned back. Those who drank of it became thirsty, while those
[551] who did not drink of it, except in the palms of their hands, had their thirst quenched.

And after he had crossed it, he and those who believed with him, and they saw Goliath, they too turned back—*they said: "We have no power this day against Goliath and his hosts." But those who knew that they would meet their Lord*—those who believed firmly—said: *"How many a little band has overcome a mighty host by God's leave! God is with the steadfast."*[716]

Three thousand six hundred and eighty-odd also turned back, so Saul departed with three hundred and nineteen, the number of the people of Badr.[717]

38; Ibn Ḥajar, *op. cit.*, XI, 440; al-Ziriklī, *op. cit.*, IX, 345.

712. ʿAbdallāh b. Wahb b. Muslim al-Fihrī al-Qurashī al-Miṣrī, Abū Muḥammad, 125–97/743–813. He was a traditionist, Qurʾān commentator, and legalist, who transmitted from Mālik b. Anas. Ibn Saʿd, *op. cit.*, VII/2, 518; *GAS*, I, 466; al-Ziriklī, *op. cit.*, IV, 289.

713. Usāmah b. Zayd b. Aslam al-Laythī, *mawlā* of ʿUmar b. al-Khaṭṭāb, Abū Zayd. He heard traditions from several Companions of the Prophet and died in Medina during the reign of al-Manṣūr, 137–58/754–75. Ibn Saʿd, *op. cit.*, V, 305.

714. Qurʾān 2:249.

715. The river of Palestine is not clear. The remainder of Qurʾān 2:249, not quoted in the text—*[except for him who takes of it in the hollow of his hand. But they drank of it, all except a few of them]*—is identical with Gideon's test of his followers at En-Harod, a spring that gives rise to a stream leading to the Jordan River. See Judges 7:1–7.

716. Qurʾān 2:249 *bis.*

717. "The people of Badr" are the small group of Muslims who defeated the more numerous Meccans at the battle of Badr, in March 2/624. For a full description, see Watt, *Muhammad in Medina,* 10–13.

Al-Muthannā[718] related to me—Isḥāq b. al-Ḥajjāj[719]—Ismāʿīl b. ʿAbd al-Karīm[720]—ʿAbd al-Ṣamad b. Maʿqil,[721] who heard Wahb b. Munabbih say: Eli,[722] who reared Samuel,[723] had two sons, young men, who did something with the sacrifice that was not appropriate.[724] The instrument with which they stirred the sacrifice consisted of two iron prongs, and whatever they took out belonged to the priest who stirred it; but Eli's sons gave it more prongs. Furthermore, whenever women came to pray in the sanctuary,[725] the two would take hold of them.

While Samuel[726] was sleeping in the front of the chamber where Eli slept, he heard a voice say: "Samuel!" and he ran to Eli saying, "Here I am! Why did you call me?" Eli replied, "No, go back to sleep." Then he heard another voice say "Samuel!" and he ran to Eli again saying, "Here I am! Why did you call me?" Eli replied, "I didn't do it. Go back to sleep. If you hear something, say 'Here I am' in your place. 'Command me and I shall do it!'" He returned and fell asleep. He heard a voice again say "Samuel!" and he replied, "Here I [552] am! It is I, so command me, I shall do it." The voice said, "Go to Eli and say to him that his paternal love has prevented him from scolding his two sons for having defiled My temple and My sacrifice and having rebelled against Me. Therefore, I shall strip the priesthood from him and from his sons, and I shall cause him and them to perish." When he arose in the morning, Eli asked Samuel [about the night], and Samuel told him; and he was very afraid because of that.

One of their enemies who surrounded them marched against them, and Eli ordered his two sons to lead the people out to fight this enemy. They went out, taking the Ark, in which were the tablets and the staff of Moses, in order to overcome the enemy by means of [the Ark].

---

718. Al-Muthannā b. Ibrāhīm. See n. 510, above.

719. Isḥāq b. al-Ḥajjāj. *Index*, 29. Not further identified.

720. Ismāʿīl b. ʿAbd al-Karīm. See n. 650, above.

721. ʿAbd al-Ṣamad b. Maʿqil. See n. 651, above.

722. Here, and hereafter, ʿAylī. See n. 695, above.

723. Shamwīl.

724. In the Bible the two sons of Eli were Hophni and Phineas. For their story, see 1 Samuel 2:12–36, 4:1–11.

725. Here *al-quds*, the usual Arabic name for Jerusalem, lit. the "holy place." Jerusalem was not yet in the hands of the Israelites at the time of Eli, but it may be meant here.

726. *Ashamwīl* or *ashmawīl*. See also nn. 727 and 728, below.

While they and their enemy lined up for battle, Eli awaited reports of what they had done. Then a man came and informed him while he was seated on his chair, "Verily your two sons have been slain, and our troops have been routed." Eli said, "What about the Ark?" The man replied, "The enemy has taken it." Eli gave the death rattle, fell out of his chair on his neck, and died. Those who had captured the Ark placed it in the house of their gods. They had an the idol they worshiped, and they placed the Ark under it, with the idol on top. But on the morning of the next day, the idol was under and the Ark on top. So they took the idol, placed it on top again, and nailed its feet to the Ark. But on the morning of the next day, the hand and two feet of the idol were cut off, and it was cast down under the Ark. They said to one another, "Have you not learned that nothing can withstand the God of the Israelites? So remove the Ark from the house of your gods." They removed the Ark and placed it in an area of their town. The people of that area suffered from pains in their necks, and they said, "What is this?" A maiden among them, one of their Israelite captives, said to them, "You will continue to witness what you
[553] do not like, as long as this Ark is among you, so remove it from your town." They said, "You lie!" She replied, "For a sign of that you should bring two oxen, both of whom have young, and upon whom no yoke has ever been placed. Then put a cart behind them, place the Ark on the cart, and make them journey while you detain their young. They will set out with [the Ark] submissively, until they have left your land and have set foot in the nearest territory of the Israelites. Then they will break their yoke and return to their young."

They did all that [she suggested], and, when the oxen left their land and set foot on the nearest territory of the Israelites, they broke their yoke and returned to their young, after having placed the Ark in a ruined place where there were Israelite reapers. The Israelites hurried toward the Ark and approached it. Yet no sooner would one of them approach it but he would die. Then their prophet Samuel said to them: "Pass in review! Whoever feels the strength in himself, let him draw near it." They passed the men by it in review, but not one was able to draw near it, except for two Israelite men whom he permitted to carry it to the house of their widowed mother. It remained in their mother's house until Saul became king. Thus did the condition of the Israelites improve with Samuel.[727] Then the Israelites said to Samuel,[728] *"Appoint for us a king who will fight for God's cause."*[729] He replied, "God is sufficient to do battle for you." They replied, "But we are afraid of those around us. If we have a king, we will take refuge in him." So God inspired Samuel thus: "Appoint for them Saul as king and anoint him with the holy oil."

Saul's father's donkeys went astray, and he sent Saul and one of his lads to find them. The two lads approached Samuel to ask him about the donkeys, and Samuel said, "God has appointed you as king over [554]
the Israelites." Saul asked, "Me?" Samuel replied, "Yes." Saul said, "Don't you know that my tribe is the lowliest tribe of the Israelites?" He said, "Certainly." Saul said, "And don't you know that my clan is the lowliest clan of my tribe?" He replied, "Certainly." He said, "Don't you know that my family is the lowliest family of my clan?" Samuel replied, "Certainly." Saul continued, "Then by what sign?" Samuel said, "By the sign that, when you return home, your father will have found his donkeys, and when you are in such-and-such a place, inspiration will descend upon you." Then he anointed him with the holy oil and said to the Israelites: *"Lo! God has raised up Saul to be a king for you." They said: "How can he have dominion over us when we are more deserving of it than he is, since he has not been given enough wealth?" He said: "Lo! God has chosen him above you and has increased him abundantly in wisdom and stature."*[730]

The account returns to al-Suddī's: *And when they went into battle against Goliath and his hosts, they said: "Our Lord! Bestow on us endurance."*[731] On that day, David's father, along with thirteen sons of his, was among those who crossed over. Now David was his youngest son. He had come to [his father] one day and said, "O my father! Whatever I throw at with my sling, I knock down." His father said, "Rejoice at that, O my son. God has placed your sustenance in your sling." Then he returned to him another time and said, "O my father! I went among the hills and found a crouching lion. I mounted

727. *Maʿa ashmawīl/ashamwīl.*
728. *Li-ashmawīl/ashamwīl.*
729. Based on Qurʾān 2:246.
730. Qurʾān 2:247.
731. Qurʾān 2:250.

it, taking hold of its two ears, and it did not throw me off." His father replied, "Rejoice at that, O my son! That is a virtue that God grants you." Then he came to him another day and said, "O my father! Verily I was walking in the hills, glorifying [God], and no hill remained that did not glorify with me." So he said, "Rejoice, O my son! That is a virtue that God has given you."

[555] David was a shepherd, and [on this day] his father had left him behind to bring food to him and his brothers. The prophet [Samuel] brought a horn in which there was oil and a breastplate[732] of iron. He sent them to Saul saying, "Verily, your companion who kills Goliath will have this horn placed on his head, and it will boil over until he will be anointed by it. But it will not flow into his face, it will just remain on his head in the shape of a crown. He will also be put in this breastplate and fill it."

Saul called the Israelites and tested them with [the horn], but none fit the description. When they were finished, Saul said to David's father, "Do you have another son who has not presented himself to us?" He replied, "Yes, there remains my son David, who brings us food." When David was returning to [his father], he passed by three stones on the road, and they spoke to him, saying, "Take us, O David, and you will kill Goliath with us!"

He picked them up and placed them in his provision bag. Saul had said: "I will marry my daughter to whoever kills Goliath, and I shall also entrust his seal with my dominion." When David arrived, they placed the horn on his head, and it boiled over until he was anointed by it. He put on the breastplate, and he filled it, even though he was a sickly, pale man. Anyone who put it on shook [loosely] in it, but when David put it on the breastplate was so tight on him that it cracked. Then he went to Goliath. Goliath was one of the stoutest and strongest of men, yet, when he looked at David, fear of him was cast into his heart. So he said to David, "O boy! Go back! I pity you lest I kill you." But David said, "No, on the contrary. I shall kill you." He took out the stones and placed them in the sling. Every time he picked up one of those stones, he gave it a name. He said, "This one is named for my father Abraham, the second for my father Isaac, and the third for my father Israel." Then he whirled the sling, and the stones became one stone. He sent it off, and it struck Goliath be-

---

732. *Tannūr* here is "breastplate," rather than the usual "oven." Cf. *Glossarium*, CLII: *lorica*.

tween the eyes, piercing his head. It killed him and kept on killing every man it struck, piercing right through him until no one remained in front of it. Then the Israelites routed them. [556]

Since David had killed Goliath, Saul returned and betrothed his daughter to David and entrusted his seal with his rule. The people were inclined toward David and loved him. When Saul saw that, he suffered anguish and envied him, desiring to kill him. David became aware that [Saul] wanted to do that, so he wrapped up a wineskin in his bed. Saul entered David's sleeping quarters after David had fled, and struck the skin with a blow that split it open, and the wine flowed. A drop of the wine fell in his mouth, and Saul said: "May God have mercy on David! How much wine he drank!"

David went into Saul's chamber the next year, while he was sleeping, and placed two arrows at his head, and at his feet, and on his right and left side two further pairs. Then he left, and when Saul awoke, he saw the arrows and recognized them. He said, "May God have mercy on David! He is better than I. I had him in my power, and I killed him [as I thought].[733] He had me in his power and refrained." Then he mounted one day, and found David walking in the wilderness, while Saul was on a horse. Saul said, "Today I shall kill David." When David became alarmed, he could not be overtaken. Saul ran at David's heels, but David became alarmed and ran faster. He entered a cave, and God inspired a spider to spin its web over it. When Saul reached the cave, he looked at the spider's web and said, "If he had entered here, he would have torn the spider's web." So he was fooled and left him.

The scholars reproached Saul in the matter of David, but Saul would kill anyone who restrained him from David, and God incited him to kill the scholars.[734] He killed every scholar among the Israelites over whom he had power, until a woman was brought to him [557]

---

733. Ibn al-Athīr, *op. cit.*, I, 221, has *fa-aradtu qatlahu* "I desired killing him"; al-Thaʿlabī, 242, has *fa-qaṣadtu qatlahu* "I intended killing him." See al-Ṭabarī, I, 556 n. *e*.

734. Here begins a version of the biblical story of the "witch" or diviner of Endor. See 1 Samuel 28:5–25. There is no mention of scholars there, but the Hebrew word *yidʿonī*, "diviner (by a familiar spirit)" is mentioned by the woman when she says to Saul (1 Samuel 28:9): "Behold, you know what Saul has done, how he has cut off those that divine by a ghost (*ōvōt*) or a familiar spirit (*yidʿonī*) . . . ." The latter word, from the Hebrew root *ydʿ*, meaning "to know," may have been mistranslated as "one who knows, a scholar." See *al-ʿarūf*, *ʿālim*, as applied to Balʿam, n. 517, above. See also Ginzberg, *op. cit.*, IV, 70–71.

who knew the most powerful name of God. He ordered the giant[735] to kill her, but the giant had pity on her, saying: "Perhaps we will need a scholar." So he left her alive. Repentance entered Saul's heart, and he regretted and wept, so that people pitied him. Every night he went out to the graves and wept. He would cry out, "I adjure by God any human who knows that there is any repentance for me to tell me." When it became too much for them, a voice called out to him from the graves, "O Saul! Are you not satisfied that you slew us when we were alive, that you wish to trouble us when we are dead?" His weeping and sadness increased until the giant pitied him and said, "What is the matter with you?" He replied, "Do you know of any scholar in the land whom I can ask whether there is any atonement for me?" The giant said to him, "Do you know what you resemble? You are like a king who lodged in a town at dusk. The cock crowed, and the king drew an evil omen from that, so he said, 'Do not leave a single cock in this town, kill them all.' Then he wanted to sleep, and he said, 'When the cock crows, awaken us so we may set out at daybreak.' They said to him, 'Have you left any cock [alive] whose crowing can be heard?' Have you left any scholar alive in the land?"

His weeping and sadness increased, and, when the giant saw that he was in earnest, he said, "Tell me, if I lead you to a scholar, will you perhaps [as I fear] kill him?" Saul replied, "No." So the giant considered him trustworthy and informed him that the woman scholar was with him. Saul said, "Take me to her. I will ask her whether there is any atonement for me." That name[736] was known only by
[558] members of a family whose men had died; then the women would know it. Then the giant said, "If she sees you, she will faint and be afraid of you." So when they reached the door, the giant left Saul behind it and entered to her, saying, "Am I not the most generous person toward you, having saved you from being killed and given you refuge with me?" She said, "Yes, of course." He said, "Then I need something from you. This is Saul who will ask you whether there is any atonement for him." She fainted out of terror, but he said, "He

735. *Al-jabbār* seems to mean "giant" here, rather than "tyrant." Jewish legend tells that the woman diviner was the mother of Abner, a cousin of Saul and a giant of extraordinary size. See Ginzberg, *op. cit.*, IV, 73. But Ibrāhīm, *op. cit.*, I, 473, reads *al-khabbāz* as "the baker."

736. *I.e.*, the ineffable name of God. See n. 518, above.

does not want to kill you, only to ask you whether there is atonement for him." She replied, "No, by God, I know of no atonement for Saul. But do you know the place of a prophet's tomb?" They said, "Yes. This is the tomb of Joshua b. Nun."[737] She went off to it, the two of them with her, and she prayed. Joshua b. Nun came out, shaking the dust off of his head. When he looked at the three of them, he said, "What is it? Has the resurrection occurred?" She said, "No. But Saul wants to ask you whether there is any atonement for him." Joshua said, "I know of no atonement for Saul, unless he divests himself of his rule and he and his sons go forth and his sons do battle before him, on God's behalf. Then, if they are slain, [Saul] will go on the offensive; if he is killed, perhaps that will be atonement for him." Then he fell down dead in the grave.

Saul returned sadder than he had ever been, for fear that his sons would not follow him. He wept until his eyelashes fell out and his body became emaciated. His thirteen sons came to him, and spoke to him, asking him about his condition. He told them his story and what had been said to him about his atonement. He asked them to do battle with him. He equipped them, and they went out together. The sons attacked before him and were killed; then he attacked and [559] was killed. David became king after that, and God made him a prophet, for that is His word: *God gave him the kingdom and the wisdom*[738]—it is said that the latter means prophecy. [God] gave him Samuel's[739] prophecy and Saul's kingship.

Saul's name in Syriac[740] is Saul b. Kish b. Abiel b. Zeror b. Becorat b. Aphiah B. Aysh b. Benjamin b. Jacob b. Isaac b. Abraham.

Ibn Isḥāq said: The prophet revived from his grave to inform Saul about his atonement was Elisha b. Akhṭūb.[741] So were we informed by Ibn Ḥumayd—Salamah—Ibn Isḥāq.

The people of the Torah assert that Saul's reign lasted forty years, from the beginning until he was slain in battle along with his sons.

---

737. In the biblical account it is the recently deceased Samuel, and not Joshua, who is raised from the dead; 1 Samuel 28:11–19.

738. Qurʾān 2:251.

739. Here Samuel is Shamʿūn.

740. Hebrew rather than Syriac, given here as Shāwul b. Qays (or Qīs) b. Abyāl b. Ḍirār b. Baḥarat b. Afīḥ/Afyaḥ b. Aysh (the latter probably in error for the Hebrew *ben ish y^{e}mini* "son of a (Ben)jaminite man," 1 Samuel 9:1. See al-Ṭabarī, I, 559 n. *f*.

741. See the discussion of this name on p. 124, and in n. 667, above.

The Account of David b. Jesse b. Obed b. Boaz b. Salmon b. Nahshon b. Amminadab b. Ram b. Hezron b. Perez b. Judah b. Jacob b. Isaac b. Abraham[742]

David was—as Ibn Ḥumayd related to us—Salamah—Ibn Isḥāq—some scholars—Wahb b. Munabbih—short, with blue eyes, little hair, and a pure and pious heart.

[560] Yūnus b. ʿAbd al-Aʿlā related to me—Ibn Wahb—Ibn Zayd related to me regarding the word of God: *"Consider those who went forth from their habitations in their thousands, fearing death"* ... to where He says ... *"God is aware of evildoers."*[743] God inspired their prophet that among the sons of so-and-so, was a man by whom

---

742. Dāwūd b. Īshā b. ʿAwbid b. Bāʿaz b. Salmūn (not Salma; cf. Ruth 4:20–21) b. Naḥshūn b. ʿAmī Nādab b. Rām b. Ḥaṣrūn b. Fāris b. Yahūdhā b. Yaʿqūb b. Isḥāq b. Ibrāhīm. The biblical story is found in 1 Samuel 16–31, 2 Samuel 1–24, and 1 Kings 1–2. The legendary accounts are in Ginzberg, *op. cit.*, IV, 81–121. See also al-Thaʿlabī, 235–60.

743. Qurʾān 2:243–46. *And God said to them: Die! And then He brought them back to life. Lo! God is a Lord of kindness to mankind, but most of mankind do not give thanks. Fight in the way of God, and know that God is Hearer, Knower. Who is it who will lend to God a goodly loan, so that He may give it manifold increase? God straitens and enlarges. To Him will you return. Consider the leaders of the Children of Israel after Moses, how they said to a Prophet whom they had: Set up for us a king, and we will fight in God's way. He said: Would you then refrain from fighting if fighting were prescribed for you? They said: Why should we not fight in God's way*

God would slay Goliath. Among his distinguishing marks is a horn which, when placed on his head, will overflow with water. So the prophet went to this man [i.e., so-and-so] and said, "God has inspired me that among your sons is a man by whom God will slay Goliath." He said, "Yes, O prophet of God!" So he brought out to him twelve men like tall columns, among whom was one who towered over the others. He tested them with the horn, but [each time] saw nothing, so he said to each big man, "Withdraw!" and tried it on the next one, but God inspired him: "Verily, We do not select men because of their forms but because of the righteousness of their hearts." The prophet said, "O Lord, he has claimed that he has no other son." God replied, "He has lied." The prophet said, "My Lord has given you the lie and said that you have a son besides them." He replied, "He is right, O prophet of God. I have a short son whom I was ashamed of having people see, so I sent him off with the herds." The prophet said, "Where is he?" The father replied, "He is within such-and-such a gorge of such-and-such a mountain."

The prophet went out to him and found that a valley had begun to flow with water between him and the plot of land where he went to rest his flocks at the end of the day. He found [this son] carrying two lambs at a time, crossing the stream with them, not making them ford it alone.[744] When the prophet saw him, he said, "This is he, no doubt about it. He is merciful to animals, so he must be even more merciful to people." He placed the horn on his head, and it overflowed.

Al-Muthannā related to me—Isḥāq—Ismāʿīl b. ʿAbd al-Karīm—ʿAbd al-Ṣamad b. Maʿqil—Wahb b. Munabbih: When the Israelites [561] surrendered rule to Saul, God inspired the prophet of the Israelites, "Say to Saul: Let him do battle with the Midianites and not leave anyone alive, killing them all, and I shall give him victory." So he went with the troops to Midian and slew those there, except their king, whom he took prisoner; he also carried off their cattle. God inspired Samuel: "Do you not wonder at Saul? I gave him My command and he violated it: he took their king prisoner and carried off their cattle. So go meet him, and say to him that I shall indeed strip dominion from his house, not to return it until the Day of Resurrec-

---

when we have been driven from our dwellings with our children? Yet, when fighting was prescribed for them, they turned away, all but a few of them.

744. Lit. *wa-lā yakhūḍu bihimā al-sayl.*

tion. For I only give honor to him who obeys Me, and I humble him who despises My command."

[Samuel] met [Saul] and said to him, "What have you done? Why did you take their king as prisoner? And why did you drive their cattle?" He replied, "I drove the cattle only in order to sacrifice them." Samuel said to him, "God has stripped rule from your house, and it will not return to it until Resurrection Day." God inspired Samuel, "Go to Jesse, and let him present his sons before you. Anoint the one whom I command you with the holy oil to be king over the Children of Israel." He went on from there until he came to Jesse and said, "Present your sons before me." Jesse called the eldest of his sons, a husky man of handsome appearance. When Samuel looked at him, he was impressed with him and said, "Praise be to God! *Lo! God is Seer of His servants.*"[745] But God inspired him, saying, "Your eyes see what is apparent, but I observe what is in the hearts. Not this one." So [Samuel] said, "Not this one. Present another before me." So he had six more pass before him, and for all of them, he said, "Not this one. Bring me another one." Finally he said, "Do you have another son besides these?" Jesse replied, "Yes, I have
[562] a red-headed boy who is herding the flocks." [Samuel] said, "Send for him!" When David, a red-headed youth, came, Samuel anointed him with the holy oil and said to his father [Jesse], "Hide this youth, for if Saul sees him, he will slay him."

Goliath and his people journeyed toward the Israelites and made camp, while Saul traveled with the Israelites and made camp. They prepared for battle, and Goliath sent to Saul, saying, "Why should my people and yours be slain? Come forth to me in single combat, or send someone out to me, whomever you want. If I slay you, dominion will be mine, while if you kill me, dominion will be yours." Saul sent a crier among his troops calling, "Who will go forth to duel with Goliath?" Then the narrator recounts the story of Saul and David's killing of Goliath and what happened between Saul and David.

Abū Jaʿfar (al-Ṭabarī) said that in this story, it becomes clear that God had already transferred kingship to [David] before he slew Goliath and before Saul's attempt to slay him had occurred. As for the remainder of those whose discourse about that we have related, they

745. Qurʾān 40:44, 3:20.

have said that David became king only after Saul and his sons were slain.

Ibn Ḥumayd has related to us — Salamah — Ibn Isḥāq, regarding what some sages have mentioned to me—Wahb b. Munabbih: When David slew Goliath and his army was routed, people said, "David has slain Goliath and has deposed Saul," and the people turned to David instead of Saul, until no mention of Saul could be heard.

When the Israelites gathered around David, God revealed the Psalms to him, and taught him ironworking,[746] making it supple for him. He also ordered the mountains and the birds to sing praise with him when he sang. According to what they have mentioned, God did [563] not give anyone of His creation a voice like his. So when David recited the Psalms, wild beasts would gaze at him with delight,[747] until they were lined up, intently listening upon hearing his voice. The demons invented flutes, lutes, and cymbals with only his voice as a model. David was extremely diligent, constant in worship, and wept much.

He was as God has described him to His prophet Muhammad, when He said, *"and remember Our servant David, possessor of might. Lo! He turned in repentance. Lo! We subdued the hills [to sing the praises] with him [at nightfall and sunrise]"*[748]—these two verses[749] mean he possessed power.

Bishr b. Muʿādh[750] related to us — Yazīd — Saʿīd — Qatādah: Regarding *And remember Our servant David, possessor of might. Lo! He turned in repentance,*[751] he said: He was granted power in worship and understanding in submission (Islam).

It has also been mentioned to us that David would stay up at night and fast half of the time. And according to what has been mentioned, four thousand men guarded him every day and night.

---

746. The connection of David with ironworking, and especially the fashioning of fine chain mail, goes back to the Qurʾānic verses 34:10–11: "... *We made iron supple to him. Saying: Make long coats of mail and measure their limbs ...*"; 21:80: "*And We taught him the art of making garments* [of mail] *to protect you in your daring.*" This association seems to antedate Islam, see *EI*², s.v. "Dāwūd."

747. Text: *tarnū*. But Ibn al-Athīr, *op. cit.*, I, 223, and al-Thaʿlabi, *op. cit.*, 244, have *tadnū* "draw near." See al-Ṭabarī, I, 563, n. *a*.

748. Qurʾān 38:18–19.

749. Qurʾān 38:18–19.

750. Bishr b. Muʿādh. See n. 98, above.

751. Qurʾān 38:18.

Muḥammad b. al-Ḥusayn[752] related to me — Aḥmad b. al-Mufaḍḍal[753]—Asbāṭ—al-Suddī, regarding His words *And We made his kingdom strong,* he said, "Four thousand men guarded him every day and night."

It is mentioned that one day, he wanted from his Lord the same status as his forefathers Abraham, Isaac, and Jacob, and he asked his Lord to test him somewhat as He had tested them and to grant him favor like that He had granted them.

Muḥammad b. al-Ḥusayn—Aḥmad b. al-Mufaḍḍal—Asbāṭ who said: al-Suddī said that David divided his time into three days: one
[564] day he would spend with people; one day he would devote to the worship of his Lord; and one day he would devote to his wives, of whom he had ninety-nine. In what he read in books, he found the excellence of Abraham, Isaac, and Jacob. When he found this in the books he read, he said: "O Lord! It seems to me that my forefathers have taken all goodness. Grant me the same as you have granted them! Do to me what you have done to them."

Then God inspired him: "Your forefathers were tried with misfortunes with which you have not been tried. Abraham was tested with the sacrifice of his son, Isaac with the loss of his sight, and Jacob with grief over his son Joseph. You have not been tried with any of that." David said, "O Lord! Test me as you have tested them, and grant me what you have given them."

God inspired him: "You are going to be tested, so be on your guard!" He waited as long as God wished him to wait, whereupon Satan came to him, taking on the shape of a golden dove. It alighted at his feet while he was standing and praying. The narrator continued: He reached out his hand to take hold of it, but it flew away. He followed it, but it distanced itself until it alighted in an aperture in the wall. He went to grab it, but it flew from the aperture. He watched to see where it would alight, so he could send after it.

He saw a woman bathing herself on her roof, one of the most beautiful women in form. She happened to turn around, and she saw him. She let down her hair, covering herself with it. That only increased his desire for her.

He asked about her and was told that she had a husband who was

752. Muḥammad b. al-Ḥusayn. *Index,* 509. Not further identified.

753. Aḥmad b. al-Mufaḍḍal, *mawlā* of Quraysh, d. 215/830. Ibn Saʿd, *op. cit.,* VI, 286.

absent at such-and-such a garrison. He sent to the garrison commander an order to send Uriah[754] against such-and-such an enemy. He therefore sent him, and [the enemy] was conquered by him. The [565] commander wrote back to David about the victory, and David wrote to him again, saying, "Send him against such-and-such an enemy, who is even stronger than they." So he sent him, and they again were conquered by him, and he wrote to David about the second victory. David wrote to him, "Send him to such-and-such an enemy." So he sent him, and on the third time, Uriah was slain.

David married Uriah's wife. When she came to him, she had been with him only a short time when God sent two angels, in human form, who requested admission to his presence. But they found that this was his day of worship, and the guards prevented them from entering. So the two scaled the wall of his private apartment to reach him.[755] He was not aware of [their arrival] while he was praying, but suddenly the two were sitting in front of him. He was startled, but they said, *"Do not be afraid.* We are *two litigants, one of whom has wronged the other, therefore judge aright between us; be not unjust"* — meaning, do not act wrongfully — *"and show us the* fair *way,* to just judgment." David said, "Tell me your story." One of them said, *"Lo! This brother of mine has ninety-nine ewes while I have one ewe.*[756] He wants to take my ewe to round out his to one hundred."

David then said to the other one, "What do you have to say?" The other replied, "I have ninety-nine ewes, and this brother of mine has one ewe, and I want to take it from him to complete my ewes to one hundred." David said, "Even though he is unwilling?" He replied, "Even though he is unwilling!" David said, "Then we cannot let you do that!" He replied, "But you are unable to [prevent] that." David said, "If you try that, then we will hit you on this and that" which Asbāṭ interprets as "the tip of the nose and the forehead." Then he said, "O David! You deserve more to be hit on this and this, since [566] you have ninety-nine wives while Uriah had only one wife. But you did not stop exposing him to slaughter until he was slain, and you married his wife."

754. Arabic: Ahriyā in al-Ṭabarī; Ibn al-Athīr, *op. cit.*, I, 224, has Awriyā; al-Thaʿlabī, *op. cit.*, 248, has Awriyāʾ.

755. This story, based on Qurʾān 38:22, reflects the biblical account of David's chastisement by the prophet Nathan; 2 Samuel 12:1–23.

756. 2 Samuel 38:23–24.

[David] looked and saw no one. Then he understood what had happened, and how he was being tested, and he fell down prostrating himself, and wept. He remained prostrate and weeping for forty days, not raising his head except for some absolute need, after which he would again fall down prostrate and weeping. He prayed until grass began to sprout from his tears.

Then after forty days passed, God inspired him "O David! Lift up your head, for I have forgiven you." He said, "O Lord! how will I know that You have forgiven me, when You are a just judge Who shows no favor in judgment? When Uriah comes on the Day of Resurrection, holding his head in his right or left hand, his neck veins gushing blood before Your Throne, he will say, 'O Lord! Ask this one why he slew me.'" God inspired him: "If that happens, I will call Uriah and ask for you as a gift from him. He will give you to Me, and I will repay him with Paradise." David said, "O Lord! Now I know that You have forgiven me." He could not raise his eyes to the heavens, because of his shame before his Lord, until he died.

ʿAlī b. Sahl[757] related to me—al-Walīd b. Muslim[758]—ʿAbd al-Raḥmān b. Yazīd b. Jābir[759]—ʿAṭāʾ al-Khurāsānī:[760] David engraved his sin on the palm of his hand, lest he should forget it. Whenever he saw it, his hand would tremble and throb.

[567] It is said that the reason for the trial with which he was tested was that his innermost feelings told him that he could spend a day without perpetrating an evil deed. It happened that the day of the trial took place on the day he thought he could spend without committing an evil deed.

Mention of who said that.

Bishr related to us—Yazīd—Saʿīd—Maṭar[761]—al-Ḥasan,[762] say-

757. ʿAlī b. Sahl al-Ramlī. *Index,* 397. Not further identified.

758. al-Walīd b. Muslim al-Umawī al-Dimashqī, Abū al-ʿAbbās, 119–95/737–810. He was the foremost scholar of Syria in his time and author of many works on tradition and history. Ibn Ḥajar, *op. cit.,* XI, 151–55; *GAS,* I, 293; al-Ziriklī, *op. cit.,* IX, 143.

759. ʿAbd al-Raḥmān b. Yazīd b. Jābir. *Index,* 353. Not further identified.

760. ʿAṭāʾ b. Abī Muslim Maysarah al-Khurāsānī, 50–140/670–757. A Damascene scholar who transmitted from Anas b. Mālik, he wrote Qurʾān commentary. Ibn Saʿd, *op. cit.,* VII/2, 369; Ibn Ḥajar, *op. cit.,* VII, 212–15; *GAS,* I, 33.

761. Maṭar b. Ṭahmān al-Warrāq. A traditionist from Khorasan, considered a weak transmitter. Ibn Saʿd, *op. cit.,* VII/2, 19.

762. Al-Ḥasan b. Abī al-Ḥasan Yasār al-Baṣrī, Abū Saʿīd, 21–110/642–728. He was a famous preacher and deeply pious personality, and his statements circulated as traditions. Ibn Saʿd, *op. cit.,* VII/1, 114ff; *EI*², s.v. "Ḥasan al-Baṣrī"; *GAS,* I, 591–94.

ing that David divided his time into four parts: one day for his wives; one day for his worship; one day for judging the Israelites; and one day during which he would exhort the Children of Israel and they him, he would bring them to tears and they him. When it was the day for the Children of Israel, he said, "Exhort me!" They said, "Is there a day in which a man does not commit a sin?" David imagined to himself that he could accomplish that, so when the day of worship came, he locked his doors, giving orders that no one was to be admitted. He devoted himself to the Torah, but while he was reading it, lo! A golden dove full of every beautiful color alighted in front of him. He reached out to seize it, but it flew off and alighted not far away, still giving him hope of reaching it. He continued following it until he looked out and saw a woman washing herself; her form and beauty pleased him. When she noticed his shadow on the ground, she covered herself with her hair, which only pleased him more. He had sent her husband to command one of his armies, and now he wrote to him to journey to such-and-such a place, a place from which he would not return.

Uriah journeyed there and was killed, so David proposed to his wife and married her. Qatādah has told us that we have heard she was Solomon's mother. When he was in his private apartment, lo! [568]
Two angels climbed the wall to him. When two litigants came to him, they usually came by way of the door of the private chamber, *so he was startled by them* when they climbed the wall of the private chamber. But *they said: "Be not afraid!* We are *two litigants, one of whom has wronged the other"* ... until where he reached—*"be not unjust"*—meaning, do not show favor—*"and show us the fair way"*—that is, the more just and better one. *"This brother of mine has ninety-nine ewes"*—and David had ninety-nine wives—*"while I have one ewe"*—and Uriah had only one wife. *"And he said: 'Entrust it to me,' and he conquered me in speech"*—that is, he wronged me and overcame me. [David] *said: "He has wronged you in demanding your ewe in addition to his ewes [and lo! Many partners oppress one another, save those who believe and do good works, and they are few.]" And David guessed*—knowing that it was secretly directed at him, that is, it was he who was meant by that—*and he fell down prostrate and he repented.*[763]

763. Qur'ān 38:23–25.

Ya'qūb b. Ibrāhīm[764] related to me—Ibn Idrīs:[765] I heard Layth[766] mention—Mujāhid: When David was overcome by this sin, he fell down, bowing to God for forty days, until herbs sprouted from his tears, covering his head. Then he called out, "O Lord! My forehead is covered with ulcers, and my eyes have dried up, but no answer has been given to David about his sin." It was proclaimed: "If [you are] hungry, you will be fed; if ill, you will be healed; or if oppressed, assistance be sought for you." He sobbed so that everything that had grown withered, and at that he was forgiven. His sin was written on his hand, so he could read it. When he was brought a vessel from which to drink, he would drink only a third or half, then he would remember his sin, and he would sob so much that his joints would be dislocated, and he would not finish drinking, until the vessel was filled with his tears. It was said one of David's tears equaled a tear of
[569] all creatures; that one of Adam's tears equaled one of David's tears and of all creatures.'

[David] will come on Resurrection Day with his sin written on his hand and will say: "Lord! My sin, my sin! Make me go ahead!" He will be sent ahead, but he will not feel secure, so he will say, "Lord! Make me stay behind!" He will then be held back, but continue to feel insecure.

Yūnus b. 'Abd al-A'lā related to me—Ibn Wahb—Ibn Lahī'ah[767] —Abū Ṣakhr[768]—Yazīd al-Raqāshī[769]—Anas b. Mālik,[770] saying: I

---

764. Ya'qūb b. Ibrāhīm b. Kathīr al-'Abdī, Abū Yūsuf, al-Dawraqī, 166–252/782–866. A leading reliable memorizer and transmitter of tradition in Iraq from whom the six codifiers received many versions. Ibn Ḥajar, *op. cit.*, XI, 381; Ibn Sa'd, *op. cit.*, VII/2, 97; *GAS*, I, 3f; al-Ziriklī, *op. cit.*, IX, 253.

765. 'Abd al-Mun'im b. Idrīs b. Sinān, Abū 'Abdallāh, d. 229/844. A grandson of Wahb b. Munabbih (n. 278, above) and leading transmitter of his grandfather's work. A native of Yemen, he died in Baghdad when he was almost one hundred years old. Ibn Sa'd, *op. cit.*, VII/2, 97; *GAS*, I, 306.

766. Al-Layth b. Sa'd. See n. 577, above.

767. 'Abdallāh b. Lahī'ah b. 'Uqbah (Fur'ān in Ziriklī) al-Ḥadramī, al-Miṣrī Abū 'Abd al-Raḥmān, 97–174/715–790. He was a *qāḍī* in Egypt and a collector of traditions who, especially during his latter days, was considered a weak authority. *GAS*, I, 94; al-Ziriklī, *op. cit.*, IV, 255–56.

768. Abū Ṣakhr, possibly Yazīd b. Abī Sumayyah, Abū Ṣakhr al-Aylī. See Ibn Sa'd, *op. cit.*, VII/2, 206. A reliable transmitter of tradition.

769. Yazīd al-Raqāshī. *Index*, 641. Possibly Yazīd b. Abān al-Raqāshī, a weak transmitter of tradition. Ibn Sa'd, *op. cit.*, VII/2, 13.

770. Anas b. Mālik b. al-Naḍr b. Ḍamḍam, al-Najārī al-Khazrajī al-Anṣarī, Abū Thamāmah (or Abū Ḥamzah) b. 612, d. 94/712, A Companion and servant of the Prophet. Al-Bukhārī and Muslim cited over two thousand traditions from him. Ibn Sa'd, *op. cit.*, VII/1, 10–16; *EI²*, s.v. "Anas b. Mālik."

heard the Messenger of God say that when David the prophet looked at the woman and became disquieted, he levied an army of the Children of Israel and gave orders to its leader, saying: "When the enemy appears, make so-and-so draw near and advance in front of the Ark." At that time, the Ark was taken as assistance: whoever advanced in front of it, would not return until he was slain or the army fled before him. Then the husband of the woman was slain, and the two angels descended and related his story to David. He understood, and bowed down, remaining so for forty nights, until plants grew up around his head from his tears, and the earth consumed part of his forehead. While he was prostrate he said—and I understood from what al-Raqāshī said only these words—"Lord! David has committed a sin beyond what is between the East and West. Lord! If You do not have mercy on David's weakness and forgive his sin, You will make his sin a subject of conversation among successive generations after him."

Gabriel went to David after forty nights and said, "O David! God has forgiven you for what you intended." David said, "I know that God is able to forgive what I intended and that God is just, not showing favor. But how about so-and-so, who will come on Resurrection Day and will say, 'O Lord! My blood is on David!'" Gabriel said, "I [570]
did not ask your Lord about that, but if you wish, I shall do so." [David] said, "Yes." Then Gabriel ascended while David prostrated himself, remaining so as long as God willed. Then [Gabriel] came down and said, "I have asked God, O David, what you sent me about, and He replied, 'Say to him, "O David! God will bring the two of you together on Resurrection Day, and He will say [to Uriah]:[771] 'Give Me your blood, which is with David' and he will reply, 'It is Yours, O Lord!' and He will say, 'You may have whatever you want in the Garden and whatever you desire in place of it.'"'"

People of the Scripture claim that David continued to rule after Saul, until the incident between him and Uriah's wife occurred. When he committed that sin, David was busied with atonement for it, according to what they claim, and the Israelites disdained him. One of his sons, named Absalom,[772] rebelled against him and called

771. Inserted by al-Thaʿlabī, *op. cit.*, 251. See al-Ṭabarī, I, 570 n. *d*.

772. Arabic: Abshā. Ibrāhīm, *op. cit.*, I, 484; Īshā, probably from MS Tn.; Ibn al-Athīr, *op. cit.*, I, 227, and al-Thaʿlabī, *op. cit.*, 254. The latter gives Shalūn as an alternative. Al-Nuwayrī has Ayshalūm.

the people to acknowledge him as ruler, and those who erred[773] among the Israelites rallied to him.

When God forgave David, some people returned to him, and David fought his son until he defeated him. He sent one of his captains to capture him, giving orders that he be careful to take him alive and show kindness in capture. As the captain sought him, he fled and was forced to run into a tree. He had luxuriant hair, and one of the branches got caught in his hair and held him. This enabled the cap-
[571] tain to overtake and kill him, contrary to David's order. David was greatly saddened over his death, and felt a hatred for the captain.

During David's time, a violent plague struck the Israelites. David took them to the place of the Temple to pray to God, asking Him to remove this misfortune from them. Their prayers were answered, and they adopted that place as a place for worship.[774] They say that this happened after David had ruled for eleven years, but that he died before he completed constructing it. So he left it to Solomon to complete, as well as to slay the captain who had killed his brother. When Solomon had buried David, he carried out his command that the captain be killed, and he completed the building of the Temple.

Regarding David's building of that Temple, there has been said what Muḥammad b. Sahl b. ʿAskar[775] reported to us — Ismāʿīl b. ʿAbd al-Karīm[776] — ʿAbd al-Ṣamad b. Maʿqil,[777] who heard Wahb b. Munabbih say that David wanted to know how many Israelites there were. To find this number, he sent out appraisers and chiefs and commanded them to bring him the number they found. But God was angry with David about this matter and said, "You know that I had promised Abraham that I would bless him and his descendants,[778] so that I would make them as numerous as the stars in heaven, and their number uncountable. Yet you wanted to know the number that I said could not be counted. So choose either that I afflict you with hunger for three years, or that I give power over you to the enemy for three months, or to death for three days." David conferred with the Israelites about this matter, and they said, "We do not have the pa-

773. *Ahl al-zaygh.*
774. *Masjidan,* lit. "a place of prostration." In Islam a mosque.
775. Muḥammad b. Sahl b. ʿAskar. See n. 649, above.
776. Ismāʿīl b. ʿAbd al-Karīm. See n. 650, above.
777. ʿAbd al-Ṣamad b. Maʿqil. See n. 651, above.
778. See the blessing of Abraham after the binding of Isaac. Genesis 22:15–18.

tience to withstand hunger for three years, nor the enemy for three months, for there would be no remnant of us. If there is no way out, then better death at His hand than at the hand of anyone else."

Wahb b. Munabbih mentioned that during one hour of the day, many thousands, the number is unknown, died among them. When David learned of the numbers of dead, he was distressed, so he devoted himself to God and prayed to Him, saying, "O Lord! I have eaten the sour sorrel, but the teeth of the Israelites are set on edge.[779] I sought this, I ordered the Israelites to do it, everything that happened is my [fault], so pardon the Children of Israel!" God responded to him by removing death from them. Then David saw the angels with their drawn swords sheathing them and climbing a golden ladder from the Rock[780] to heaven, and David said, "This is a site on which a place of worship[781] should be built." David wanted to begin its construction, but God inspired him: "This is a holy house, and you have stained your hands with blood. You are not to be its builder, then, but a son of yours, whom I shall make king after you, whom I shall name Solomon, [and] whom I shall keep safe from bloodshed."[782] When Solomon became king, he built the place of worship and ennobled it. David's life, according to the accounts that came from the Messenger of God, lasted one hundred years, whereas one of the Scriptuaries claims that he lived for seventy-seven years[783] and reigned for forty years. [572]

---

779. *Anā ākil al-ḥummāḍ wa-banū Isrā'īl yaḍrasūna.* In 2 Samuel 24:17 (repeated in 1 Chronicles 21:17) David asks God to end the plague, saying: "Lo, I have sinned, and I have acted iniquitously; but these sheep, what have they done? Let Thy hand be against me, and against my father's house." A phrase closer to the one used here occurs in Jeremiah 31:29: "The fathers have eaten sour grapes, and the children's teeth are set on edge." The same occurs in Ezekiel 18:2.

780. *Al-ṣakhrah,* presumably the rock over which the Dome of the Rock was later built on the Temple Mount in Jerusalem.

781. Once again, *masjid,* but it may be taken as "a place of prostration" or "temple."

782. Compare the play on the root letters of Solomon's name in Arabic and Hebrew, here: *S*u*l*ay*m*ān u*s*a*ll*i*m*uhu: "I shall name *Solomon* whom *I shall keep safe*"; 1 Chronicles 22:9: *sh*ᵉ*lo*m*o* yihyeh shemo we-*sh*a*lo*m . . . "his name shall be *Solomon,* and I will give *peace* . . . ."

783. See 2 Samuel 5:4, 10: "David was thirty years old when he began to reign, and he reigned forty years." Hence he was seventy years old at his death.

The History of Solomon b. David[784]

Solomon b. David ruled over the Israelites after his father David. God compelled the jinn, men, birds, and wind to serve him. In addition, He gave Solomon prophecy, and he asked his Lord to give him dominion that would not be appropriate to anyone after him, and He responded, giving him that.

According to what we were told by Ibn Ḥumayd—Salamah—
[573] Muḥammad b. Isḥāq—some scholars—Wahb b. Munabbih: When he left his dwelling for his council chamber, the birds would stay close to him, while men and jinn would arise for him until he was seated on his throne.

He was—they assert—pale, corpulent, clean, and hairy, and wore white garments. During the days of his father's rule, after Solomon had reached mature manhood, his father would consult with him, according to what is recorded, about his affairs. One of his and David's concerns involved giving judgment about sheep who had wandered by night by themselves into the fields of people, an account of whom—as well as the account of the two of them—God related in His Book, saying: *And David and Solomon, when they gave judgment concerning the field, when people's sheep had pastured therein by night; and We were witnesses to their judgment. And We*

784. See the biblical account in 1 Kings 2–11. Jewish legendary accounts are to be found in Ginzberg, *op. cit.*, IV, 125–76; al-Thaʿlabī, *op. cit.*, 257–92; *Shorter Encyclopaedia of Islam*, s.v. "Sulaimān."

made Solomon understand; and to each of the two We gave judgment and knowledge.[785]

Abū Kurayb and Hārūn b. Idrīs al-Aṣamm,[786] related to us—al-Muḥāribī[787]—Ashʿath—Abū Isḥāq—Murrah—Ibn Masʿūd: Regarding His words: *And David and Solomon, when they gave judgment concerning the field, when people's sheep had pastured therein by night,*[788] he said: It was a vineyard, whose clusters had sprouted, and [the sheep] had ruined them. David passed judgment on the sheep in favor of the owner of the vineyard, but Solomon said: "Not that, O prophet of God!" He replied, "Why is that?" He said, "Hand over the vineyard to the owner of the sheep, so that he may take care of it until it returns to its former condition, and give the sheep to the owner of the vineyard, so that he may gain from them until the vineyard has returned to its previous state, then hand it over to its owner and the sheep to their owner. For that is His saying: *We made Solomon understand* [the case].[789] [574]

He was a warfaring man, who rarely ceased his constant campaigning. No sooner would he hear about a ruler in some part of the world, but he would go to him to humble him. It was as Ibn Ḥumayd related to us—Salamah—Ibn Isḥāq, as they claim, that when he desired to do battle, he would command his army[790] to be mustered, and wood would be cut for it. It would be set upon [the wood], and people, draft animals, weapons of war, everything, was loaded on it. As soon as it carried what he wanted, he commanded the violent wind to enter under the wood and raise it up. When it had been lifted, he commanded the light breeze, which carried them [the distance of] a month in one night, and [the distance of] one month in one morning, to wherever he wished. God says: *So We made the wind subservient to him, that ran at his command softly, wherever he might light upon*[791]—meaning, wherever he wished. And God

785. Qurʾān 21:78–79.

786. Hārūn b. Idrīs al-Aṣamm. *Index,* 604. Not further identified.

787. ʿAbd al-Raḥmān b. Muḥammad, Abū Muḥammad, al-Muḥāribī, d. 196/811, a Kūfan who was considered trustworthy but made many errors in transmission. Ibn Saʿd, *op. cit.,* VI, 273.

788. Qurʾān 21:78.

789. Qurʾān 21:79.

790. Ibn al-Athīr, *op. cit.,* I, 230, has instead: "He commanded the making of a carpet of wood to accommodate his army." Cf. al-Ṭabarī, I, 574 n. *b.*

791. Qurʾān 38:37.

said: *And unto Solomon (We gave) the wind, of which the morning's course was a month's journey, and its evening course a month's journey.*[792]

The narrator continued: It was mentioned to me that there is an inscription, written by one of Solomon's companions, either a jinni or one of mankind, in a dwelling in the vicinity of the Tigris: "We dwelt in it, but we did not build it; we found it already built. We came early in the morning from Iṣṭakhr[793] and spent the midday rest in it. We will go from it in the evening, if God wills, and spend the night in Syria."

[575] According to what I have heard, the wind carried his army, and the light breeze blew him wherever he wished, yet it could move over a sown field and not make it move.

Al-Qāsim b. al-Ḥasan[794] related to us—al-Ḥusayn—Ḥajjāj—Abū Maʿshar[795]—Muḥammad b. Kaʿb al-Quraẓī:[796] We have heard that Solomon's army [stretched] one hundred parasangs: twenty-five of them consisted of humans, twenty-five of jinn, twenty-five of wild animals, and twenty-five of birds. He possessed one thousand houses of glass on the wooden [carpet], in which there were three hundred wives[797] and seven hundred concubines.[798] Solomon ordered the violent wind, and it lifted all this, and ordered the gentle breeze and it transported them. God inspired him while he was journeying between heaven and earth: "Lo! I have increased your rule so that no creature can say anything without the wind bringing it and informing you."

Abū al-Sāʾib related to me—Abū Muʿāwiyah—al-Aʿmash—al-Minhāl b. ʿAmr—Saʿīd b. Jubayr—Ibn ʿAbbās: "Solomon b. David had six hundred thrones set out. The noblest humans would come

---

792. Qurʾān 34:12.

793. In Iran. See n. 133, above.

794. Al-Qāsim b. al-Ḥasan. See n. 243, above.

795. Abū Maʿshar Najīḥ b. ʿAbd al-Raḥmān al-Sindī, d. 170/786, a younger contemporary of Ibn Isḥāq from Yemen, who later lived in Medina and Baghdad. He was more highly regarded as a historian than as a reliable transmitter of tradition. Ibn Saʿd, *op. cit.*, V, 309; *EI²*, s.v. "Abū Maʿshar"; al-Ziriklī, *op. cit.*, VIII, 328.

796. Muḥammad b. Kaʿb al-Quraẓī. See n. 385, above.

797. *Ṣarīḥah*, lit. "pure, unmixed, (f.) of race or genealogy." See Lane, *op. cit.*, 1675. Usage unclear.

798. *Thalāthumiʾatu ṣarīḥatin wa-sabʿumiʾatu surriyatin*, but al-Thaʿlabī has *thalāthumiʾatu surriyatin wa-sabʿumiʾatin imratin*, i.e., three hundred concubines and seven hundred wives.

and sit them near him, then the noblest jinn would come and sit near
the humans." He continued: "Then he would call the birds, who [576]
would shade them, then he would call the wind, which would carry them." He went one: "During one morning, they would all travel the distance of a month's journey."

What We Have Heard about Solomon's Campaigns, among Them His Raid during Which He Corresponded with Bilqīs

Who was, according to what the genealogists say, Yalmaqah bt. al-Yashraḥ—some say, bt. Aylī Sharḥ, and others say, bt. Dhī Sharḥ—b. Dhī Jadan b. Aylī Sharḥ b. al-Ḥārith b. Qays b. Ṣayfī b. Saba᾿ b. Yashjub b. Yaʿrub b. Joktan [Qaḥṭān],[799] after which she came to Solomon peacefully, without warfare or battle.

He corresponded with her, according to what is said, because he had missed the hoopoe bird one day during a journey. He needed water, but no one with him knew how far away it was. He was told that the hoopoe possessed such knowledge, so he asked for the hoopoe, but could not find it. Someone said that, on the contrary, Solomon had asked about the hoopoe because it missed its shift.[800]

Regarding his story, the story of that journey, and the story of

---

799. These names seem generally to be South Arabian. For similar genealogies, see nn. 154, 539, above. The name Bilqīs itself has been linked with Naukalis, given by Josephus as the name of the Queen of Egypt and Ethiopia; with the Greek *phallaxis* and Hebrew *pilegesh* "concubine." See *Shorter Encyclopaedia of Islam,* 63, s.v. "Bilkīs"; see also Newby, *History,* 132 n. 1.

800. Text has *bi-al-nabwa,* lit. "tell news," comparing it to *bi-nabā᾿in* "tidings," in Qur᾿ān 27:22, but this hardly fits. MS BM and Ibrāhīm have *nawba* "(its) shift, turn," which is translated here. See al-Ṭabarī, I, 576 n. *i*.

Bilqīs, there is what al-ʿAbbās b. al-Walīd al-Āmulī[801] related to me — ʿAlī b. ʿĀṣim[802] — ʿAṭāʾ b. al-Sāʾib[803] — Mujāhid — Ibn ʿAbbās: When Solomon b. David went on a journey or wanted to travel, he [577] would sit on his throne with seats placed to his right and left. He would give permission to the humans to enter, and permitted the jinn to enter behind them. Then he gave permission to the demons, after the jinn. He would then send for the birds to give them all shade from above, and for the wind to carry them, while he sat on his throne and the people in their seats. The wind carried them, *the morning's course was a month's journey, and its evening course was a month's journey,*[804] *softly wherever he might light [upon].*[805] It was neither a violent nor a light wind, but one in the middle between the two.

While Solomon was traveling, he always chose one bird that he made the chief of all the birds. If he wanted to ask a bird about anything, he would ask its chief. While Solomon was traveling, he alighted in a desert and asked about the distance to water from there. The humans said, "We do not know," so he asked the jinn. They said, "We do not know." Then Solomon asked the demons, and they said, "We do not know." So he became angry and said, "I shall not leave until I know how far away water is from here."

The demons said to Solomon: "O Messenger of God! Do not be angry, because if there is anything to be known, the hoopoe knows it." Solomon said, "Bring the hoopoe to me!" But it could not be found, so Solomon became angry and said, *"How is it that I do not see the hoopoe, or is he among the absent? Verily I will punish him with hard punishments, or I will slay him, or he will bring me a clear authority"*[806] — meaning, a clear excuse — "for being absent from this journey of mine." His punishment for a bird's absence was to pluck out its feathers and to place it in the sun; it would be unable

801. Al-ʿAbbās b. al-Walīd. See n. 53, above.

802. ʿAlī b. ʿĀṣim b. Ṣuhayb al-Wāsiṭī, Abū al-Ḥasan. 105–201/723–816. He was a leading memorizer of traditions of Iraq in his time. Ibn Saʿd, *op. cit.*, VII/2, 61; al-Ziriklī, *op. cit.*, V, 110.

803. ʿAṭāʾ b. al-Sāʾib al-Thaqafī, Abū Zayd, d. 136/753. He was a trusted transmitter of the earliest traditions until later in his life, when some confusion occurred. Ibn Saʿd, *op. cit.*, VI, 235.

804. Qurʾān 34:12.

805. Qurʾān 38:37.

806. Qurʾān 27:20–21.

to fly and would become one of the insects of the earth if [Solomon] wished so. Or he would slay it, and that would be its punishment.

The hoopoe passed over Bilqīs' palace and saw one of her gardens
[578] behind the palace. It inclined toward the greenness and alighted on it, and lo! There was one of [Bilqīs'] hoopoes in the garden. Solomon's hoopoe said: "Where are you [so far] from Solomon? And what are you doing here?" Bilqīs' hoopoe replied, "And who is Solomon?" He replied, "God sent a man named Solomon as a messenger, and humbled before him the wind, the jinn, humans, and birds."

Bilqīs' hoopoe said to the other, "What are you saying?" It replied, "I am saying to you what you have heard." [Bilqīs' hoopoe] said, "This is indeed a wonder, but more wonderful than that is that all of these many people, a woman rules *over them, and she has been given [abundance] of all things, and hers is a mighty throne.* They replaced thanks to God by *worshiping the sun instead of God.*"[807] When the hoopoe had mentioned Solomon, it flew off. When it reached the army, the other birds met it and said, "The Messenger of God has threatened you," and they informed it of what Solomon had said.

Solomon's punishment of the birds was to pluck their feathers and to spread them in the sun, so that they would never fly again and would become like the insects of the earth. Or he would kill them and they would never have posterity.

The hoopoe said, "But did the Messenger of God make no exception?" They replied, "Yes, he did, saying, '*Or let him bring me a clear* excuse.'"[808] When the hoopoe went to Solomon, he asked it, "What has caused you to be absent from my journey?" The hoopoe responded, *"I have found out a thing that you do not apprehend, and I come to you from Sheba with sure tidings"*—to where He reached—*"and see what [answer] they return."*[809]

---

807. Qur'ān 27:23–24.

808. Qur'ān 27:21; see above.

809. Qur'ān 27:22–28. The verses omitted in the text are: *Lo, I found a woman ruling over them, and she has been given (abundance) of all things, and hers is a mighty throne. I found her and her people worshiping the sun instead of God; and Satan makes their deeds seem fair to them, and debars them from the way (of truth), so they do not go aright. So they do not worship God, who brings forth the hidden in the heavens and the earth, and knows what you hide and what you proclaim. God; there is no god besides Him, the Lord of the tremendous throne. (Solomon) said: We*

The hoopoe pleaded excuses and related to him of Bilqīs and her people as the other hoopoe had told him. Solomon responded, "You have pleaded an excuse. *We shall see whether you speak the truth or whether you are a liar. Go with this letter of mine, and throw it down to them.*[810]

The hoopoe met her while she was in her palace and threw the letter to her, and it came into her mind[811] that this was *a noble letter.*[812] She was worried about it, so she took it and threw her garments over it, ordered her throne be brought out, then went to sit upon it and proclaimed to her people, saying to them: *"O chieftains! Lo! There has been thrown to me a noble letter. Lo! It is from Solomon, and it is: 'In the name of God the Beneficient, the Merciful. Exalt not yourselves against me, but come to me as those who surrender.'*[813] I am accustomed not to decide a matter until you bear witness to me."[814] *They said: "We are lords of might and lords of great prowess, but it is for you to command; so consider what you will command." [She said: "Lo, when kings enter a town, they ruin it, and make the honor of its people shame. Thus will they do.] But lo! I am going to send a present to them.*[815] If he accepts it, then he is an earthly king, and I am more powerful and stronger than he. But if he does not accept it, then this is something from God." When the present reached Solomon, he said to them, *"Would you help me with wealth? That which God has given me is better than what He has given you. [Nay it is you (not I) who exult in your gift. Return to them. We shall surely come to them with hosts that they cannot resist, and we shall drive them from there with shame] and they will be abased"*[816]—that is, they are not praiseworthy. [579]

She sent him an unpierced gem and told him: "Pierce it!" Solomon asked people, but they had no knowledge about that, then he

---

shall see whether you speak the truth or whether you are a liar. Go with this letter of mine and throw it down to them; then turn away.

810. Qur'ān 27:27–28.

811. *Saqaṭa fī ḥijriha.* For *ḥijr* as "understanding, intelligence, intellect, mind, or reason." See Lane, *op. cit.*, II, s.v. *ḥjr*. Some versions have *suqiṭa fi khaladiha,* which means "she was nonplused." See *Glossarium*, CCCXCIII, s.v. *sqṭ;* and al-Ṭabarī, I, 579 n. *a*.

812. Qur'ān 27:29.

813. Qur'ān 27:29–31.

814. A paraphrase of Qur'ān 27:32.

815. Qur'ān 27:33–35.

816. Qur'ān 27:36–37.

asked the jinn, but they had no knowledge of that. Then he asked the demons, who said, "Send for the termite." So the termite came, placed a hair in her mouth, entered into [the gem], and after a while, pierced it. When her messengers returned to her, [Bilqīs] left her people hurriedly at the break of day with her people following after her.

[580] Ibn ʿAbbās said, "She had one thousand *qayls*[817] with her." Ibn ʿAbbās said, "The people of Yemen call their leader *'qayl,'* and with each *qayl* were ten thousand men." Al-ʿAbbās said, "ʿAlī said, ten thousand thousand."

Al-ʿAbbās[818] said—ʿAlī[819]—Ḥuṣayn b. ʿAbd al-Raḥmān[820] related to us—ʿAbdallāh b. Shaddād b. Alhād:[821] Bilqīs proceeded to Solomon with three hundred and twelve *qayls,* each with ten thousand men.

ʿAṭāʾ — Mujāhid — Ibn ʿAbbās: Solomon was an awe-inspiring man. No enterprise was undertaken unless he was responsible for it. On that day, he went out to sit upon his throne and saw a cloud of dust near him. He asked, "What is this?" They told him, "Bilqis, O Messenger of God!" He said, "She has encamped near us in this place!"

Mujāhid said that Ibn ʿAbbās described that for us, "I estimated [the distance] as that between al-Kūfah and al-Ḥīrah, the distance of one parasang." He continued: [Solomon] addressed his troops and said: *"Which of you will bring me her throne before they come to me, surrendering?" An 'ifrīt of the jinn said: "I will bring it to you before you rise from your place"*[822]—in which you are now until the time you rise for your morning meal.

Solomon said, "Who will bring her throne to me before that?" *One who had knowledge of Scripture said: "I will bring it to you*
[581] *before your gaze returns to you."*[823] Solomon looked at him, and when he had finished speaking, Solomon returned his gaze to the throne.[824] He saw that her palanquin[825] had come and emerged from

817. *Qayl,* pl. *aqyāl,* the minor or petty kings of pre-Islamic Arabia.
818. *I.e.,* al-ʿAbbās b. al-Walīd. See n. 53, above.
819. *I.e.,* ʿAlī b. ʿĀṣim. See n. 802, above.
820. Ḥusayn b. ʿAbd al-Raḥmān, Abū al-Hudhayl, al-Sulamī. Ibn Saʿd, *op. cit.,* VI, 236.
821. ʿAbdallāh b. Shaddād. See n. 397, above.
822. Qurʾān 27:38–39.
823. Qurʾān 27:40. See n. 845, below.
824. *ʿArsh,* usually treated by Muslim commentators as the divine throne. Hence

beneath his throne.[826] *And when he saw it set in his presence, (Solomon) said: "This is of the bounty of my Lord, that He may try me, whether I give thanks* ... when He brings it to me before my gaze even returns to me ... *or am ungrateful*[827] ... for He has made one in my power more able to bring it than me."

They set up her throne for her. He said further: *When she came,* she sat next to Solomon, and *it was said* to her: *"Is your throne like this?"* So she looked at it, and *she said: "It is as though it were the very one."*[828] Then she said: "I left it in my fortress with troops surrounding it, so how was this brought, O Solomon? I should like to ask you something, so you may tell me about it." He said: "Ask!" She said: "Tell me about sweet water that is from neither heaven nor earth." The narrator said: When Solomon was faced with something he did not know, he began by asking humans about it. If humans had knowledge of it, [good], otherwise he asked the jinn. If the jinn had no knowledge about it, he asked the demons. The demons said to him: "How easy that is, O Messenger of God! Command the horses and make them run, then fill a vessel with their sweat." So Solomon said to her, "The sweat of horses." She said, "You are right. Then tell me about the color of the Lord." Ibn ʿAbbās said that Solomon rose up from his throne and fell down prostrating himself. Al-ʿAbbās said — ʿAlī — ʿAmr b. ʿUbayd[829] told me — al-Ḥasan: "Solomon was thunderstruck and fainted and fell down from his throne." Then we [582]
return to the original account, which says: She arose, and his troops scattered from him, while a messenger arrived, saying, "O Solomon! Your Lord says to you, 'What is wrong with you?'" He replied, "She has asked me something that I am reluctant to repeat."[830] [The messenger] said, "God commands you to return to your throne and sit upon it. Send for her, those of her troops who were with her, and all

the common word for throne. See n. 826, below.

825. *Sarīr,* "couch or bedstead," sometimes used as a symbol of royalty. See Lane, *op. cit.,* s.v. *srr.*

826. *Kursī,* sometimes used for throne, when used together with *ʿarsh,* it is treated as the footstool. See *EI²,* s.v. "Kursī."

827. Qurʾān 27:40 *bis.*

828. Qurʾān 27:42.

829. ʿAmr b. ʿUbayd b. Bāb al-Taymī, Abū ʿUthmān, 80–144/699–761. A leading Muʿtazilite Qurʾān commentator, noted for his piety, asceticism, and learning. *EI²,* s.v. "ʿAmr b. ʿUbayd" *GAS,* I, 597.

830. *Yukabidunī an uʿīdahu.* See *Glossarium,* CDLXIV, s.v. *kbd.*

of your troops who were present. Let them all come to you, while you ask her and them what she had asked you."

He did that, and when they had all entered to his presence, he said to her, "About what did you ask me?" She replied, "I asked you about sweet water that is from neither heaven nor earth." He said, "And I answered you that it was horse's sweat." She said, "And you were right." He said, "And what else did you ask me?" She said, "I did not ask you anything but that." The narrator went on: Solomon said to her, "Then why did I fall from my throne?" She said, "That is something I know nothing about."

Al-ʿAbbās said—ʿAlī: "I forgot it." He went on, "So he asked her troops, and they said what she had said." [Solomon] asked his own troops, jinn, birds, and whoever of his troops had been present, and they all said, "She asked you, O Messenger of God, only about sweet water." The narrator said: The messenger had said, "God says to you, 'Return to your place, for I have taken care of them for you.'"

Solomon said to the demons, "Build me a castle in which Bilqīs will enter to me." He continued: The demons turned to one another and said, "Solomon is the Messenger of God, and God has humbled
[583] to him whatever He has humbled. Bilqīs is the queen of Sheba, whom he will marry, and she will bear him a boy, and we shall never be freed from slavery."

Bilqīs was a woman with hairy legs, so the demons said, "Build a structure for him that will show him that, so that he will not marry her." They built him a castle of green glass, making floor tiles[831] of glass that resembled water. They placed within those tiles every kind of sea creature, fish, and the like, then they covered it up. They said to Solomon, "Enter the castle."

A throne was set up for Solomon at the far end of the castle. When he entered, he looked around, went to the throne, sat upon it, and said: "Let Bilqīs enter to me." *"She was told, "Enter the castle!"* When she began to enter, she saw the forms of the fish and creatures in water, so *she thought it was a pool,* i.e., she thought it was water, *and she bared her legs* to enter it. The hair was twisted around her legs, and when Solomon saw this, he called to her, averting his glance: *"Lo! It is a hall, made smooth, of glass."* She let down her

---

831. *Ṭawābiq.* See *Glossarium,* CCCXXXVIII, s.v. *ṭbq*: *largae tegulae soli in aedificio.*

garment, and *she said: "My Lord! Lo! I have wronged myself, and I surrender with Solomon to God, the Lord of the Worlds."*[832]

Then Solomon called the humans and said, "How ugly this is! What can remove it?" They said, "O Messenger of God! The razor." He said, "Razors will cut the woman's legs." So he called the jinns and asked them. They said, "We do not know." Then he called the demons and said, "What will remove this?" They said likewise, "The razor." He replied, "Razors will cut the woman's legs." He [584] continued: They apologized to him, then made a depilatory paste for him.

Ibn ʿAbbās said, "It was the first day on which depilatory paste was mixed. Then Solomon married her."

Ibn Ḥumayd related to us — Salamah — Ibn Isḥāq — a scholar — Wahb b. Munabbih: When the messengers brought back to Bilqīs what Solomon had said, she said, "By God! I had known that this is no ordinary king and that we have no power to oppose him and will not accomplish anything by vying with him." So she sent to him, saying, "I am coming to you with the kings of my people, so that I may see your situation and your religion to which you are inviting [me]." She then ordered her royal palanquin, upon which she used to sit, made of gold inlaid with sapphire, topaz, and pearls, and it was placed within seven structures, each within another, then she had their doors locked. She was served only by women, of whom there were six hundred with her. Then she said to the one whom she had appointed over her domain, "Guard what is in your hands and the palanquin of my rule, and do not let anyone reach it or even see it until I return." Then she went off to Solomon with twelve thousand *qayls* from the kings of Yemen, and under the authority of each of them were many thousands. Solomon began sending out the jinns, who would bring him [word] of her travel and how far she reached each day and night. When she drew near, he assembled all the jinns and men under his command and said, *"O you chiefs! Who will* [585] *bring me her throne before they come to me submitting?"*[833] The narrator said: "She submitted [to Islam], and her Islam was sincere."

It is claimed that Solomon said to her, when she had accepted Islam and he had completed the matter with her, "Choose a man from

832. Qurʾān 27:44.
833. Qurʾān 27:38.

your people to whom I will marry you." She replied, "Shall men marry someone like me, O Prophet of God, when I have had dominion and power among my people such as I have had?" He said, "Yes. In Islam, there can only be the like of that. It is not fitting for you to forbid that which God has made permissible for you." So she said, "Then marry me, if it must be so, to Dhū Tubbaʾ, king of Hamdān."[834] So Solomon married her to him, returned her to Yemen, and gave rule over Yemen to her husband Dhū Tubbaʾ. Solomon called Zawbaʿah, prince of the jinns of Yemen, and said, "Do for Dhū Tubbaʾ whatever he asks you to do for his people."

So Zawbaʿah carried out construction projects in Yemen for Dhū Tubbaʾ, and Dhū Tubbaʾ remained there as king, having whatever he wanted done for him, until Solomon b. David died. Then, when a year had passed and Solomon's death[835] became clear to the jinn, one of them journeyed through Tihāmah[836] until, in the midst of Yemen, he shouted at the top of his voice, "O assemblage of jinn! King Solomon has died, so stop working." The demons directed themselves to two large stones, upon which they wrote an inscription in Himyarite script:[837] "We built Salḥīn in seventy-seven years,[838] striv-
[586] ing steadily. And we built Ṣirwāḥ, Marāḥ, and Baynūn by the sweat of [our] hands;[839] and Hind and Hunaydah and seven cisterns[840] in a paved court, and Talthūm in Raydah. Were it not for the one who shouted in Tihāmah, we would have left in al-Bawn[841] a sign."

The narrator explains: Salḥīn, Ṣirwāḥ, Marāḥ, Baynūn, Hind, Hu-

---

834. Although the text has Dhū Bataʿ, Ibrāhīm, *op. cit.*, I, 495, has Dhū Tubbaʿ, basing this on other MSS, as noted by the editor. See al-Ṭabarī, I, 585 n. *c*. See also Yāqūt, *op. cit.*, I, 115, and al-Thaʿlabī, *op. cit.*, 286.

835. See the story of Solomon's death, pp. 173–74, below.

836. The central area of western Arabia between Yemen and the Ḥijāz. See Yāqūt, *op. cit.*, I, 901–3.

837. *I.e.*, the South Arabian alphabet. The inscription is written in *sajʿ*, rhymed prose.

838. *Kharīfan*, lit. "autumns," South Arabian: "years." See al-Ṭabarī, I, 585 n. *e*.

839. Written *aydīn(a)*, it should have long ā, but it is probably written to rhyme with *dāʾibīn(a)*. See the correct form in Yāqūt, *op. cit.*, III, 115, s.v. "Salḥīn."

840. *Amjilah*, pl. of *majil*, for *maʾjil*. *Glossarium*, CDLXXXI, s.v. *mjl*. Written *amḥilah* in another version. See n. 806, above.

841. Bawn, a town in Yemen. See Yāqūt, *op. cit.*, I, 763–64, supposedly the site of the "deserted well and lofty tower" (Arberry: "a ruined well, a tall palace") mentioned in Qurʾān 22:45.

naydah, and Talthūm are fortresses in Yemen[842] that the demons built for Dhū Tubba'. Then they stopped work and left. The rule of Dhū Tubba' and Bilqīs ended with the rule of Solomon b. David.

---

842. Yāqūt lists some but not all of these fortresses separately and in most cases attributes their building to Solomon or to the devils. E.g., Yāqūt, *op. cit.*, III, 115, s.v. "Salḥīn": A great fortress in Yemen of the Tubbaʿs (kings of Yemen). It is claimed that the devils built the castles and buildings for Dhū Tubbaʿ, king of Hamdān, when Solomon married Bilqīs." He then gives the inscription as follows: "We built Baynūn and Salḥīn, Ṣirwāḥ and Mirwāḥ, with the weakness (*rijājah*; Lane, *op. cit.*, s.v. *rjj*) of our hands. And Hindah and Hunaydah, Qalsūm and Buraydah, and seven *amḥilah* (?) in a courtyard." See also al-Ṭabarī, 586 nn. *b–f*. Al-Thaʿlabī, *op. cit.*, 286, has Salḥīn, Ghamdān, Banyūn; on 287 he has Salḥīn, Abnujīn, Ṣirwāḥ, Marwaḥ, Fanqūn, Hindah, Hunaydah, and Dalūm.

Solomon's Campaign against the Father of His Wife, Jarādah, and the Story of the Devil Who Took Solomon's Signet Ring

Ibn Ḥumayd related to us—Salamah—Ibn Isḥāq—a scholar—Wahb b. Munabbih: Solomon heard of a city, named Sidon,[843] on one of the
[587] islands of the sea, in which was a mighty powerful king. People had no access to him because of his situation in the sea. However, God had given to Solomon within his dominion, power to which nothing on land or sea would be inaccessible. He needed only to ride to it when he rode on the wind. He set out for that city, the wind carrying him over the water, until he landed there together with his troops of men and jinns. He killed its king and took everything as booty. Among those items he seized was a daughter of that king, the like of whose comeliness and beauty he had never seen. He chose her for himself and invited her to become a Muslim. She accepted Islam, but reluctantly and doubtfully. He loved her with a love he had never shown to any of his wives and became obsessed with her.[844] But despite her standing with him, her sadness did not leave her, nor did her

843. Ṣaydūn, Ṣīdūn, perhaps for Hebrew *ṣīdōn,* the seaport in Phoenicia, although its usual Arabic name is Ṣaydā'.

844. *Waqaʿat nafsuhu ʿalayhā.* See *Glossarium,* DLXIV, s.v. *wqʿ: amor ejus occupavit animum.*

tears stop. When he saw how [sad] she was, distressed by what he saw, he said to her, "Woe is you! What is this sadness that does not leave you? And these tears that do not stop?" She replied, "It is my father. I remember him and his dominion. I remember what his position was, and what happened to him. It makes me sad." He said, "God has exchanged it with a dominion for you that is greater than his, and power greater than his power. He has guided you to Islam, which is better than all of that." She said, "Certainly that is so, but whenever I remember him, sadness overcomes me, as you have seen. Perhaps you could command the demons to make a likeness of my father in my dwelling, so that I may see it in the morning and evening. I hope this will take away my sadness and divert me somewhat from what I feel." So Solomon commanded the demons, saying, "Make for her a likeness of her father in her dwelling in which nothing would be unrecognizable for her." They made his likeness for her so that she (seemed to) look at her father himself, except that there [588] was no soul in him. After they had made him for her, she directed herself to him, wrapping him in a girdle, putting a shirt and a turban on him, and restored him to the kind of clothing he used to wear and the sort of appearance he used to have. Then, when Solomon would leave her dwelling, she would enter to [the image] early in the morning with her slave girls. She and the slave girls would bow down to him, as they used to do for him in his dominion. Every evening she would go to him in the same way, and Solomon knew nothing of that for forty days.

Word of that reached Asaph b. Berechiah,[845] a trusted counselor who was never turned back from Solomon's gates, and at any hour he desired to enter any of his apartments, he entered, whether Solomon was present or not. He went to Solomon and said, "O Prophet of God! I have become old, my bones have become frail, and my time is running out. It is time for me to pass on. I should like to stand in a place before my death in which I might mention those of God's prophets who have passed on and praise them with my knowledge of them,

845. Asaph b. Berechiah is mentioned in 1 Chronicles 6:24 and 15:17 as one of the Levites who sang and played before the Ark when it was brought into Jerusalem at David's command. In Islamic lore he is supposed to be the one referred to (though not by name) in Qurʾān 27:40: *One with whom was knowledge of the scripture* (see n. 817, above), who brought the throne of Bilqis to Solomon in the twinkling of an eye. He is known in Islamic tradition and folklore. See *EI*², s.v. "Asaf b. Barkhyā."

and teach the people something of what they have not known of many things about them." Solomon said, "Do so!" Solomon gathered the people to him, and he stood among them as a preacher, mentioning God's prophets who had passed on. He praised each prophet for what he had been and mentioned in what way God had made him excel, until he came to Solomon's name, and mentioned him, saying, "How forbearing you were—in your youth, and how pious you were—in your youth, and how virtuous you were—in your youth, and how wise you were—in your youth, and how far you were from everything disapproved—in your youth!" Then he left, and Solomon
[589] grew angry until he was filled with rage. He entered his dwelling and sent for Asaph, saying, "O Asaph! You mentioned the prophets of God who have passed on, and you praised their goodness throughout their lives and in every state of their affair. But when you mentioned me, you began to praise my goodness in my youth, but you remained silent about everything else in my case after I matured and what I have done in my latter days." Asaph responded, "Verily, someone other than God has been worshiped in your dwelling during the last forty days in the passion of a woman." Solomon said, "In my dwelling?" He replied, "In your dwelling!" Solomon said, *"Verily, we are God's, and lo! To Him do we return.*[846] I know that you spoke only about something that has reached you." Then Solomon returned to his dwelling, broke the image, and punished that woman and her slave girls.

Then [Solomon] ordered garments of purification to be brought to him. They are garments spun by none but virgins, woven by none but virgins, washed by none but virgins, and no woman who had menstruated may touch them. He put them on, then went out to a deserted piece of land by himself. He ordered ashes to be brought and spread out for him. Then he came, repenting to God and sat on those ashes, rolling in them in his garments, humbling himself before God and entreating him, weeping, praying, asking forgiveness for what had happened in his dwelling, saying among the things he said [as was mentioned to me, but God knows best], "Lord, why do You afflict the family of David so that they worship other than You, and that they permit in their dwellings and among their family the worship of other than You." He remained thus until the evening came,

846. Qur'ān 2:156.

weeping to God, imploring Him, and asking His forgiveness. Then he returned to his dwelling.

He had a chief concubine named al-Āminah to whom, when he entered his privy or when he wished to have intercourse with one of [590] his wives, he would give his signet ring until he purified himself, because he would not touch his signet ring unless he was [ritually] pure.[847] His dominion was in his signet, and one day, he gave it to her, as he used to do, then he entered his privy. The Devil who was master of the sea, who was named Ṣakhr, came to her in Solomon's form. Āminah saw nothing unlike Solomon in him, and when he said, "My signet ring, O Āminah!" she gave it to him. He put it on his hand, went out, sat on Solomon's throne, and the birds, jinns, and men surrounded him.

Solomon came out and went to al-Āminah, but his condition and appearance had changed for everyone who saw him. When he said, "O Āminah, my signet ring!" she replied, "And who are you?" He said, "I am Solomon b. David." She said, "You lie! You are not Solomon b. David. Solomon came and took his signet ring. He is that one, sitting on his throne in his dominion."

Solomon realized that his sin had overtaken him. He went out and began to stand at one of the houses of the Israelites, saying, "I am Solomon b. David," but they would throw dirt on him and insult him, saying, "Look at this madman! What does he say? He claims that he is Solomon b. David." When Solomon saw that, he turned to the sea, and would carry fish to the market for the seafaring men. Each day, they would give him two fish. When evening came, he would sell one fish for some loaves of bread, and grill the other and eat it. He remained thus for forty days—the same amount of time that the idol had been worshiped in his dwelling. Asaph and the powerful men of the Israelites found fault in the judgment of God's enemy, the Devil, during those forty days. Asaph said, "O assembly of the Children of Israel! Have you noticed the same change in the [591] judgment of the son of David that I have noticed?" They said, "Yes." He said, "Give me time to enter to his wives so that I may ask them whether they have found the same fault in his private affairs that we

---

847. In Islam ritual purity after sexual intercourse involving seminal emission requires *ghusl,* complete immersion (*EI*[2], s.v. "Ghusl"), whereas defecation or urination requires *wuḍūʾ*, the minor ablution (hands, feet, etc.). See *Shorter Encyclopaedia of Islam,* s.v. "wuḍūʾ."

have found with his public affairs with the people and his outward behavior." He went in to Solomon's wives and said, "Woe unto you! Have you found something wrong in Solomon's behavior as we have found wrong?" They said, "The worst of it is that he will not leave any woman of us who is menstruating alone,[848] and he does not wash himself from impurity."[849] Asaph said: *"Verily we are God's, and to Him do we return!*[850] *Verily that is a clear test."*[851] Then he returned to the Israelites and said, "What he does in private is worse than what he does in public."

When forty days had passed, the Devil flew away from his council chamber. As he passed over the sea, he threw the signet ring into it, and a fish swallowed it. One of the fishermen saw that fish and caught it. Solomon had worked for him from the beginning of that day until evening, so he gave Solomon his two fish, [including] the one that had taken the signet ring. Solomon went out with his two fish and sold the one in whose stomach there was no signet ring for some loaves of bread. He then applied himself to the other fish, cutting it open in order to grill it, and was confronted by his signet ring in its stomach. He took it, placed it on his hand, and fell down, prostrating himself to God. The birds and jinns surrounded him, and people approached him, and he knew that what had come upon him was only because of what he had let happen in his household. He returned to his dominion and manifested repentance for his sin. He commanded the demons, saying, "Bring [Ṣakhr] to me!" The demons sought him until they caught him, and he was brought. Solomon bored a hole in a stone for him and put him inside. Then he closed it up with another [stone], bound it with iron and lead, and gave orders for it to be cast into the sea.

[592] Muḥammad b. al-Ḥusayn[852] related to us—Aḥmad b. al-Mufaḍḍal—Asbāṭ—al-Suddī said about [God's] word: *And verily We tried Solomon, and set upon his throne a body*[853]—he said, [this was] the devil, when he sat on [Solomon's] throne for forty days. He contin-

848. Sexual intercourse with menstruating women is forbidden by the Qurʾān (2:222), but the rules forbidding contact are less stringent in Islam than in Judaism. See *EI*[2] s.v. "Ḥaiḍ."

849. See n. 845, above.

850. Qurʾān 2:156.

851. Qurʾān 37:106.

852. Muḥammad b. al-Ḥusayn. See n. 752, above.

853. Qurʾān 38:35.

ued: Among Solomon's one hundred wives, was one called "Jarādah." She was his favorite wife and the most trusted. When he was impure or went out for his need, he would take off his ring, and he would trust no one of the people but her with it. She went to him one day and said, "My brother has a dispute with so-and-so, and I should like you to settle it for him when he comes to you." He said, "Of course." But he did not do it, and he was afflicted. He gave her his signet ring and entered the toilet. But the devil came out in his form. He said, "Give me the ring!" and she gave it to him. Then he went and sat on Solomon's seat. Afterward, Solomon came out and asked her for his signet ring, and she said, "Did you not take it before?" He said, "No," and went out of his place bewildered.

The devil continued judging the people for forty days. The people found fault with his judgments, and the readers and scholars of the Children of Israel assembled, and came and entered to [Solomon's] wives and said, "We find fault with this, and if it is Solomon, then he has lost his senses. We disapprove of his judgments." [Al-Suddī] continued: The women wept upon [hearing] this. The people approached them on foot until they reached [the devil] and surrounded him. Then they unrolled and read the Torah. He flew from before them until he rested upon an embattlement with the signet ring. Then he flew until he reached the sea, and the signet ring, falling from him into the sea, was swallowed by one of the fish.

[Al-Suddī] continued: Solomon approached in the state in which he was, until he reached one of the fishermen of the sea, and he was [593] hungry. Solomon's hunger had become very strong, and he asked [the fisherman] for food from their catch, saying, "Verily I am Solomon." One of the fishermen arose and struck him with a staff, cutting open his head. Solomon began to wash off his blood—he was on the seashore—and the fishermen blamed their companion who had struck him, saying: "How bad was what you did when you struck him!" He said, "It was because he claimed that he was Solomon."

They gave him two of the fish they had caught, but he did not busy himself with what he had of the catch until he stood at the seashore and split open the two [fish], beginning to wash them, and found his signet ring in the stomach of one. He took it, put it on, and God restored his glory to him and his dominion. The birds came so that they hovered over him, and the people knew that he was Solomon. The people rose and asked his pardon for what they had done. He said, "I shall not praise you for your asking pardon, nor will I blame you for what you did. This matter had to be."

He went until when he reached his dominion, he sent for the devil, and he was brought to him. The wind and the demons were made to work for him on that day; they had not been subordinated to him before then, for that is His word: *"Bestow upon me sovereignty such as shall not belong to anyone else after me. Lo! You are the Bestower."*[854]

He sent for the devil, and he was brought. [Solomon] gave orders to
[594] place him in a chest of iron, then it was shut and locked with a lock. He sealed it with his signet ring, then he gave orders to cast it into the sea. The devil will be in it until the Hour arrives. His name was Ḥabaqīq.

Abū Jaʿfar said: Then Solomon continued in his sovereignty after God had returned him to it, the jinn making for him *what he willed: places of worship and statues, basins like water troughs and anchored cooking pots*[855] and his other projects.

He punished those demons he wished, and set free those he liked, so that when he neared his term and God wanted to take him to Him, his matter was as was told to me, as Aḥmad b. Manṣūr[856] related about him—Mūsā b. Masʿūd Abū Hudhayfah[857]—Ibrāhīm b. Ṭahmān[858]—ʿAṭāʾ b. al-Sāʾib—Saʿīd b. Jubayr—Ibn ʿAbbās—the Prophet: When Solomon, the Prophet of God, was praying, he would see a tree sprouting in front of him, and he would say to it: "What is your name?" It said, "Such-and-such." Then he said, "For what purpose are you?" If it was for planting, it would be planted; if it was for a remedy, it would be written down. One day while he was praying, suddenly he saw a tree in front of him, and he said to it, "What is your name?" It said, "Carob (*kharrūb*)." He said, "For what purpose are you?" It said, "For the destruction (*kharāb*) of this house." Sol-

---

854. Qurʾān 38:36.

855. Qurʾān 34:13.

856. Aḥmad b. Manṣūr b. Sayyār al-Ramādī, Abū Bakr, 182–265/798–877. A trustworthy memorizer of traditions, he traveled widely seeking their sources and wrote many books, including collections of traditions. Ibn Ḥajar, *op. cit.*, I, 83; *GAS*, I, 41; al-Ziriklī, *op. cit.*, I, 244.

857. Mūsā b. Masʿūd al-Nahdī al-Baṣrī, Abū Ḥudhayfah, d. 240/854. He was one of the authorities of al-Bukhārī. Ibn Ḥajar, *op. cit.*, X, 370–71; *GAS*, I, 41.

858. Ibrāhīm b. Ṭahmān b. Shuʿbah al-Khurasānī, Abū Saʿīd, d. 164/780. Born in Herat, he journeyed to Nishapur, Baghdad, and Mecca, where he died. He was considered one of the best traditionists of Khurāsān. Ibn Ḥajar, *op. cit.*, I, 129–31; *GAS*, I, 92–93.

omon said, "O my God! Blind the jinn to my death, so that men may know that the jinn do not know what is hidden." He hewed [the tree] into a staff and was supported upon it for a year after he had died, while the jinn continued to work. Then, a termite ate it, and he fell. Thus, humans perceived that *the jinn, if they had known the unseen, would not have continued in despised toil.*[859]

He said: Ibn ʿAbbās used to read it "for a year in despised toil." He [595] continued: The jinn thanked the termite and used to bring it water.

Mūsā b. Hārūn[860] related to me—ʿAmr[861]—Asbāṭ—al-Suddī, in an account that he related—Abū Mālik; and Abū Ṣāliḥ—Ibn ʿAbbās; and Murrah al-Hamdānī—Ibn Masʿūd; and people among the companions of the Prophet: Solomon would isolate himself in the Temple for a year or two years, for a month or two months, or for more or less time. His food and drink would be brought in to him, as it was at the time he died. From the beginning, there was not a day when he woke [early], but a tree had sprouted in the Temple. He would go to it and ask it, "What is your name?" And the tree would say, "My name is such-and-such." He would say to it, "Why have you sprouted?" And it would say, "I sprouted for such-and-such [a purpose]." He would give orders regarding it, and it would be cut down. If it sprouted for planting, he would plant it. If it sprouted as a remedy, it would say, "I have sprouted as a remedy for such-and-such," and he would use it for that. Then a tree sprouted that is called the carob, and he asked it, "What is your name?" It replied, "I am the carob tree." He said, "Why did you sprout?" It replied, "I have sprouted for the destruction of this place of worship." Solomon said, "God would not destroy it while I am alive. You [are the one] upon whose face is my death and the destruction of the Temple." He pulled up the tree and planted it in a wall of his. He then entered the prayer chamber and stood praying, leaning on his staff, and he died. The demons did not know of this, and they were working for him at that time, fearing that he would come out and punish them. They would [596] gather around the prayer chamber, with its openings in front and back. Any devil who wanted to disobey would say, "Am I not strong if I enter (here) and depart from that side?" So he would enter and depart from the other side. Then one devil entered and passed by. No

859. Qurʾān 34:14.
860. Mūsā b. Hārūn. See n. 174, above.
861. ʿAmr b. Muḥammad. See n. 506, above.

devil could look at Solomon in the prayer niche without being burned. But as this one passed by, he did not hear Solomon's voice. When he returned, he still did not hear it. Then he returned again and stood in the Temple and was not burned. He looked at Solomon, who had fallen down dead, and went out, informing the people that Solomon had died. They opened up the Temple and brought him out. They found that his stick (*minsa'ah*)[862]—which is a staff in the Ethiopian language—had been eaten by a termite. They did not know how long he had been dead. So they placed the termite on the staff, and it ate of it for one day and night. Then they reckoned, on the basis of that, that he had died a year previously. This is, in the reading of Ibn Masʿūd:[863] "They continued to submit to him for a whole year after his death." People determined thereby that the jinn had been lying, for if they had known the unseen, they would have known of Solomon's death and would not have remained in toil for a year working for him.[864] For that is God's word: *Nothing showed him his death but a creeping creature of the earth [which gnawed away his staff (minsaʿatahu). And when he fell the jinn saw clearly how, if they had known the unseen, they would not have contin-*
[597] *ued] in despised toil*[865]—meaning, that their situation made clear to the people that they had been lying.

Then the demons said to the termite, "If you ate food, we would bring you the best food. If you drank wine, we would bring you the best wine. But we will bring [you] water and clay."

They [would] bring the termite water and clay, wherever it was. The narrator went on: Have you not seen the clay that is within wood? That is what the demons bring the termite out of gratitude.

Solomon b. David's life span, according to what they say, was some fifty-odd years,[866] and in the fourth year of his reign, he began building the Temple, as it is said.

---

862. Not of Arabic origin. See *Glossarium*, DXI, s.v. *nsʾ: baculus* (a staff, or scepter). It occurs in Qurʾān 34:14, below.

863. See al-Ṭabarī, 496 n.*b*. Ibn Masʿūd, see n. 179, above.

864. The jinn, therefore, do not possess the superhuman power of foretelling the future or even knowing what was generally unknown. Had they been aware of Solomon's death, they would not have continued their toil for him.

865. Qurʾān 34:14. The words in brackets are omitted in text.

866. The length of Solomon's life is not specified in the Bible, but he reigned for forty years, 1 Kings 11:42; 2 Chronicles 9:30. Al-Thaʿlabī, *op. cit.*, 260, says that Solomon was thirteen years old when he succeeded his father.

Bibliography of Cited Works

Abū al-Faraj al-Iṣfahānī. *Kitāb al-aghānī.* Cairo: al-Hay'ah al-miṣriyyah al-ʿāmmah li-al-ta'līf wa-al-nashr, 1963.

Addenda. See al-Ṭabarī.

Alram, M. *Nomina Propria Iranica in Nummis. Materialgrundlagen zu den iranischen Personennamen auf antiken Münzen.* Iranisches Personennamenbuch IV. Vienna: Verlag der österreichischen Akademie der Wissenschaften, 1986.

Anklesaria, B. T. *Zand-Ākāsīh: Iranian, or Greater Bundahišn.* Bombay: Rahumae Mazdayasnan Sabha, 1956.

Bartholomae, C. *Altiranisches Wörterbuch.* Strassburg: Verlag Karl J. Trübner, 1904; repr. Berlin: Walter de Gruyter & Co., 1961.

al-Bayḍāwī, ʿAbdallāh b. ʿUmar. *Anwār al-tanzīl.* Cairo: Dār al-kutub al-ʿarabiyyah al-kubrā, 1330/1912.

Ben Zeev (Wolfensohn), I. *Kaʿb al-Aḥbār.* Jerusalem: Maṭbaʿat al-sharq al-taʿāwuniyyah, 1976.

al-Bīrūnī, Abū Rayḥān Muḥammad. *Kitāb al-athār al-bāqiyah ʿan al-qurūn al-khāliyah,* trans. C. E. Sachau as *The Chronology of Ancient Nations.* London: W. H. Allen and Co., 1879

Boyce, M. *A History of Zoroastrianism.* Vol. II. *Under the Achaemenians.* Handbuch der Orientalistik, Abteilung I, Band VIII, Abschnitt I, Lieferung 2, Heft 2a. Leiden: E. J. Brill, 1982.

Brinner, W. M., trans. *Prophets and Patriarchs.* The History of al-Ṭabarī II. Albany: State University of New York Press, 1987.

Bundahishn. See Anklesaria.

Christensen, A. *Les Kayanides.* Historisk-filologiske Meddelelser XIX/2. Copenhagen: Det Kongeliger Danske Videnskabernes Selskab, 1932.

———. *Les types du premier homme et du premier roi dans l'histoire légendaire des Iraniens.* 2 vols. Archives d'Études Orientales 14/1–2. Stockholm: P. A. Norstaedt & Söner, 1917–34.

Darmesteter, J. *Le Zend-Avesta.* Vol. II. *La loi (Vendidad) — l'épopée (Yashts) — le livre de prière (Khorda Avesta).* Annales du Musée Guimet 22. Paris: Leroux, 1893. Repr. Paris: Adrien-Maisonneuve, 1960.

Dodge, B., ed. and trans. *The Fihrist of al-Nadīm: A Tenth-Century Survey of Muslim Culture.* 2 vols. New York: Columbia University Press, 1970.

Dozy, R. *Supplément aux dictionnaires arabes.* 2 vols. Leiden: E. J. Brill, 1881. Repr. Beirut: Librairie du Liban, 1968.

Eilers, W. *Der Name Demawand.* Hildesheim: Georg Olms Verlag, 1988.

Friedlaender, I. *Die Chadirlegende und der Alexanderroman.* Leipzig: B. G. Teubner, 1913.

Ginzberg, L. *The Legends of the Jews.* 7 vols. Philadelphia: Jewish Publication Society, 1909–36.

Glossarium. See al-Ṭabarī.

Goodenough, E. R. *Jewish Symbols in the Greco-Roman Period.* 13 vols. New York: Pantheon Books, 1953–68.

Ibn al-Athīr, ʿIzz al-Dīn. *al-Kāmil fī al-taʾrīkh,* ed. C. Tornberg. 13 vols. Leiden: E. J. Brill, 1867. Repr. Beirut: Dār Ṣādir, 1965.

Ibn Ḥajar al-ʿAsqalānī. *Tahdhīb al-tahdhīb.* Ḥyderabad: n.p., 1325–27/1907–8.

Ibn Khaldūn, ʿAbd al-Raḥman b. Muḥammad. *Kitāb al-ʿibār,* ed. M. de Slane as *Histoire des Berbères et des dynasties musulmanes de l'Afrique septentrionale.* Vol. I. Algiers: Imprimerie du gouvernement, 1847.

———. *al-Muqaddimah,* trans. F. Rosenthal as *The Muqaddimah: An Introduction to History.* 3 vols. Bollingen Series XLVIII. New York: Pantheon Press, 1958.

Ibn Saʿd, Abū ʿAbdallāh Muḥammad. *Kitāb al-ṭabaqāt al-kabīr,* ed. E. Sachau as *Biographien Muhammeds.* 9 vols. Leiden: E. J. Brill, 1904–21.

Ibrāhīm. See al-Ṭabarī.

Index. See al-Ṭabarī.

Jarīr b. ʿAṭiyyah. *The Nakaʾiḍ of Jarir and al-Farazdaḳ,* ed. A. A. Bevan. 3 vols. Leiden: E. J. Brill, 1905–12.

Justi, F. *Iranisches Namenbuch.* Hildesheim: Georg Olms Verlag, 1963.

Juynboll, G. H. A. *The Authenticity of the Tradition Literature: Discussions in Modern Egypt.* Leiden: E. J. Brill, 1969.

Khaṭīb al-Tibrīzī, Muḥammad b. ʿAbdallāh. *Mishkāt al-masābīḥ,* trans. J. Robson. 2 vols. Lahore: Sh. Muhammad Ashraf, 1981.

Khoury, R. G. *Wahb ibn Munabbih.* Wiesbaden: Otto Harrassowitz, 1972.

Lane, E. W. *An Arabic-English Lexicon.* 2 vols. London: Williams and Norgate, 1863. Repr. in 8 vols., Beirut: Librairie du Liban, 1968.

Lassner, J. *The Topography of Baghdad in the Early Middle Ages.* Detroit: Wayne State University Press, 1970.

Le Strange, G. *Palestine under the Moslems.* London: A. P. Watt, 1890.

Mayrhofer, M. *Die altiranischen Namen.* Iranisches Personennamenbuch I. Vienna: Verlag der österreichischen Akademie der Wissenschaften, 1979.

Mujmal al-tawārīkh wa-al-qiṣaṣ, ed. M.-T. Bahār. Tehran: Khāwar, 1318 Sh./1939.

Newby, G. D. *A History of the Jews of Arabia.* Columbia: University of South Carolina Press, 1988.

______. *The Making of the Last Prophet.* Columbia: University of South Carolina Press, 1989.

Nissim b. Jacob b. Shahin. *al-Faraj baʿd al-shiddah,* trans. W. M. Brinner as *An Elegant Composition Concerning Relief after Adversity.* Yale Judaica Series XX. New Haven: Yale University Press, 1978.

Perlmann, M., trans. *The Ancient Kingdoms.* The History of al-Ṭabarī IV. Albany: State University of New York Press, 1987.

Popper, W. *Egypt and Syria under the Circassian Sultans, 1362–1468 A.D.* 2 vols. University of California Publications in Semitic Philology XV–XVI. Berkeley: University of California Press, 1955–57.

Rowson, E. K., trans. *The Marwānid Restoration: The Caliphate of ʿAbd al-Malik.* The History of al-Ṭabarī XXII. Albany: State University of New York Press, 1989.

Schützinger, H. "Die arabische Bileam-Erzählung," *Der Islam,* 59 (1982): 195–221.

Schwarzbaum, H. "The Jewish and Moslem Versions of Some Theodicy Legends," *Fabula,* 3 (1959): 119–69.

______. "Jewish, Christian, Moslem and Falasha Legends of the Death of Aaron, the High Priest" *Fabula,* 5 (1962): 185–227.

Shorter Encyclopaedia of Islam, ed. H. A. R. Gibb and J. H. Kramers. Leiden: E. J. Brill, 1961.

al-Ṭabarī, Abū Jaʿfar Muḥammad b. Jarīr. *Taʾrīkh al-rusul wa-al-mulūk,* ed. M. J. de Geoje as *Annales.* 3rd series, 4 vols. Leiden: E. J. Brill, 1883–84; *Indices,* 1901; *Introductio, Glossarium, Addenda et Emendanda,* 1901. Ed. M. A. Ibrāhīm as *Taʾrīkh al-Ṭabarī.* 14 vols. Cairo: Dār al-maʿārif, 1960.

al-Thaʿlabī, Aḥmad b. Muḥammad. *Qiṣaṣ al-anbiyāʾ: al-Musammā ʿarāʾis al-majālis.* Beirut: al-Maktabah al-thaqafiyyah, n.d.

A Tourist's Handbook for Egypt. London: Cook's, 1897.

Watt, W. M. *Muhammad in Medina.* Oxford: Oxford University Press, 1962.

West, E. W. trans. *The Bundahis-Bahman Yast, and Shāyast Lā-Shāyast* (Indian Bundahishn). Sacred Books of the East V. Pahlavi Texts 1. Oxford: Clarendon Press, 1880–97.

Wilkinson, I. G. *A Handbook for Travellers to Egypt.* London: 1858.

Yāqūt al-Ḥamawī. *Kitāb muʿjam al-buldān,* ed. F. Wüstenfeld as *Jacut's Wörterbuch.* 6 vols. Leipzig: F. A. Brockhaus, 1866. Repr. Tehran: Maktabat al-asadī, 1965.

al-Ziriklī, Kh. *al-Aʿlām: Qāmūs al-tarājim.* 2nd ed. 10 vols. Cairo: n.p., 1954.

Translations of the Qurʾān

Arberry, A. J. *The Koran Interpreted.* New York: Macmillan, 1955.

Dawood, N. J. *The Koran.* Harmondsworth, U.K.: Penguin Books, 1956.

Kasimirski, (A.) *Le Coran.* Paris: Charpentier, 1840. Repr. with chronology and preface by M. Arkoun. Paris: Garnier-Flammarion, 1976.

Pickthall, M. M. *The Meaning of the Glorious Koran.* London: George Allen & Unwin, 1957.

Rodwell, J. M. *The Koran.* 2nd ed. London: B. Quartich, 1876. Repr. London: J. M. Dent & Sons Ltd., 1943.

Sale, G. *The Koran.* New York: A. L. Burt, n.d.

Index

Included are names of persons, groups, and places, as well as Arabic words that recur often in the text or are discussed in the footnotes. Entries that are mentioned in both text and footnotes on the same page are listed by page number only. Finally, the Arabic definite article al- *and the abbreviations* b. (ibn) *and* bt. (bint) *have been disregarded in the alphabetizing of entries.*

A

B

C

J

N

R

S

U

V

W

Y

Z